Industrial Organization

Industrial Organization

A European Perspective

Stephen Martin

OXFORD
UNIVERSITY PRESS

OXFORD
UNIVERSITY PRESS

Great Clarendon Street, Oxford OX2 6DP

Oxford University Press is a department of the University of Oxford.
It furthers the University's objective of excellence in research, scholarship,
and education by publishing worldwide in

Oxford New York

Athens Auckland Bangkok Bogotá Buenos Aires Cape Town
Chennai Dar es Salaam Delhi Florence Hong Kong Istanbul Karachi
Kolkata Kuala Lumpur Madrid Melbourne Mexico City Mumbai Nairobi
Paris São Paulo Shanghai Singapore Taipei Tokyo Toronto Warsaw

with associated companies in Berlin Ibadan

Oxford is a registered trade mark of Oxford University Press
in the UK and in certain other countries

Published in the United States
by Oxford University Press Inc., New York

British Library Cataloguing in Publication Data

Data available

Library of Congress Cataloging in Publication Data

Data available

ISBN 0–19–829728–9

Typeset by RefineCatch Limited, Bungay, Suffolk
Printed in Great Britain on acid-free paper by
Bath Press Ltd., Bath, Somerset
10 9 8 7 6 5 4 3 2 1

Contents

List of Figures

List of Tables

Preface

It is a foolish thing to make a long prologue, and to be short in the story itself.

  Second Book of the Maccabees 2:32

I have tried to follow two guidelines in writing this book. The first is to know my audience, or more precisely, to know those who I hope will make up my audience. The second is to keep in mind not how much I think I have to teach, but rather how much those in my audience have to learn.

I have tried to write an introductory textbook in the field of industrial organization. Most of the students who use this book will not become professional industrial economists,[1] and I have tried to present the material in a way that is accessible to them. For the most part, I use a modelling approach—to do otherwise would be unfaithful to the field— but in the text I rely on minor variations of a single basic model. Some end-of-chapter problems present extensions of this basic model; I make no attempt to hint at the wonderland of models that one encounters at the research level in industrial organization.

I am grateful to several cohorts of students at the Copenhagen Business School and at the University of Amsterdam, who served as guinea pigs for early versions of the book. I would also like to thank Inés Macho Stadler, Peter Møllgaard, David Perez-Castrillo, Bruno Versaevel, and four anonymous reviewers for comments on various parts of the manuscript, without implicating them in remaining shortcomings.

I have had the temerity to entitle this book *Industrial Organization: A European Perspective*. It is not, of course, a European's perspective: I still carry a passport that requires me to stand in the long and slow-moving line at customs counters when I move in and out of the EU and in and out of the Schengen zone, and I carry the mental baggage that goes with the passport. I should like to dedicate this book to all those who have helped me and my family during our extended European vacation. You know who you are.

---

[1] Not everyone can be lucky.

Chapter 1
Background

A hard beginning maketh a good ending.

John Heywood

1.1 **Subject matter**

Industrial organization is an imperialist field. Its origin lies in the study of imperfectly competitive markets and the felt need to inform government policy toward such markets, but the insights generated by the study of imperfectly competitive markets have caused it to extend its reach to touch on almost all branches of economics.

The first analytical framework of industrial organization, the structure-conduct-performance approach, drew on differences in market structure and business behaviour to explain differences in market performance. The aspects of market performance that attracted the most attention were (as with the standard comparison of perfect competition and monopoly) output levels, the relation of price to marginal cost, consumers' surplus, and the amount of economic profit. These are shown in the upper left-hand corner of Figure 1.1.

As the name suggests, the structure-conduct-performance paradigm emphasized structure as the determinant of business conduct and business conduct, within a given market structure, as the determinant of market performance. At the same time, the S-C-P approach recognized that market structure and business behaviour are themselves the products of economic forces.[1] The analysis of the determinants of market structure and of firm conduct is thus also part of the subject matter of industrial organization.

Work on mergers and merger policy led naturally to the question of the structure within firms,[2] and to what might be called the structure between firms: vertical relationships, joint ventures, and strategic alliances.

Going in one direction, the analysis of firm conduct led to the investigation of collu-

---

[1] See Scherer's classic (1970, 1980) treatment of the structure-conduct-performance framework.

[2] Industrial economists studying firm structure drew on streams of research originating with Coase (1937) and Chandler (1962, 1977, 1990); on current work, see Hart (1995).

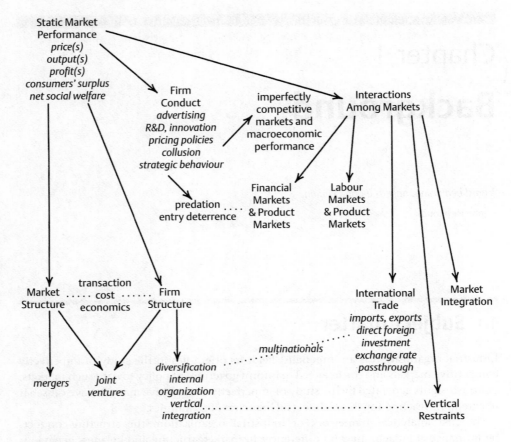

Fig. 1.1 Topics in industrial organization

sion and of strategic behaviour by dominant firms. The analysis of pricing policies in imperfectly competitive markets links industrial organization and macroeconomics.

Going in another direction, the analysis of firm conduct led to the topic of technological progress and dynamic market performance.[3] Drawing on applications of game theory to the analysis of strategic behaviour in situations of imperfect information, the analysis of firm conduct led to the study of strategic behaviour intended to influence market structure and rivals' conduct. This in turn leads to questions that focus on relationships between product markets and other types of markets—financial markets, labour markets, markets for wholesale and retail distribution services. Relations among imperfectly competitive international markets also fall within the field of industrial organization. So do questions of market integration, a topic of particular importance for the European Community.[4]

---

[3] On which, see Schumpeter (1934, 1943/1975) and more popularly Galbraith (1952).

[4] Formally, the European Union is a broader entity of which the European Community is a part. It is the European Community that administers economic and competition policy, and for that reason we will generally refer to the EC rather than the EU in this book.

We will not attempt to cover all the topics indicated in Figure 1.1.[5] In the remainder of this chapter, we examine the concepts of markets and market structure, review the basic microeconomic models of perfect competition and of monopoly, and introduce EC competition policy. In Chapter 2 we introduce the oligopoly models that are the building blocks of the analysis of imperfectly competitive markets. Chapters 3 and 4 deal with collusion and dominant firm behaviour, respectively. Chapter 5 looks at the determinants of technological progress. Chapter 6 examines the determinants of market structure, as well as mergers and joint ventures and their implications for market performance. Chapters 7, 8, and 9 examine the implications of imperfectly competitive international markets for market performance and for public policy. Finally, Chapter 10 takes up questions related to market integration in the European Community.

1.2 Markets and market structure

It would not be quite right to say that "market" is an undefined term in economics, but it is often an unexamined one.[6] Here we discuss how one might draw market boundaries from a general economic point of view; in Section 3.6 we take up the same question in the context of EC competition policy.

In an early and influential discussion, Cournot (1838; 1927, pp. 51–2) characterized the geographic bounds of the market in terms of the tendency of price to converge to a single value:

It is well known that by market economists mean, not a certain place where purchases and sales are carried on, but the entire territory of which the parts are so united by the relations of unrestricted commerce that prices there take the same level throughout, with ease and rapidity.

Cournot's approach of defining the geographic market as the area within which price assumed a single value was taken up by Marshall (1920, p. 325), who brought differences in the cost of servicing different regions into the picture:

Thus the more nearly perfect a market is, the stronger is the tendency for the same price to be paid for the same thing at the same time in all parts of the market: but of course if the market is large, allowance must be made for the expense of delivering the goods to different purchasers; each of whom must be supposed to pay in addition to the market price a special charge on account of delivery.

What Marshall offers is not a standard for defining the geographic scope of markets in general, but rather a standard for defining the geographic scope of what we would now call a perfectly competitive market. For Marshall (1920, p. 112):

A perfect market is a district, small or large, in which there are many buyers and sellers all so keenly

---

[5] In particular, we will not discuss the interaction between product markets and labour markets or the impact of imperfect competition on macroeconomic performance.

[6] See, however, Phlips (1962), who considers the question of market definition in the context of integrating markets, and Fingleton et al. (1999, pp. 66–76) for a survey.

on the alert and so well acquainted with one another's affairs that the price of a commodity is always practically the same for the whole of the district.

As a field, industrial organization interests itself particularly in imperfectly competitive markets. For many purposes, it might be sensible to regard regions with different net prices (that is, after making adjustments for different costs of supply) as part of a single *imperfectly competitive* market. Marshall's approach does not come to grips with the need to define the scope of imperfectly competitive markets.

In one of the seminal works on product differentiation, Robinson (1933, p. 17) broached the subject of product market definition, but in the end fell back on homogeneity—that is, the lack of differentiation—as an essential characteristic of a product market:

(a) A *commodity* is a consumable good, arbitrarily demarcated from other kinds of goods, but which may be regarded for practical purposes as homogeneous within itself.

(b) An *industry* is any group of firms producing a single commodity. The correspondence of such an industry to the industries of the real world is not perhaps very close. But in some cases, where a commodity in the real world is bounded on all sides by a marked gap between itself and its closest substitutes, the real-world firms producing this real-world commodity will conform to the definition of an industry sufficiently closely to make the discussion of industries in this technical sense of some interest.

For many purposes, insistence on homogeneity as a characteristic of a product market will lead to excessively narrow definitions of the product market.

Chamberlin (1933, pp. 56–7), Robinson's great contemporary, writes of products rather than markets, and essentially defines product differentiation by negation: products are differentiated if they are not standardized. Thus (1933, p. 57) "virtually all products are

Table 1.1 NACE Industry 15.5.

Code	Title
15	Manufacture of food products and beverages
15.5	Manufacture of dairy products
15.51	Operation of dairies and cheese making;
includes:	production of fresh liquid milk, pasteurized, sterilized, homogenized and/or ultra heat treated
	production of cream from fresh liquid milk, pasteurized, sterilized, homogenized
	manufacture of dried or concentrated milk whether or not sweetened
	production of butter
	production of yoghurt
	production of cheese and curd
	production of whey
	production of casein or lactose
15.52	Manufacture of ice cream
includes	production of ice cream and other edible ice such as sorbet

Source: EC Commission (1996)

differentiated, at least slightly". For Chamberlin, when products are differentiated (1933, p. 10) "each producer throughout the group has a market at least partially distinct from those of the others". In the presence of product differentiation, each variety has a market that is to some extent its own.

> *Market definition: a market* is usually defined as a region within which and a group of varieties for which prices tend to equality, adjusting prices for differences in cost of supply and for differences in product characteristics.

1.2.1 Industry classification schemes

For many practical purposes, one will wish to compare the structures of several different product or geographic markets, or examine changes over time in the structure of a single market. What is called for then are measures of market structure that are collected, classified, and reported in a consistent way for a wide range of comparably-defined industries.

To meet this need, government statistical agencies report descriptive information about economic activity, including market structure, according to standardized systems of classifying the activities of firms into industries. For the European Union, it is the NACE classification scheme that provides such a framework.[7]

To illustrate the structure of the NACE classification, Table 1.1 lists descriptive information for NACE category 15, manufacture of food products and beverages. NACE category 15 is divided into nine three-digit subcategories, one of which is NACE category 15.1, operation of dairies and cheese making. This in turn is further subdivided into two sub-categories. One of these, 15.52 (manufacture of ice cream) is fairly homogeneous and might very well correspond to a market, at the manufacturing level, in an economic sense. The other category, 15.51 (operation of dairies and cheese making) includes products which for most purposes would probably be considered part of distinct economic markets (milk and cheese, for example).

As this example illustrates, government industry classification schemes tend to be highly aggregated. They also tend to be defined in terms of factors related to the supply side of markets. This is natural, given that it is businesses, suppliers, that provide the underlying information from which official statistics are prepared. But the proper definition of economic markets involves interactions between consumers and suppliers, and in many cases official industry statistics, even those available at the least aggregated level, combine activities of suppliers that operate in what must by any reasonable standard be considered different economic markets.[8]

---

[7] NACE is an acronym for "nomenclature générale des activités économiques dans les Communautés Européennes". It is described in EC Commission (1996). The corresponding scheme for the United States, the Standard Industrial Classification, is described in US Department of Commerce (1987).

[8] Sutton (1997, p. 50) writes that "at the [4- or 5-digit] level of aggregation, markets tend to contain large numbers of more or less independent submarkets". See also Werden (1988).

1.2.2 **Measures of supply-side market structure**

We now look at the way economists describe the supply side of imperfectly competitive markets. The elements of market structure that we consider—principally, market share, the seller concentration ratio, and the Herfindahl index—are important factors explaining market performance. They are also widely used in empirical research and in competition policy guidelines.

In principle, market share is measured in terms of physical units. If crude oil is a homogeneous commodity, if q_1 is Exxon's output of crude oil over a certain time period, and if Q is world output of crude oil over the same time period, then Exxon's share of the world oil market is[9]

$$s_1 = \frac{q_1}{Q}. \tag{1.1}$$

Very often products are not homogeneous and physical measures of output are unavailable. When products are differentiated, even if physical measures of output were available, they would not be directly comparable. It would not make sense to add together the number of apples and the number of oranges sold in a given area over a given time period and call the sum the supply of fruit.

As a practical matter, market shares are often measured in terms of value. Thus if n firms supply a market, selling amounts $q_1, q_2, \ldots, q_n$, at prices $p_1, p_2, \ldots, p_n$, respectively, it will often be possible to measure the sales revenue of each firm, $p_1 q_1, p_2 q_2, \ldots, p_n q_n$, and then to calculate the market share of firm 1 as[10]

$$\sigma_1 = \frac{p_1 q_1}{p_1 q_1 + p_2 q_2 + \ldots + p_n q_n}. \tag{1.2}$$

For some industries—those with active trade associations that collect and publish sales data, those that are the objects of government investigation, or regulated industries—it is possible to identify virtually all supplying firms and measure their physical output and/or sales revenue. For such industries, it is possible to construct an essentially complete description of the distribution of firms' market shares.

For example, Table 1.2 lists 1997 sales revenue and market shares of cars and light trucks by supplier in three regional markets—Western Europe, Japan, and North America. When this sort of information is available, it provides a complete description of the structure of the supply side of a market.[11]

When such detailed information about the output of individual firms is not available, public sources of data often resort to summary descriptive measures of the distribution of firm size and market shares on the supply side of a market. Even when more detailed information is available, summary measures of supply side market structure are useful for comparisons across time or across industries.

---

[9] For this example, assume that if the product market is crude oil, the appropriate geographic market is the world.

[10] This is what is done for Table 1.2. What is reported there is the market share of each auto manufacturer in each region, based on revenue for sales of the many differentiated models produced by that manufacturer.

[11] We continue the discussion of firm size distributions in particular industries in Section 6.4.1.

Table 1.2 1997 new car and light truck sales (1,000s) and regional shares.

Western Europe			Japan			North America		
Firm	Sales	%	Firm	Sales	%	Firm	Sales	%
VW	2296	17.11	Toyota	1991	29.59	GM	4713	31.09
Fiat	1631	12.16	Nissan	1034	15.36	Ford	3817	25.18
GM/Opel	1601	11.93	Honda	772	11.47	Chrysler	2304	15.20
PSA	1510	11.26	Mitsubishi	679	10.09	Toyota	1230	8.11
Ford	1505	11.22	Suzuki	596	8.85	Honda	940	6.20
Renault	1320	9.84	Daihatsu	448	6.66	Nissan	728	4.80
BMW	819	6.10	Mazda	316	4.69	Mazda	222	1.46
Mercedes	492	3.67	Fuji	305	4.54	VW	172	1.13
Nissan	399	2.97	Isuzu	123	1.83	Subaru	134	0.88
Toyota	373	2.78	Imports	365	5.43	BMW	122	0.81
Volvo	231	1.72	Hino	45	0.66	Mercedes-Benz	122	0.81
Honda	215	1.60	Nissan Diesel	30	0.45	Volvo	91	0.60
Mazda	186	1.39	Other	26	0.39	Saab	28	0.19
Mitsubishi	176	1.31				Other Japanese	310	2.04
Hyundai	147	1.10				Korean	169	1.11
Suzuki	120	0.89				Other European	58	0.38
Chrysler	88	0.66						
Subaru	45	0.34						
Kia	37	0.28						
Daihatsu	35	0.26						
Porsche	17	0.13						
Lada	14	0.10						
Other	160	1.18						
Total	13417		Total	6370		Total	13918	
H		0.1011	H		0.1543	H		0.1970
1/H		9.89	1/H		6.48	1/H		5.08

Source: Automotive News 1998 Market Data Book

The most commonly reported summary measures of supply-side market structure are the m-firm seller concentration ratio and the Herfindahl index. The m-firm seller concentration ratio is the combined market share of the largest m firms in the market. If s_i is firm i's market share, and firms are numbered so that firm 1 is the largest firm, firm 2 the second largest, and so on, then the m-firm seller concentration ratio is the sum of the market shares of the largest m firms:

$$CRm = s_1 + s_2 + \ldots + s_m. \tag{1.3}$$

Governments commonly report the combined market shares of several firms as a way of providing some information about supply-side market structure without revealing the market shares of individual firms. This commitment to confidentiality makes it easier to get the cooperation of firms in providing information to the government. But a result is that much detail about the size distribution of firms is masked within the single number that is reported.

For example, an industry supplied by one firm with 65 per cent of the market, three firms with 5 per cent each, and 20 firms each with 1 per cent market shares would have a four-firm seller concentration ratio $CR4 = 80$. But $CR4 = 80$ could also mean that an industry is supplied by five firms, each with a 20 per cent market share. The implications of the two alternative market share distributions for market performance would be quite different, the first case a market with a dominant firm and the second a small-numbers oligopoly.

The Herfindahl or H-index[12] is the sum of squares of market shares of all firms in the industry:

$$H = s_1^2 + s_2^2 + \ldots + s_n^2, \tag{1.4}$$

where n is the total number of firms in the industry. The H-index has the desirable characteristic of combining information about the market shares of all firms in the industry without revealing the market share of any individual firm. The H-index arises naturally in many oligopoly models (see equation 2.36 and the associated text).

To understand some of the properties of the seller concentration ratio and the H-index, consider two industries, each supplied by 10 firms, with the market share distributions given in Table 1.3.

The first industry is supplied by ten firms, each with a 10 per cent market share. The 4-firm seller concentration ratio is 40 per cent. This conveys some information: if $CR4 = 40$, we can be reasonably sure that there is no dominant firm, and we also know that there is not atomistic competition. But if $CR4 = 40$, it might be that the industry is supplied by one firm with $\frac{1}{3}$ or more of the market and a host of small firms, or it might be that the industry is supplied by 10 firms of the same size (as is the case in this example). If all we know is that $CR4 = 40$, we are not able to say which case is more likely.

When there are 10 equally-sized firms, the H-index is $\frac{1}{10}$ and $\frac{1}{H} = 10$. If there are n equally-sized firms in an industry, then $H = \frac{1}{n}$ and $\frac{1}{H} = n$. For this reason, the inverse of the H-index is said to be a *numbers-equivalent* measure of seller concentration.

If there are two equally sized firms, $H = \frac{1}{2}$ and $\frac{1}{H} = 2$. If there are three equally-sized firms, $H = \frac{1}{3}$ and $\frac{1}{H} = 3$. If the H-index for an industry is $\frac{1}{3}$, we can say that the industry is as concentrated as an industry with three equally-sized firms, even though many other combinations of market shares can produce an H-index of $\frac{1}{3}$.

Table 1.3 Seller concentration measures examples.

Industry	Market Shares	CR4	H	$\frac{1}{H}$
1	$s_1 = s_2 = \ldots = s_{10} = 10\%$	40	0.100	10.000
2	$s_1 = 91\%, s_2 = \ldots = s_{10} = 1\%$	94	0.829	1.206

---

[12] The H-index is due, in economics at least, to Hirschman (1945) and Herfindahl (1950); see Hirschman (1964).

Thus if $s_1 = s_2 = s_3 = \frac{1}{3}$, $H = \frac{1}{3}$ and $\frac{1}{H} = 3$. But if there are four firms in the industry, firm 1 with a market share of 0.4, firms 2 and 3 with identical market shares of 0.2943 each, and firm 4 with a market share of 0.0012, the H index is also $\frac{1}{3}$ and $\frac{1}{H} = 3$. From a numbers-equivalent point of view, we would say that an industry supplied by four firms with the indicated market shares is as concentrated as an industry supplied by three equally-sized firms.

For the second industry in Table 1.3, the information that $CR4 = 94$ allows a wide range of possibilities. The industry could be supplied by four firms of roughly equal size and a fringe of small firms or (as in this example) by a dominant firm and a fringe of small firms. The H-index, 0.829, is close to 1, and $\frac{1}{H} = 1.206$. This allows us to say that the industry is as concentrated as an industry supplied by 1.2 equally-sized firms, and by this we mean that supply-side concentration is closer to monopoly than duopoly, even though there are 10 active firms in the market.

Table 4.1 reports approximate concentration measures for several EC 2-digit NACE industries. The concentration measures are constructed using data for a sample of 309 large EC firms. Despite that fact that most industrial economists would not consider 2-digit classifications to represent industries in an economic sense, concentration measures were calculated at the two-digit industry to allow for the fact that most of the firms are diversified into several less aggregated (three- or four-digit) industries.[13]

The concentration measures given in Table 1.4 suggest that even among large firms, there is typically substantial inequality in firm size. In NACE industry 22, for example,

Table 1.4 Concentration statistics for selected NACE industries, EC, 1994.

NACE code	Title	C1	C4	C10	H	$\frac{1}{H}$	n
22	Production and preliminary processing of metals	17.2	41.6	69.4	0.069	14.4	28
24	Manufacture of non-metalic mineral products	25.2	59.3	86.7	0.119	8.4	16
25	Chemical industry	9.0	29.9	53.5	0.040	24.7	50
31	Manufacture of metal articles	20.3	54.5	82.0	0.105	9.5	18
32	Mechanical engineering	21.0	47.1	69.9	0.089	11.3	27
34	Electrical engineering	24.9	62.1	87.4	0.127	7.9	22
35	Manufacture of motor vehicles and of motor vehicle parts and accessories	19.5	56.7	89.5	0.108	9.2	22
41/42	Food, drink and tobacco industry	16.1	43.2	62.2	0.067	15.9	51
47	Manufacture of paper and paper products, printing and publishing	7.9	28.2	55.5	0.043	23.3	32
50	Building and civil engineering	17.0	41.5	62.6	0.063	15.8	40

Source: EC Commission (1997)

[13] Publishing *C1*, the market share of the largest firm supplying the market, defeats the purpose of maintaining confidentiality about information pertaining to individual firms. The statistics in Table 1.4 were assembed from publicly available data sources (EC Commission, 1997, p. 70).

the largest of the 28 large firms in the sample has a market share of slightly more than 17 per cent. The 10 largest firms have a combined market share of nearly 70 per cent, indicating that the smallest 18 firms divide the remaining 30 per cent of sales.

The numbers-equivalent measure for industry 22 is 14.4, roughly half the number of firms in the sample. The numbers-equivalent measures reported in Table 1.4 are all substantially less than the actual number of firms. Industries 25 and 47 are the least concentrated, and industries 24 and 34 the most concentrated.[14]

Table 1.2 reports Herfindahl indices and numbers-equivalents for three regional markets in the world automobile industry. Although there are more than 22 active suppliers in Western Europe, the market has an H-index of about $\frac{1}{10}$, the same as an industry supplied by 10 equally-sized firms. The Japanese market, with more than 10 domestic suppliers, has the H-index of an industry supplied by between six and seven equally-sized firms. In terms of the H-index, the North American market is the most concentrated of the three, with a numbers-equivalent of slightly more than 5.[15]

Supply side market structure: summary measures of *the number and size distribution of firms* include *concentration ratios* (the combined market shares of the largest firms in the industry) and the *H*-index (the sum of squares of the market shares of all firms in the industry).

1.3 Perfect competition and monopoly

1.3.1 Perfect competition

The abstract model of a perfectly competitive market makes the assumptions that:

(a) there are many small buyers and sellers;

(b) with complete and perfect knowledge of market conditions;

(c) dealing in a standardized product;

(d) with free and easy entry into and exit from the market.

Market demand

We also assume that each individual consumer maximizes his or her own welfare, subject to a budget constraint. With the kind of partial equilibrium analysis that is typical of

---

[14] The industries used in Table 1.4 are defined at a highly aggregated level in terms of products and their geographic coverage is the EU as a whole. It seems likely that seller concentration in less aggregated product and geographic markets will be higher than the figures reported in Table 1.4.

[15] The H-index for Western Europe was computed assuming that "Other" sales were by firms the same size as Lada, the smallest identified firm. The H-index for Japan was computed treating "Imports" sales as if made by a single firm and "Other" sales as if made by a single firm. The H-index for the United States was computed treating "Other Japanese" sales as if made by a single firm and "Other European" sales as if made by a single firm.

industrial organization, we usually summarize the demand side of the market with an aggregate demand function showing the relationship between price p and quantity demanded Q. In general, such an aggregate demand function can be written

$$p = f(Q). \qquad (1.5)$$

The demand function in equation (1.5) is said to be written in *inverse form* because it shows the price that corresponds to each quantity demanded, not the quantity demanded for each price.

As an example, a linear demand function (shown in Figure 1.2) is

$$p = 100 - Q. \qquad (1.6)$$

In this case, 10 units of output are demanded if $p = 90$, 20 units of output are demanded if $p = 80$, and so on.

For any particular demand function, *the price elasticity of demand*—loosely, the percentage change in quantity demanded in response to a given percentage change in price—tells us how sensitive the quantity demanded is to price:

$$\varepsilon_{Qp} = -\frac{\Delta Q / Q}{\Delta p / p} \approx -\frac{p}{Q} \frac{dQ}{dp}. \qquad (1.7)$$

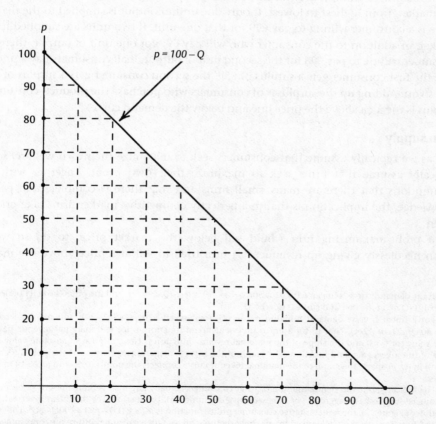

Fig. 1.2 Linear market demand curve

Here $-dQ/dp$ is the absolute value of the slope of the inverse demand curve.[16]

Marginal revenue is the change in total revenue in response to a small change in output,

$$MR = \frac{d(pQ)}{dQ} = p + Q\frac{dp}{dQ}.$$ (1.8)

Intuitively, marginal revenue is the revenue received from selling an extra unit of output at price p minus (the slope of the demand curve, dQ/dp, is negative) the revenue given up on units of output that could have been sold at a slightly higher price.

From (1.7) and (1.8), there is a relationship between marginal revenue and the price elasticity of demand:[17]

$$MR = p + Q\frac{dp}{dQ} = p\left(1 + \frac{Q\,dp}{p\,dQ}\right) = p\left(1 - \frac{1}{\varepsilon_{Qp}}\right).$$ (1.9)

Consumers' surplus is the difference between the maximum amount consumers would pay for a given amount of output and the amount that they actually pay.

For the linear inverse demand function (1.6), holding incomes and the prices of all other goods constant, think of consumers as being placed along the quantity axis in order of the maximum amount they would be willing to pay for the next unit of output put on the market, from highest to lowest. If only one unit of output is supplied to the market, there is a consumer willing to pay €99 for that one unit. If two units are supplied to the market, in addition to the consumer who will pay €99 for one unit of output, there is a consumer willing to pay €98 for the second unit of output. If all consumers pay a price of €40, the first consumer gets a surplus of €59, the second consumer gets a surplus of €58, and so on. Adding up the surpluses of consumers who purchase the product, consumers' surplus is the area above the price line and below the demand curve.[18]

Firm supply

Just as we typically assume that consumers seek to maximize their own welfare, so we typically assume that firms seek to maximize their own profit. Together with the assumptions that there are many small firms and that there is complete and perfect knowledge, the implication is that in a perfectly competitive market firms take price as given.

No profit-maximizing firm would sell below the market price; to do so would mean needlessly giving up revenue. If a firm tried to sell at a price above the market

---

[16] If the demand curve is linear, with equation $p = a - bQ$, then $dQ/dp = -b$ and the price-elasticity of demand at a point (Q,p) on the demand curve is $\varepsilon_{Qp} = bp/Q$.

[17] For a linear inverse demand function $p = a - bQ$, total revenue is $pQ = aQ - bQ^2$ and marginal revenue $MR = d(pQ)/dQ = a - 2bQ$. That is, for a linear inverse demand function, price and marginal revenue have the same value for $Q = 0$ and the slope of the marginal revenue function is twice as great in absolute value as the slope of the inverse demand function. The graph of the inverse demand curve connects the points $(0, a)$ and $(a/b, 0)$ in (Q, p)-space; the graph of the marginal revenue curve connects the points $(0, a)$ and $(a/2b, 0)$ in (Q, p)-space.

[18] Heuristically, one can define the sum of what consumers actually pay for a certain amount of output and consumers' surplus as an aggregate or representative consumer utility function. For the linear inverse demand function of Figure 1.2, the representative consumer utility function is $pQ + \frac{1}{2}(100 - p)Q = 100Q - \frac{1}{2}Q^2$. The market demand function can then be derived by maximizing the representative consumer utility function subject to a budget constraint.

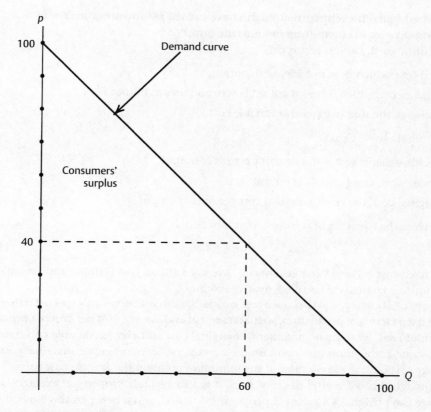

Fig. 1.3 Consumers' surplus, $p = 40$

level, consumers would simply go elsewhere (consumers have complete and perfect knowledge) so the firm would sell nothing. A profit-maximizing firm picks the output that maximizes its own profit, taking market price as given.

Since the firm is a price taker, its revenue, pq, depends on the amount it sells. Since profit is the difference between revenue and economic cost,

$$\pi = pq - C(q), \tag{1.10}$$

what the profit-maximizing output level is for a particular firm depends on the way its economic costs $C(q)$ vary with its output q.

A firm's cost of supplying a particular output level includes all its payments to inputs used to produce the output. This includes wages paid to workers, the cost of supplies (fuel, raw materials), and the rental cost of fixed assets. The latter cost includes a normal rate of return on investment, which marks a difference between economic cost and accounting cost.

Thus if the rate of return on investment in a safe asset is 10 per cent, and the accounting rate of return on stockholders' equity for a firm is 9 per cent, the economic rate of return on stockholders' equity in the firm is −1 per cent: stockholders are losing money compared with the return they might have earned by investing in a safe asset, the opportunity cost of committing funds to the firm.[19]

We distinguish various cost types:[20]

- fixed cost, which does not vary with output;
- variable cost, which is zero if output is zero and rises as output rises;
- total cost, the sum of fixed and variable cost;

and from these we derive:

- average variable cost, variable cost per unit of output;
- average cost, cost per unit of output; and
- marginal cost, the change in total cost per unit of output.[21]

If we write the equation of the firm's cost function as

$$C(q) = F + c(q), \tag{1.11}$$

then fixed cost is F and variable cost $c(q)$. Average variable cost is $c(q)/q$, and average cost $[F + c(q)]/q$. Marginal cost is the derivative $dc(q)/dq$.

Figure 1.4 shows typical ∪-shaped cost curves.[22] Such cost curves are expected if there are some fixed factors of production, so that marginal and average cost per unit of output rise as output rises. By standard arguments, marginal cost and average variable cost have the same value at the minimum point on the average variable cost curve; marginal cost and average cost have the same value at the minimum point on the average cost curve.[23]

Although this is a matter of economics, it is also a simple property of averages. If the average (say) height of a group of people is calculated, and a new person who is shorter than the previous average is added to the group, the new average height will be less than the old average height. If a new person who is taller than the previous average height is added to the group, the new average height will be greater than the old average height. If a new person who is exactly the average height is added to the group, the new average will be the same as the old average height. In the same way, if marginal cost is below average cost, average cost is falling; if marginal cost is above average cost, average cost is rising; and if marginal cost equals average cost, average cost is at its minimum value. Similar arguments apply to average variable cost.

The short-run output decision of a profit-maximizing firm involves the relationship between marginal cost, average variable cost, and price (which the firm takes as given). If a firm is producing an output that makes its marginal cost less than price, the firm will increase profit by expanding output. If a firm is producing an output that makes its

---

[19] The opportunity cost of investing in a firm also depends on the economic rate of depreciation of the firm's assets, the rate of change of the price of capital assets, and various aspects of the tax system.

[20] For some purposes, particularly the analysis of entry and exit decisions, we need to consider whether costs are sunk or not. The cost of investing in a tangible or intangible capital asset is sunk if the value of the asset cannot be recovered by resale upon exit from the market. Costs may be fixed but not sunk or sunk but not fixed; see Problems 6–1 and 6–2.

[21] Since variable cost is the only portion of total cost that changes as output changes, it is also correct to define marginal cost as the change in variable cost as output changes.

[22] Figure 1.4 is drawn for the cubic cost function $C(q) = 1 + 9q - q^2 + q^3$.

[23] This is what Samuelson calls the Viner-Wu theorem; see Viner (1931).

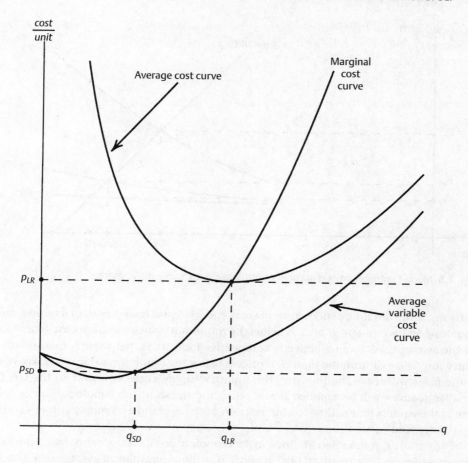

Fig. 1.4 Firm cost curves

marginal cost greater than price, the firm will increase profit by reducing output. When the firm produces an output that makes its marginal cost equal to price, it is maximizing its short-run profit.

This conclusion holds provided price is greater than average variable cost, in which case the firm will make enough money selling the product to pay all its variable costs and at least some of its fixed cost. If price is below the minimum value of average variable cost, the firm's profit-maximizing choice is to shut down (to produce zero output). The short-run supply function of a firm in a perfectly competitive industry is the firm's marginal cost function, for prices at or above the minimum value of average variable cost. For lower prices, the quantity supplied by a profit-maximizing firm is zero.

In any short-run time period, the industry supply function is the sum of the supply functions of the firms in the industry. Figure 1.5 shows three short-run industry supply curves, for 25, 50, and 90 firms respectively, if all firms have cost curves of the kind shown in Figure 1.4. The short-run equilibrium price, the price that clears the market, is the price at which the demand curve and the short-run supply curve intersect.

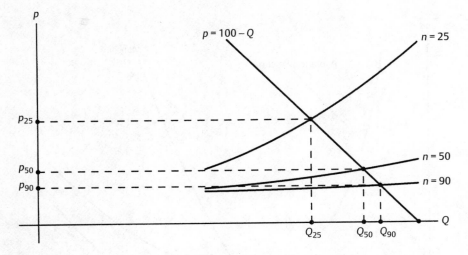

Fig. 1.5 Market equilibrium and number of firms, perfectly competitive market

In any short-run time period, firms make economic losses (earn less than a normal rate of return on investment) if price is below the minimum value of average cost. Since one of the assumptions about a perfectly competitive industry is that there is free and easy entry into and exit from the market, if price is below the minimum value of average cost some firms will leave the industry, the industry supply curve will shift to the left (a smaller quantity will be supplied at any price) and the short-run equilibrium price will rise as the equilibrium point—the intersection of the demand and supply curves—shifts up the demand curve.

In any short-run time period, firms make economic profits (earn more than a normal rate of return on investment) if price is above the minimum value of average cost. Short-run economic profits will attract new firms into the industry, the industry supply curve will shift to the right (a greater quantity will be supplied at any price) and the short-run equilibrium price will fall as the equilibrium point shifts down the demand curve. The equilibrating process of exit or entry ends—firms earn a normal rate of return on investment and only a normal rate of return on investment—when equilibrium price equals the minimum value of average cost.

In the long-run equilibrium of a *perfectly competitive market*, each firm produces an output that makes its marginal cost equal to price (each firm maximizes profit), and price equals average economic cost, which includes a normal rate of return on investment (no incentive for entry or exit).

1.3.2 **Monopoly**

A market is a monopoly if it is supplied by a single firm, without the possibility of entry. With one difference, the logic behind a monopolist's output decision is the same as the logic behind the output decision of a firm in a perfectly competitive industry. The difference is that a firm in a perfectly competitive industry is a price taker: if it sells one unit more or less, its revenue changes by the price of the good.

A monopolist is a price maker: if it sells one unit more or less, its revenue changes by marginal revenue, which is less than price. Thus if the monopolist is producing an output that makes its marginal cost less than its marginal revenue, the monopolist will increase profit by expanding output; if the monopolist is producing an output that makes its marginal cost greater than its marginal revenue, the monopolist will increase profit by reducing output; if the monopolist is producing an output that makes its marginal revenue equal to its marginal cost, the monopolist is maximizing its profit.

Compared with the long-run equilibrium of an otherwise identical perfectly competitive industry, the monopolist restricts output and raises price. One result is that the monopolist earns economic profit

$$\pi_m = p_m q_m - C(q_m) \tag{1.12}$$

(where q_m is profit-maximizing monopoly output and p_m is the corresponding monopoly price).

This monopoly profit is an income transfer from consumers to the owners of firms. If consumers and owners are both members of the same society and if the income of all citizens is given equal weight, this monopoly profit is not a welfare loss from a social point of view.[24]

Another result of monopoly output restriction is that consumers do not spend

$$c(Q_c - q_m) \tag{1.13}$$

in the monopolized industry (where Q_c would be long-run output if the market were perfectly competitive). Instead, they spend this amount in other markets. If other markets are perfectly competitive, this is not a welfare loss from a social point of view, it is simply a transfer of spending from one market to others.[25]

Consumers also lose the consumers' surplus that they would have enjoyed on the output,

$$Q_c - q_m, \tag{1.14}$$

that would have been produced in long-run perfectly competitive equilibrium but is not produced under monopoly. Graphically (Figure 1.6), this lost consumers' surplus is the area below the demand curve, above the marginal cost curve, and to the right of monopoly output. If consumers and producers are all members of the same society and

---

[24] It should be kept in mind that in modern industrial societies, business ownership and economic profits are often widely distributed among a large group of shareholders, each one of which has only a small ownership share (Berle and Means, 1932/1968). "Consumers" and "owners" are overlapping groups.

[25] We usually assume that other markets can be treated as if they are perfectly competitive, which allows us to take a partial equilibrium approach. If other markets are not perfectly competitive, we are in the world of second-best welfare economics; see Lipsey and Lancaster (1956–57).

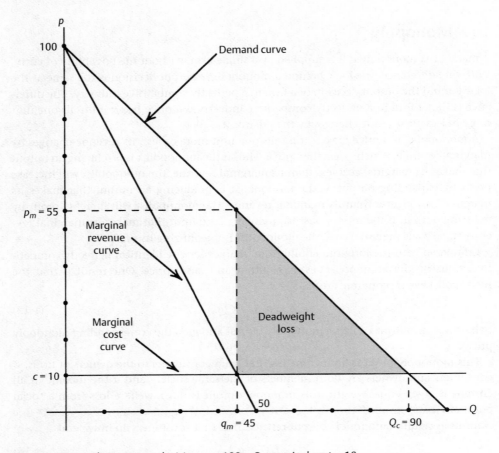

Fig. 1.6 Monopolist's output decision, $p = 100 - Q$, marginal cost $= 10$

the interests of consumers and producers are given equal weight, it is this lost consumers' surplus that is the social welfare loss due to monopoly, and it is called the *deadweight welfare loss* (DWL) due to the exercise of monopoly power.[26,27]

Since price is equal to marginal cost in the long-run equilibrium of a perfectly competi-

[26] The origin of the adjective *deadweight* in the term deadweight welfare loss is unclear. Hotelling (1938, p. 256) refers to "dead loss"; Hicks (1941, p. 332) to "social loss"; Harberger (1954, p. 78) to "welfare loss". The term "deadweight welfare loss" does not seem to appear in the first or fourth editions of Samuelson's *Economics*, perhaps reflecting his reservations about the notion of consumers' surplus (1947, pp. 194–5); it is in the seventh edition (1967, p. 492).

[27] Empirical estimates of the deadweight welfare loss due to the exercise of market power in industrial economies are typically small; see Harberger (1954) for a seminal study, and Cowling and Mueller (1978), who attempt to take costs of acquiring and maintaining market power into account, and obtain somewhat larger estimates. Another static consequence of market power may be to permit firms to operate inefficiently; see Leibenstein (1966) and a large follow-on literature. Dynamically, there is the possibility that income transfers from consumers to the owners or shareholders of firms with market power would alter the distribution of wealth. Work by Siegfried and Roberts (1991), Blitz and Siegfried (1992), Siegfried and Round (1994), Siegfried, Blitz and Round (1995), and Hazledine and Siegfried (1997) suggests that the income redistribution effects of market power are not large in practice.

tive industry and price is greater than marginal cost under monopoly, it is natural to measure the impact of the exercise of market power on market performance by looking at the difference between monopoly price and marginal cost, $p - c$.

Measured in this way, the difference between price and marginal cost depends on currency units; to correct for this, it is usual to look at the ratio of price minus marginal cost to price,

$$\frac{p - c}{p}, \tag{1.15}$$

called the Lerner index of market power after Abba P. Lerner (1934), who first analyzed monopoly distortions in this way.

A monopolist maximizes profit by picking an output that makes marginal revenue equal to marginal cost,

$$MR = c. \tag{1.16}$$

From equation (1.9), we know that marginal revenue is related to price in terms of the price elasticity of demand,

$$MR = p\left(1 - \frac{1}{\varepsilon_{Qp}}\right). \tag{1.17}$$

Hence at the profit-maximizing monopoly output

$$p\left(1 - \frac{1}{\varepsilon_{Qp}}\right) = c, \text{ so that } \frac{p - c}{p} = \frac{1}{\varepsilon_{Qp}}. \tag{1.18}$$

A monopolist maximizes profit by producing an output that makes the Lerner index—the price-cost margin as a fraction of price—equal to the inverse of the price elasticity of demand.

The price elasticity of demand measures the sensitivity of the quantity demanded to changes in price. If the price elasticity of demand is high, a profit-maximizing monopolist will not raise price very much above marginal cost, because to do so would cause the quantity sold to fall a great deal. If the price elasticity of demand is low, the quantity demanded is not very sensitive to price, and a profit-maximizing monopolist will raise price substantially above marginal cost.

A profit-maximizing monopolist—a single supplier that does not face the threat of entry by competitors—maximizes profit by producing an output that makes marginal cost equal to marginal revenue. The resulting social cost is the deadweight welfare loss, consumers' surplus on output that would be produced in long-run competitive equilibrium but is not produced under monopoly.

1.4 **EC competition policy**

Since before the founding of the European Community, competition policy has been thought to be essential to European market integration, and therefore to European integration overall. In 1956, the Spaak Report, which anticipated the EC Treaty, said that (p. 55)

the treaty should provide the means to avoid situations in which monopoly practices block the fundamental objectives of the common market. In this regard, it is appropriate to prevent:

- market division by agreement among firms . . .;
- agreements to limit output or restrict technical progress . . .;
- the absorption or domination of the market for a product by a single firm . . .

In the beginning, the fundamental objection of EC competition policy to monopoly practices was not their economic effects—deadweight welfare loss—but the perception that they would block the process of market integration.

Provisions aiming to block collective monopoly practices appear in Article 81 of the EC Treaty.[28] Article 81(1) prohibits agreements that affect trade between the Member States and have the object or effect of preventing, restricting, or distorting competition on the ground that they are incompatible with the common market. Article 81(3) allows exceptions to the Article 81(1) prohibition for agreements that improve production or distribution, or promote technical or economic progress, provided among other conditions that a fair share of the benefits generated by the agreement goes to consumers. Under the EC Treaty, it is not illegal to have a dominant market position, but it is illegal, under Article 82, for one or more firms to abuse a dominant market position. Examples of behaviour that has been found to constitute such abuse include restricting output, price discrimination, and using a dominant position in one market to limit competition in another market.

The European Commission may fine firms that violate Article 81 or 82 up to 10 per cent of their annual turnover. The Commission may also order that offending behaviour be stopped.

Articles 81 and 82 of the EC Treaty deal with business conduct. The 1989 Merger Control Regulation[29] deals with market structure. It gives the European Commission authority over mergers and related types of business combinations that meet specified size and multinationality conditions. Under the merger control regulation, the Commission may block a proposed merger entirely, or permit a merger to go forward on terms different from those originally proposed.

Articles 86, 87, and 88 of the EC Treaty set rules for actions of the Member States toward the business sector. Article 86 says that EC competition policy applies to public enterprises

---

[28] The paragraphs of the EC Treaty were renumbered by the Treaty of Amsterdam. The current Articles 81 and 82 were originally Articles 85 and 86. In this book, we refer to treaty provisions by their current numbers, changing the text of older decisions and documents as necessary.

[29] Regulation (EEC) No 4064/89 OJ L395 30 December 1989, p. 1, amended by Regulation (EC) No 1310/97, OJ L180, 9 July 1997.

and to private enterprises that are given specific missions by a Member State. Article 87(1) prohibits Member State aid to business, if the aid distorts or threatens to distort competition. Article 87(3) allows exceptions to the Article 87(1) prohibition for aid that promotes regional and other specified types of development. Article 88 requires the Commission to monitor Member State aid systems to ensure continued compatibility with the common market.

The formal provisions of EC competition policy are enforced by the European Commission and interpreted by decisions of the Court of First Instance and the European Court of Justice, to which Commission decisions may be appealed. Important changes in the infrastructure for enforcement of competition policy are being implemented as the EU prepares for expansion to the East and for the deepening of integration with the single European currency.

The *EC Treaty* lays out the basic provisions of EC competition policy toward cooperative business behaviour (Article 81), dominant firm behaviour (Article 82), and Member State aid to business (Articles 87 and 88). The Merger Control Regulation provides for EC control of some kinds of changes in market structure.

Study points

- structure-conduct-performance paradigm (page 1)
- market definition (page 3)
- NACE industry classification (page 5)
- market share (page 6)
- seller concentration ratio (page 7), Herfindahl index (page 8)
- perfect competition (page 10)
- price elasticity of demand (page 11)
- marginal revenue (page 12)
- consumers' surplus (page 12)
- cost concepts (page 14)
- deadweight welfare loss (page 18)
- Lerner index of market power (page 19)
- Spaak Report (page 20), EC Treaty (page 20)

Problems

1-1 Find monopoly output, price, deadweight welfare loss, and the Lerner index if the market inverse demand curve is

$$p = 100 - Q \qquad (1.19)$$

and marginal cost is 10.

1-2 (a) Graph the average variable, average, and marginal cost curves if the cost function is

$$C(q) = 1 + 9q. \qquad (1.20)$$

1-3 (b) Graph the average variable, average, and marginal cost curves if the cost function is

$$C(q) = 1 + 9q - q^2 + q^3. \qquad (1.21)$$

Chapter 2
Oligopoly markets: noncooperative behaviour

Between the perfect competition and monopoly of theory lie the actual cases.

Hotelling (1929, p. 44).

2.1 Introduction

We begin with the first and still most common model of an imperfectly competitive market, the Cournot model of quantity-setting oligopoly, and its mirror-image counterpart, the Bertrand model of price-setting oligopoly. These models are the foundation of a vast library of models used to study specific types of markets, and the intuitions they support will carry us far in understanding the factors that determine the nature of market performance when markets are imperfectly competitive.

2.2 Cournot oligopoly

2.2.1 The basic model

The seminal model of oligopoly is due to Cournot (1838). He analyzed a very simple imperfectly competitive market: two producers of a standardized product—in Cournot's example, mineral water drawn from a common underground source. In this model, each firm knows the market demand curve, the two firms have identical costs, and each firm knows that the other firm knows as much about the market as it does.

Each firm picks its own output to maximize its own profit, knowing that the other firm acts in the same way and with the same information.[1]

Within this framework, Cournot began by asking the same questions that economists ask about perfectly competitive markets and about monopoly: what outputs will the firms produce, and at what price will the product sell?

What we require of an equilibrium pair of outputs is that each firm's equilibrium output maximizes its profit, given the equilibrium output of the other firm.[2] For such an output pair, each firm is making as large a profit as it possibly can, given what the other firm does. In view of Cournot's assumption that each firm seeks to maximize its own profit, neither firm would wish to alter its own part of such an output pair.

We begin the task of finding equilibrium outputs by characterizing the output that will maximize a firm's profit for an arbitrary output level of the other firm. The schedule of all such output pairs is called the firm's *best response function*. We then look for mutually consistent output levels on the best response functions of the two firms.

2.2.2 Best response functions

We will use a specific example to illustrate the Cournot model. In this example, the market inverse demand curve is

$$p = 100 - Q = 100 - (q_1 + q_2), \tag{2.1}$$

where q_1 is the output of firm 1 and q_2 is the output of firm 2.

The firms have identical cost functions, with constant average and marginal cost, 10 per unit of output:

$$C(q_1) = 10q_1 \qquad C(q_2) = 10q_2. \tag{2.2}$$

For simplicity, we assume that there are no fixed costs.

If firm 2 produces an arbitrary output level q_2, the relation between firm 1's output level q_1 and the market-clearing price p is

$$p = (100 - q_2) - q_1. \tag{2.3}$$

(2.3) is the equation of firm 1's *residual demand function*, so-called because it gives the relation between the quantity supplied by firm 1 and price in the part of market left for firm 1 after firm 2 has disposed of its output.

In this left-over part of the market, firm 1 is a monopolist, or at least, it acts as a monopolist, since firm 2's output is assumed to be fixed at the arbitrary level q_2. The output that maximizes a monopolist's profit is that which makes its marginal revenue equal to its marginal cost.

For a linear demand curve, the marginal revenue curve has the same price axis intercept

---

[1] As we will see, the Cournot model can be generalized to allow for more than two firms, for differentiated products, and in many other ways. Of Cournot's assumptions, the ones that are in some sense fundamental to the nature of the model are that firms have the same knowledge and unlimited analytical ability and the assumption that each firm independently maximizes its own profit.

[2] This is the Nash (1950) equilibrium. On the relation between the Cournot and Nash equilibrium concepts, see Leonard (1994).

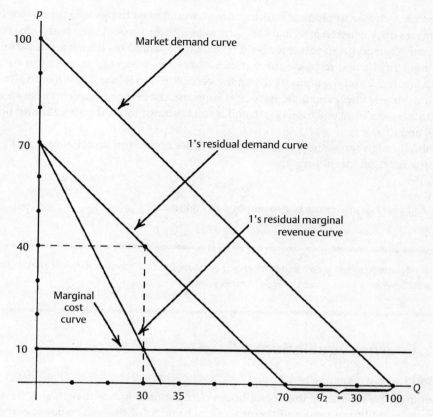

Fig. 2.1 Firm 1's output decision, $q_2 = 30$

as the demand curve (this is $100 - q_2$ for the residual demand curve (2.3)) and a slope that is twice as great in absolute value as the slope of the demand curve. The equation of firm 1's residual marginal revenue function is therefore

$$MR_1 = (100 - q_2) - 2q_1.$$ (2.4)

Firm 1's profit-maximizing output makes its marginal revenue equal to its marginal cost,

$$MR_1 = (100 - q_2) - 2q_1 = 10 = MC.$$ (2.5)

This is shown in Figure 2.1, which is drawn for $q_2 = 30$.

Equation (2.5) can be rewritten as

$$q_1 = \frac{1}{2}(90 - q_2) = 45 - \frac{1}{2}q_2.$$ (2.6)

Equation (2.6) is the equation of firm 1's *best response function* for this example: it gives the profit-maximizing output of firm 1 for any output level of firm 2.

To understand the shape of the best response curve, note that if firm 2 produces nothing, firm 1 is a monopolist, and maximizes profit by producing the monopoly output. To make firm 1 choose to produce nothing, firm 2 would need to produce the output level that makes price equal to marginal cost. Any sales by firm 1 would then push price below marginal cost and mean losses for both firms; firm 1 would maximize profit by selling nothing. Firm 1's best response curve thus includes the points $(q_m, 0)$ on the horizontal axis in Figure 2.2 and the point $(0, Q_c)$ on the vertical axis in Figure 2.2. When the inverse demand curve is linear and marginal cost is constant, the best response curve is a straight line (this is clear from equation (2.6)), and it can be drawn by connecting the two points $(q_m, 0)$ and $(0, Q_c)$.

Going through the same procedure for firm 2, we obtain the equation of firm 2's best response function for this example,

$$q_2 = 45 - \tfrac{1}{2}q_1. \tag{2.7}$$

Firm 2's best response curve is also graphed in Figure 2.2.

> *Best response function*: a firm's (quantity) *best response function* specifies its profit-maximizing output level for arbitrary output levels of other firms.

2.2.3 Cournot equilibrium

Outputs

When firms are producing their equilibrium outputs, each firm is maximizing its profit, given the equilibrium output of the other firm. In terms of the best response curve diagram (Figure 2.2), the equilibrium outputs are found at the intersection of the best response curves.

For this combination of outputs—and only at this combination of outputs—each firm is maximizing its own profit, given the output produced by the other firm.

Analytically, the values of the Cournot equilibrium outputs are found by solving the equations of the best response functions, here (2.6) and (2.7); this gives the coordinates of the point where the two best response curves intersect. Since this example is symmetric, in the sense that the two firms have identical cost functions and identical beliefs each about the other, the firms will produce identical output levels in equilibrium. Call this common equilibrium output q_{Cour} and set $q_1 = q_2 = q_{Cour}$ in (2.6) (the same result would be reached if we made the substitution in (2.7)). This allows us to find the Cournot equilibrium output per firm:

$$2q_{Cour} + q_{Cour} = 3q_{Cour} = 90,$$
$$q_{Cour} = 30. \tag{2.8}$$

Other characteristics of Cournot equilibrium

Other aspects of Cournot equilibrium that are of interest, in addition to the outputs of the individual firms, are:

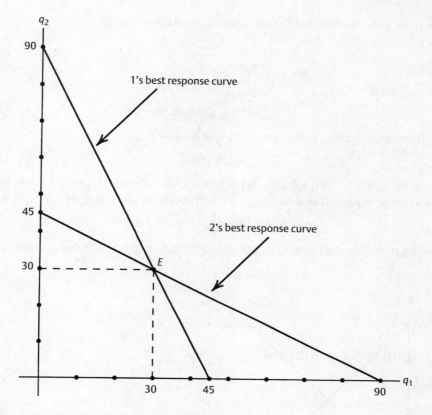

Fig. 2.2 Best response curves, Cournot duopoly

- total output;
- price;
- the degree of market power;
- economic profit;
- consumers' surplus;
- deadweight welfare loss.

These can all be determined in a straightforward way from the equilibrium outputs.

Adding the outputs of the two firms gives total output:

$$Q_{Cour} = 2q_{Cour} = 60. \tag{2.9}$$

Cournot equilibrium output is greater than monopoly output (45), but less than long-run competitive equilibrium output (90).

From the equation of the inverse demand curve, the Cournot equilibrium price is

$$p_{Cour} = 100 - 60 = 40 = 10 + 30. \tag{2.10}$$

This is greater than marginal cost (10), but less than the monopoly price (55).

In Cournot equilibrium, the Lerner index of market power is

$$\frac{p_{Cour} - c}{p_{Cour}} = \frac{40 - 10}{40} = \tfrac{3}{4}. \tag{2.11}$$

Profit per firm is

$$\pi_{Cour} = (p_{Cour} - 10)q_{Cour} = (30)(30) = 900. \tag{2.12}$$

Since there are two firms, total economic profit is twice π_{Cour}:

$$2\pi_{Cour} = 1800. \tag{2.13}$$

Consumers' surplus (CS) is the area of the triangle the sides of which are formed by the demand curve, the horizontal line $p_{Cour} = 40$, and the price axis (see Figure 2.3). This area is

$$CS = \tfrac{1}{2}(100 - 40)(60) = \tfrac{1}{2}(60)^2 = 1800. \tag{2.14}$$

Deadweight welfare loss (DWL) is the area of the triangle with sides formed by the

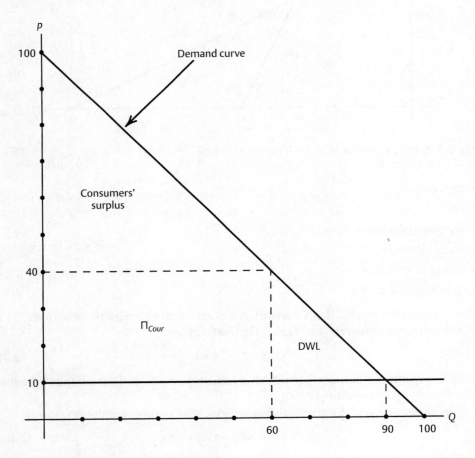

Fig. 2.3 Market equilibrium, Cournot duopoly

demand curve, the marginal and average cost line, and the vertical line $Q_{Cour} = 60$. This area of this triangle is

$$DWL = \tfrac{1}{2}(40 - 10)(90 - 60) = \tfrac{1}{2}(30)^2 = 450.$$ (2.15)

2.2.4 **Taxes**

It is useful to think about oligopoly interactions in terms of best response functions because the impact of changes in the market can be determined by examining how those changes move the best response functions and, therefore, the equilibrium outputs of firms.

To illustrate this approach, suppose that the government imposes a tax t on every unit of output. What are the consequences for equilibrium outputs and for the other aspects of Cournot equilibrium? How, for example, would a tax affect consumers' surplus? How would the tax affect the price consumers pay and firms' profit? How much revenue would the government collect?

As far as a firm is concerned, a tax t per unit of output increases the firm's marginal cost from 10 to $10 + t$. Setting firm 1's marginal revenue equal to this new, higher marginal cost gives

$$MR_1 = (100 - q_2) - 2q_1 = 10 + t = MC_t,$$ (2.16)

writing MC_t for firm 1's marginal cost with the tax.

The equation of firm 1's best response function becomes

$$q_1 = \tfrac{1}{2}(90 - t - q_2).$$ 2.17

For any output level of firm 2, taxes mean firm 1 will produce less to maximize its profit, because its marginal cost is higher with the tax than without it. Graphically, firm 1's best response curve shifts toward the origin.

The same is true for firm 2's best response curve (see Figure 2.4, which is drawn for the case $t = 30$). Because of the tax, the intersection of the best response curves—the equilibrium point—moves toward the origin.

How much do equilibrium outputs change? The equation of firm 1's best response function can be written

$$2q_1 + q_2 = 90 - t.$$ (2.18)

Since both firms pay the tax, they have the same costs and produce the same output in equilibrium; set $q_1 = q_2 = q_t$ in (2.18) and solve for equilibrium firm output with the tax:

$$q_t = 30 - \tfrac{1}{3}t.$$ (2.19)

If the tax is sufficiently high (in this example, if $t = 90$), equilibrium firm output is zero, the firms shut down, and the industry goes out of existence.

Total output is lower with than without a tax,

$$Q_t = 60 - \tfrac{2}{3}t,$$ (2.20)

and total price higher with than without a tax:

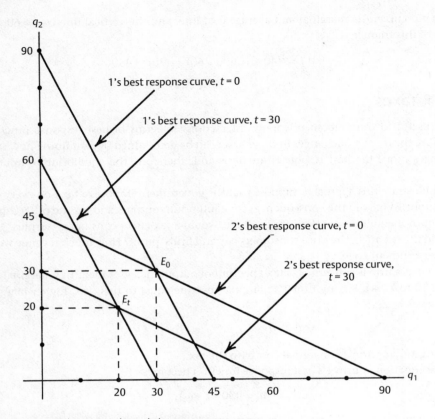

Fig. 2.4 Taxes and Cournot duopoly best response curves

$$p_t = 40 + \tfrac{2}{3}t. \tag{2.21}$$

With a tax, the difference between price and marginal cost is

$$p_t - 10 - t = 30 - \tfrac{1}{3}t, \tag{2.22}$$

compared with a price-marginal cost difference of 30 without a tax.

In imperfectly competitive markets, part of any cost increase, including a tax increase, is absorbed by producers in the form of a lower price-cost margin and part is passed on to consumers in the form of a higher price.

The equilibrium Lerner index of market power is

$$\frac{p_t - 10 - t}{p_t} = \frac{40 + \tfrac{2}{3}t - (10 + t)}{40 + \tfrac{2}{3}t} = \frac{30 - \tfrac{1}{3}t}{40 + \tfrac{2}{3}t} = \frac{1}{2}\left(\frac{150}{60 + t} - 1\right). \tag{2.23}$$

The equilibrium degree of market power falls as taxes rise.

Economic profit per firm also falls as the tax rises:

$$\pi_t = (p_t - 10 - t)q_t = (30 - \tfrac{1}{3}t)^2. \tag{2.24}$$

Taxes reduce firms' profits. This is one reason why firms oppose taxes on their products, even though in a formal sense they are able to pass part of the tax along to consumers in the form of higher prices.

Since the tax reduces equilibrium output, it also reduces consumers' surplus:

$$CS_t = \tfrac{1}{2}(100 - 40 - \tfrac{2}{3}t)\, 2\, (30 - \tfrac{1}{3}t) = 2\, (30 - \tfrac{1}{3}t)^2 \qquad (2.25)$$

Deadweight welfare loss rises with the tax:

$$DWL_t = \tfrac{1}{2}(40 + \tfrac{2}{3}t - 10)\, [90 - (60 - \tfrac{2}{3}t)] = \tfrac{1}{2}(30 + \tfrac{2}{3}t)^2. \qquad (2.26)$$

Market equilibrium with a tax $t = 15$ is shown in Figure 2.5.

Net social welfare, the sum of economic profit, consumers' surplus, and tax revenue, is

$$NSW_t = 2(30 - \tfrac{1}{3}t)^2 + 2(30 - \tfrac{1}{3}t)^2 + t(60 - \tfrac{2}{3}t) = 3600 - 20t - \tfrac{2}{9}t^2. \qquad (2.27)$$

This compares with net social welfare of 3600 without the tax (set $t = 0$ in (2.27), or alternatively add (2.13) and (2.14)). The higher the tax rate, the lower is net social welfare (falling to zero for $t = 90$).

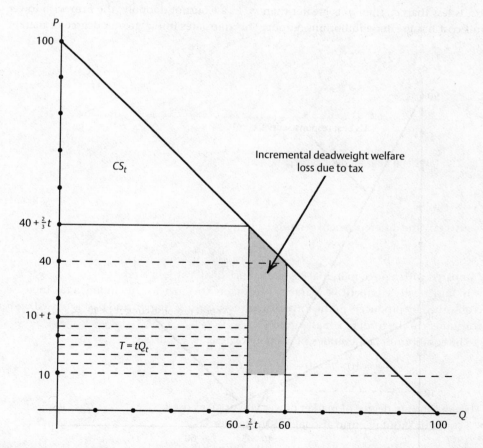

Fig. 2.5 Market equilibrium, Cournot duopoly, per unit tax $t = 15$; CS_t = consumers' surplus with tax

2.2.5 **Cost differences**

If we continue to suppose that each firm has constant marginal cost, but allow different firms to have different marginal costs, the equations of the best response functions become

$$2q_1 + q_2 = 100 - c_1 \tag{2.28}$$

$$q_1 + 2q_2 = 100 - c_2. \tag{2.29}$$

The best response curves are shown in Figure 2.6. Equilibrium outputs (found by solving equations (2.28) and (2.29)) are

$$q_1 = \tfrac{1}{3}(100 - 2c_1 + c_2), \tag{2.30}$$

$$q_2 = \tfrac{1}{3}(100 + c_1 - 2c_2), \tag{2.31}$$

and it follows that

$$q_1 - q_2 = c_2 - c_1. \tag{2.32}$$

If c_1 is less than c_2, then q_1 is greater than q_2. In a Cournot duopoly, the firm with lower unit cost has greater equilibrium output. This translates into a greater degree of market

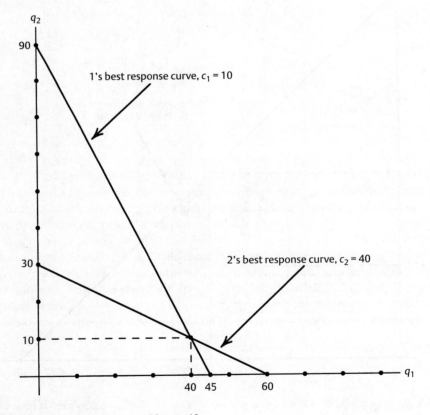

Fig. 2.6 Best response curves, $c_1 = 10$, $c_2 = 40$

power for the firm with lower unit cost. Using the equation of firm 1's best response function, (2.28), in this example

$$p = 100 - q_1 - q_2 = c_1 + q_1,\tag{2.33}$$

in equilibrium, so

$$\frac{p - c_1}{p} = \frac{q_1}{p} = \frac{q_1 Q}{Q p} = \frac{s_1}{\varepsilon_{Qp}},\tag{2.34}$$

where $s_1 = 81/Q$ is firm 1's market share and ε_{Qp} is the absolute value of the price elasticity of demand.[3]

Equation (2.34) generalizes the Lerner index of market power from monopoly to Cournot oligopoly with cost differences. If firm 1 has lower unit cost than firm 2, it will have greater equilibrium output than firm 2, and will exercise more equilibrium market power than firm 2.

It is equally true that lower cost improves market performance, in the sense of leading to greater equilibrium output and lower equilibrium price. This is most easily seen by adding equations (2.28) and (2.29), which shows that equilibrium total output

$$Q = q_1 + q_2 = \tfrac{1}{3}[200 - (c_1 + c_2)]\tag{2.35}$$

rises as c_1 falls. If output rises as c_1 falls, then equilibrium price falls as c_1 falls.

If we multiply equation (2.34) by s_1, multiply the corresponding expression for firm 2 by s_2, and add the results, we obtain

$$\frac{p - \hat{c}}{p} = \frac{H}{\varepsilon_{Qp}},\tag{2.36}$$

where $\hat{c}$ is the market-share weighted average of the unit costs[4] of the two firms and $H = s_1^2 + s_2^2$ is the Herfindahl index of seller concentration.

We thus obtain the result that in Cournot oligopoly with cost differences, the noncooperative equilibrium industry-average price-cost margin is higher where seller concentration as measured by the Herfindahl index is higher, all else equal.

Figure 2.7 illustrates the welfare effects of imperfect competition in Cournot duopoly with cost differences. Firm 1's unit cost is less than firm 2's unit cost ($c_1 < c_2$). If firms acted as price takers, firm 1 would supply the entire market at a price slightly less than c_2. In Cournot duopoly equilibrium, price is greater than c_2. The net loss of social welfare is the deadweight welfare loss from output restriction, plus the extra social cost of producing firm 2's output at unit cost c_2 rather than unit cost c_1; this amount is $(c_2 - c_1)q_2$. The higher-cost firm has positive output only because the lower-cost firm does not act as a price-taker. Economic profits are $\pi_1 = (p_{Cour} - c_1)q_1$ and $\pi_2 = (p_{Cour} - c_2)q_2$. These are income transfers from consumers to producers. The amount $(c_2 - c_1)q_1$, shown as the shaded

---

[3] In general, the absolute value of the price elasticity of demand is

$$\varepsilon_{Qp} = -\frac{p}{Q}\frac{dQ}{dp}.$$

When (as at present) the slope of the market demand curve is -1, the price elasticity of demand is simply p/Q. See footnote 16, Chapter 1.

[4] That is, $\hat{c} = s_1 c_1 + s_2 c_2$.

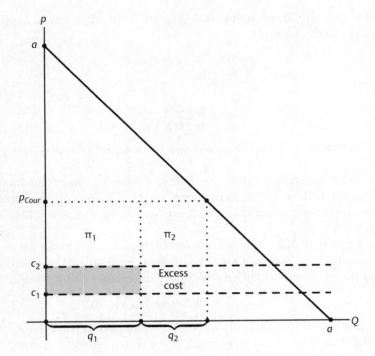

Fig. 2.7 Market power and welfare losses with efficiency differentials; shaded area is an efficiency rent

area in Figure 2.7, is an efficiency rent collected by firm 1 on the output that it does produce.

In the classic formulation, associated with Malthus and Ricardo, a rent is an income stream that need not be received in order for the services of a factor of production to be provided. Rent is a residual determined by the price of output. The efficiency rent is also an income transfer, from consumers to firm 1.

2.2.6 Conjectural variations

Thinking about the way best response curves shift is also a way to understand what happens if the Cournot behavioural assumption—that each firm maximizes its own profit, given the equilibrium output of the other firm—is changed. This leads to a simple way of modelling dynamic interactions among firms in imperfectly competitive markets using the static Cournot model.

Suppose that firm 1 expects that for every 1 per cent change in its own output q_1, there will be an α% change in q_2:

$$\alpha = \frac{\Delta q_2/q_2}{\Delta q_1/q_1}. \tag{2.37}$$

Then the equation of firm 1's best response function becomes

$$2q_1 + (1 + a)q_2 = 90, \qquad (2.38)$$

or

$$q_1 = 45 - \tfrac{1}{2}(1 + a)q_2. \qquad (2.39)$$

With Cournot conjectures, $a = 0$ and the slope of the best response curve is $-1/2$.

If $a > 0$, firm 1 expects that if it reduces its own output, firm 2 will reduce output as well, so that both firms act to reduce total output. Then for any level of output of firm 2, firm 1 produces less than it would with Cournot conjectures. Firm 1's best response curve rotates around the q_1-axis intercept toward the origin.

Best response curves for different values of a are graphed in Figure 2.8. If $a < 0$, firm 1 expects that if it reduces output, firm 2 will increase its output, partially neutralizing the effort to reduce total output. For any output level of firm 2, firm 1 will produce more than it would with Cournot conjectures. Firm 1's best response curve rotates around its q_1-axis intercept away from the origin.

As long as firms have identical conjectures, equilibrium outputs are the same for both firms. Setting $q_1 = q_2 = q_a$ in (2.38) gives an expression for equilibrium output with identical conjectures:

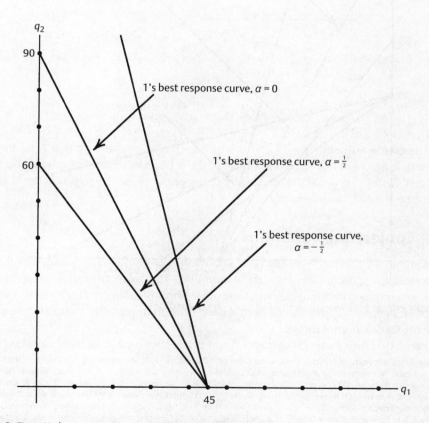

Fig. 2.8 Firm 1's best response curve, alternative conjectures

$$q_a = \frac{90}{3+a}.$$
(2.40)

Equilibrium outputs are smaller (total output is closer to the monopoly level) for match-ing conjectures ($a > 0$) and equilibrium outputs are larger (total output is closer to the long-run competitive equilibrium level) for contrarian conjectures ($a < 0$). Matching con-jectures move the market toward the kind of outcome associated with collusion; contrar-ian conjectures move the market toward the kind of outcome associated with perfect competition (Figure 2.9). Smaller values of a mean tougher rivalry between the two firms.[5]

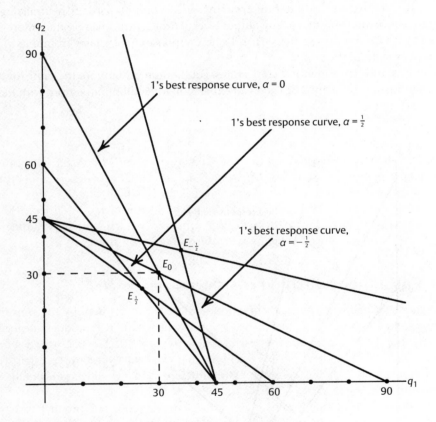

Fig. 2.9 Cournot equilibrium, alternative conjectural variations

[5] If $a = 1$, then from (2.40) in equilibrium each duopolist produces half the monopoly output. For this reason, $a = 1$ is sometimes referred to as the case of collusive conjectures (although if firms make output decisions independently they would not normally be considered to have colluded in a legal sense). If $a = -1$, then from (2.40) in equilibrium each firm produces half the perfectly competitive output. Total output is what it would be in long-run perfectly competitive equilibrium, with only two firms supplying the market. As we will see in Section 2.3.1, this is the same result as in the Bertrand model of price-setting duopoly with standardized products. For this reason, $a = -1$ is sometimes referred to as the case of Bertrand conjectures.

2.2.7 **Product differentiation**

How do the results of the basic Cournot model change if products are not standardized? To work out the answer to this question, suppose that each firm has its own inverse demand curve, with

$$p_1 = 100 - (q_1 + \theta q_2), \tag{2.41}$$

$$p_2 = 100 - (\theta q_2 + q_1), \tag{2.42}$$

where the product differentiation parameter θ is a number between zero and one.[6]

These kinds of market demand would arise, for example, if firm 1 produces flat mineral water, firm 2 produces fizzy mineral water, $\theta = \frac{1}{2}$, and consumers will trade off two units of one type of mineral water for one unit of the other.

Setting marginal revenue along the inverse demand curve for each firm equal to its marginal cost, we find the equations of the best response functions:

$$2q_1 + \theta q_2 = 90 \tag{2.43}$$

$$\theta q_1 + 2q_2 = 90. \tag{2.44}$$

For values of θ less than one, best response curves become steeper, compared with the standardized product case (Figure 2.10).[7]

Smaller values of θ correspond to cases in which each variety is a poorer substitute for the other. Smaller values of θ mean that each producer is closer to being a monopolist. In the extreme case $\theta = 0$, each firm is a monopolist. Firm 1's best response curve is then vertical at $q_1 = 45$ and firm 2's best response curve is horizontal at $q_2 = 45$. When $\theta = 0$, the two products are independent in demand. Each firm produces the monopoly output, and charges the monopoly price, no matter what the output of the other.

2.2.8 **Consumer switching costs**[8]

There are many markets where consumption involves an investment by the consumer. The investment may be intangible, such as learning where particular products are located in a neighbourhood supermarket or learning how to use a software package. It may be tangible, such as the cost of music recordings that can be played only in a particular format. Consumption of music recordings in a different format would require purchase of a compatible player.

Such consumer investments create a cost of changing from one product variety to another—the cost of learning how to use an alternative variety, the cost of replacing complementary products. These switching costs create differences in imperfectly competitive markets.

Suppose that in our basic Cournot example

---

[6] This way of modelling product differentiation is due to Bowley (1924), and more recently used by Spence (1976), Dixit (1979).

[7] For very high levels of q_2, $p_2 = 0$ and firm 1's quantity best response curve is constrained to run along the $p_2 = 0$ line. For simplicity, this segment of the best response curve is not shown in Figure 2.10.

[8] See Klemperer (1987, 1989).

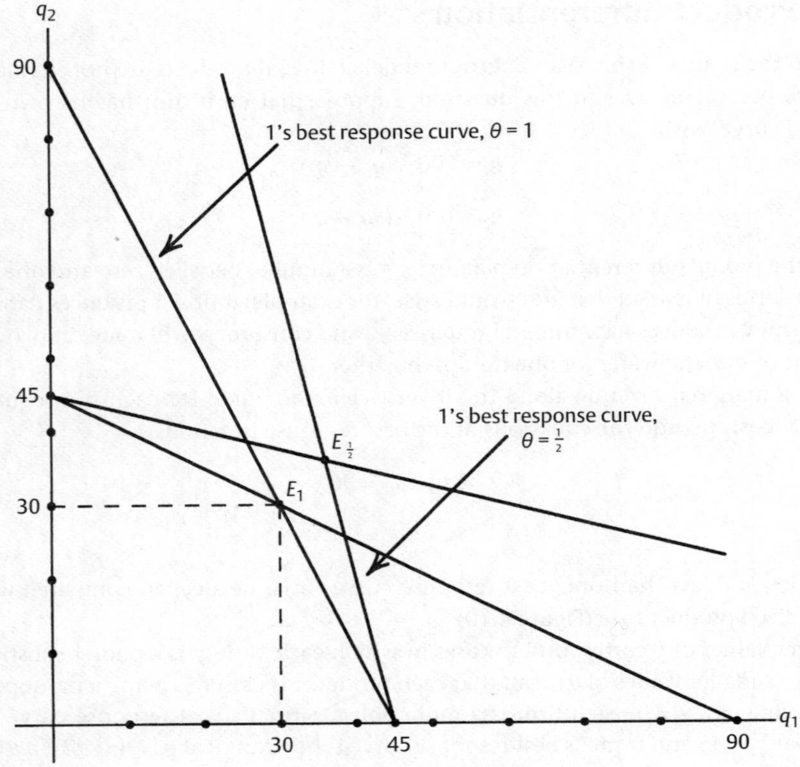

Fig. 2.10 Cournot best response curves with product differentiation

$$p = 100 - Q = 100 - (q_1 + q_2)$$

$$C(q_1) = 10q_1 \qquad C(q_2) = 10q_2$$

there is a switching cost τ per unit of changing from the product of firm 1 to the product of firm 2. Consumers who purchase variety 1 will switch to variety 2 only if the price of variety 2 is low enough to balance out the switching cost they will need to cover because of the switch. Then it is as if the demand curve for the product of firm 2 has become

$$p_2 = p - \tau = 100 - \tau - (q_1 + q_2). \qquad (2.45)$$

Firm 2's profit is

$$\pi_2 = (100 - \tau - q_1 - q_2 - 10)q_2 = (90 - \tau - q_1 - q_2)q_2. \qquad (2.46)$$

Consumer switching costs τ per unit of output have the same effect on firm 2's profit as a cost increase—for firm 2 alone—of τ per unit.

In the usual way, we can find the equation of firm 2's best response function:

$$q_1 + 2q_2 = 90 - \tau \qquad (2.47)$$

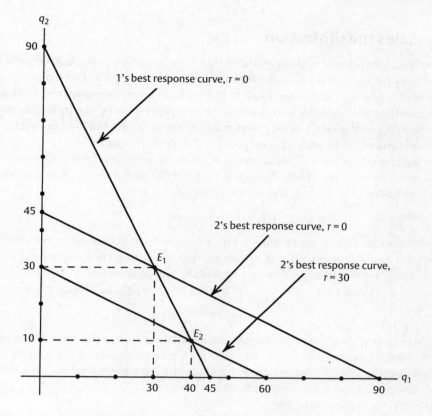

Fig. 2.11 Consumer switching costs and Cournot best response curves

As shown in Figure 2.11, the effect of consumer switching costs is to move firm 2's best response curve toward the origin. Compared with the no-switching-cost case, the equilibrium point slides down firm 1's best response curve; firm 1 produces more in equilibrium, and firm 2 less, than in the absence of switching costs.

The equation of firm 1's best response function is unchanged from the basic model; it is (2.6):

$$2q_1 + q_2 = 90.$$

Solving the equations of the best response functions gives expressions for equilibrium outputs:

$$q_1 = 30 + \tfrac{1}{3}\tau \tag{2.48}$$

$$q_2 = 30 - \tfrac{2}{3}\tau \tag{2.49}$$

The larger are consumer switching costs, the smaller is firm 2's equilibrium output. If consumer switching costs are sufficiently great (45, in this example), firm 2's equilibrium output would be zero—it would go out of business.

2.2.9 **Sales maximization**

Economists give priority to the hypothesis that firms maximize profit, but for some markets it may be appropriate to suppose that firms have other goals. Government-owned firms may have a legal obligation to act in the public interest. Labour-owned firms might maximize the total return to worker-owners: wages plus profit. Private firms, particularly those with some degree of market power, may engage in empire-building or deviate from profit maximization in other ways for considerable periods of time.

We can extend the basic Cournot model to allow the analysis of goals other than strict profit maximization. For example, suppose that in a Cournot duopoly, firm 1 maximizes a weighted average of profit π_1 and sales revenue pq_1,

$$g_1 = (1 - \sigma)\pi_1 + \sigma pq_1. \tag{2.50}$$

If $\sigma = 0$, firm 1 maximizes profit. If $\sigma = 1$, firm 1 maximizes its sales revenue. For values of σ between 0 and 1, larger values of σ indicate that the firm gives more weight to sales revenue and less weight to profit when it makes its output decision.

Since firm 1's profit is $\pi_1 = pq_1 - cq_1$ and its sales revenue pq_1, the objective function g_1 is

$$g_1 = [p - (1 - \sigma)c]q_1. \tag{2.51}$$

A greater weight given to sales maximization—a larger σ—has the same effect on the firm's objective function as a cost reduction for a profit-maximizing firm. Just as a cost reduction shifts a firm's best-response curve outward, so a greater value of σ causes the firm's best response curve to shift outward.

With inverse demand function

$$p = 100 - q_1 - q_2 \tag{2.52}$$

and unit cost $c = 10$, firm 1 picks its output to maximize

$$g_1 = (90 + 10\sigma - q_1 - q_2)q_1. \tag{2.53}$$

The equation of the best response function giving the output level q_1 that maximizes g_1 for any output level q_2 of firm 2 is

$$q_1 = \tfrac{1}{2}(90 + 10\sigma - q_2) = 45 + 5\sigma - \tfrac{1}{2}q_2. \tag{2.54}$$

The more weight firm 1 gives to sales maximization, the more it will wish to sell, for any output level of firm 2. In terms of the best response curve diagram, firm 1's best response curve moves away from the origin as σ increases (Figure 2.12, drawn for $\sigma = \tfrac{4}{5}$).

Compared with the pure profit maximization case, the equilibrium point slides down firm 2's unchanged best response curve, from E_0 to $E_{\frac{4}{5}}$. Firm 1 takes a larger share of the market, directly because it offers more for any output supplied by the other firm, and strategically because firm 2 reacts to the greater supply of firm 1 by reducing its own output.

These direct and strategic effects of sales-maximizing behaviour lead to the counterintuitive result that the sales-maximizing firm's profit increases, the greater the weight it gives to sales maximization. Firm 1's equilibrium payoff is

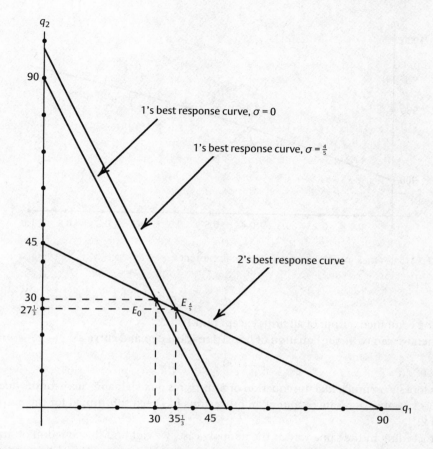

Fig. 2.12 Cournot best response curves, partial sales maximization by firm 1, $\sigma = \frac{4}{5}$

$$\pi_{1\sigma} = (30 - \tfrac{10}{3}\sigma)(30 + \tfrac{20}{3}\sigma),$$

and this increases steadily as σ rises from 0 to 1 (Figure 2.13).[9]
At the same time, the profit of the other firm is lower than it would be if both firms were strict profit maximizers.

2.2.10 Many firms

The general Cournot model—n firms rather than two—cannot be illustrated graphically. Particularly in the symmetric firm case, however, the generalization from two to n firms is straightforward.

If there are n identical Cournot firms in the industry, write

---

[9] It is essential for this result that the direct and the strategic effects of sales maximization work in the same direction. If the product is differentiated and firms set price rather than quantity, direct and strategic effects work in opposite directions, and a sales-maximizing firm makes lower profit, all else equal, than a strictly profit-maximizing firm. See Problem 2–2.

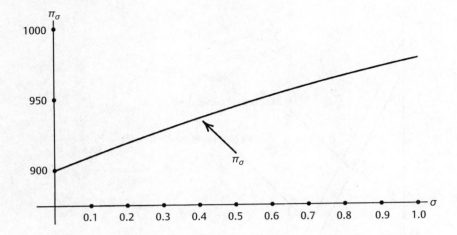

Fig. 2.13 Sales maximization and equilibrium firm profit

$$Q_{-1} = q_2 + \ldots + q_n \qquad (2.55)$$

for the combined output of all firms except firm 1.

Then we can write the equation of firm 1's residual demand curve as

$$p = (100 - Q_{-1}) - q_1. \qquad (2.56)$$

This looks very much like the equation of firm 1's residual demand curve for the duopoly case, (2.3); the aggregate output of all other firms has been substituted for the output of firm 2.

Proceeding in the same way as the duopoly case, we can find the equation of firm 1's best response curve by setting its marginal revenue along the residual demand curve (2.56) equal to its marginal cost:

$$100 - Q_{-1} - 2q_1 = 10, \qquad (2.57)$$

or

$$2q_1 + Q_{-1} = 90. \qquad (2.58)$$

In the symmetric firm case, all firms will produce the same output in equilibrium. (2.58) becomes

$$2q_{Cour} + (n-1)q_{Cour} = 90, \qquad (2.59)$$

so that

$$q_{Cour} = \frac{90}{n+1}. \qquad (2.60)$$

If $n = 2$, (2.60) reduces to (2.8).

From the equilibrium output of a single firm, we can work out all the other characteristics of n-firm equilibrium. Here we note two of these, total output and price, which are

$$Q_{Cour} = \frac{n}{n+1}90 = \left(1 - \frac{1}{n+1}\right)90 \tag{2.61}$$

and

$$p_{Cour} = 10 + \frac{90}{n+1} \tag{2.62}$$

respectively.

If $n = 1$, these are the monopoly output and price. As n increases, Cournot equilibrium output increases toward the long-run competitive equilibrium output level, and Cournot equilibrium price approaches marginal cost. The symmetric Cournot model predicts that market performance will improve as the number of firms increases, and in fact that market performance will approach that of long-run competitive equilibrium as the number of firms approaches infinity.[10]

2.3 **Bertrand duopoly**

In 1883, the French mathematician Bertrand wrote a review of Cournot's 1838 book, criticizing Cournot in particular for assuming that firms picked outputs and that price adjusted so that consumers would willingly demand the total quantity supplied. Since that time, Bertrand's name has been associated with models of imperfectly competitive markets in which firms pick prices and sell whatever amount of output is demanded at those prices.

2.3.1 **Standardized product**

Keeping all the other assumptions of the basic Cournot model, firm 1's residual demand curve looks quite different if firms set prices rather than quantities.

This is shown in Figure 2.14. If firm 2 has set a price $p = 40$, firm 1 will sell nothing if it sets a price greater than 40, and will supply the entire market if it sets a price below 40. There is a discontinuity in firm 1's residual demand curve at $p = 40$, with the quantity demanded jumping from 0 to 60 as price falls from above 40 to below 40.

Firm 1 can sell up to 60 units of output at a price slightly below 40. For outputs less than 60 units, firm 1's marginal revenue is slightly less than 40. To sell more than 60 units of output, firm 1 must reduce price and move down the market demand curve. For outputs greater than 60 units, firm 1's marginal revenue curve is the same as the market marginal revenue curve. The horizontal break in firm 1's residual demand curve at a price just less than 40, $p = 40 - \varepsilon$ for some small number ε, means that there is a vertical break in firm 1's marginal revenue curve at an output level slightly greater than $Q = 60$.

---

[10] As we have seen in Chapter 1 for the case of perfect competition, and as we will see in Chapter 6 for oligopoly, the long-run equilibrium number of firms is itself determined by market forces.

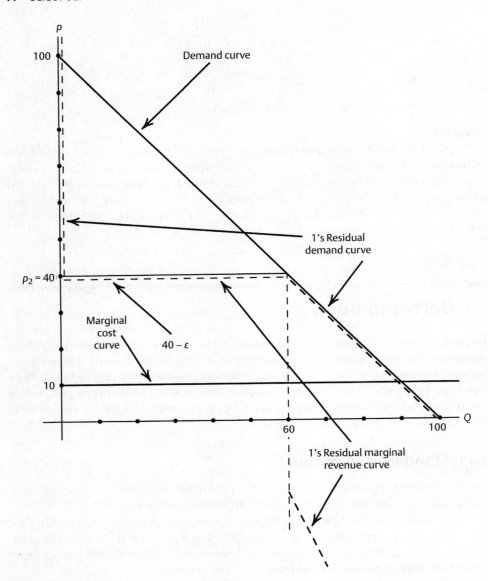

Fig. 2.14 Firm 1's price decision, $p_2 = 40$

For outputs less than 60, firm 1's marginal revenue ($40 - \varepsilon$) is greater than its marginal cost (10). For outputs greater than 60, firm 1's marginal revenue is less than its marginal cost.[11] To maximize its profit, firm 1 will set a price just a little below 40 and supply the entire quantity demanded at that price. Firm 2 will sell nothing.

---

[11] As drawn in Figure 2.14, firm 1's marginal revenue is negative for outputs greater than 60, and therefore certainly less than firm 1's marginal cost, which is positive. For higher values of p_2, firm 1's marginal revenue could be positive for some output levels greater than the critical level.

This cannot be an equilibrium, however. Firm 2 would have an incentive to undercut firm 1's price slightly, thus recapturing what would be a slightly larger market demand at a slightly lower price. And if firm 2 did this, firm 1 would once again have an incentive to set a price slightly below firm 2's new, lower, price.

If either firm sets a price above marginal cost, the other has an incentive to set a lower price. Neither firm would set a price below marginal cost, because that would mean losing money.

These arguments show that the Bertrand equilibrium price is $p = 10$. When each firm sets a price equal to marginal cost, each firm is maximizing its own profit, given that the other firm sets a price equal to marginal cost.

The Bertrand model therefore predicts that when the product is standardized, market performance is the same as in the long-run equilibrium of a perfectly competitive market, provided there are at least two firms supplying the market.

2.3.2 **Differentiated products**

The assumption that the product is standardized is essential for the result that the Bertrand equilibrium price equals marginal cost with at least two price-setting suppliers. To see this, we introduce product differentiation to the model of price-setting duopoly.

Suppose that the two firms produce differentiated brands of mineral water, with the inverse demand curves used for the discussion of Cournot oligopoly with product differentiation:

$$p_1 = 100 - (q_1 + \theta q_2) \qquad p_2 = 100 - (\theta q_1 + q_2).$$

If, for example, $\theta = \frac{1}{2}$, the equations of the inverse demand functions are

$$p_1 = 100 - (q_1 + \tfrac{1}{2}q_2) \qquad p_2 = 100 - (\tfrac{1}{2}q_1 + q_2). \tag{2.63}$$

If we solve these two equations for outputs in terms of prices, we obtain the equations of the demand functions:

$$q_1 = \tfrac{2}{3}(100 - 2p_1 + p_2) \qquad q_2 = \tfrac{2}{3}(100 + p_1 - 2p_2). \tag{2.64}$$

Firm 1's profit as a function of p_1 and p_2 is

$$\pi_1 = (p_1 - 10)q_1 = \tfrac{2}{3}(p_1 - 10)(100 - 2p_1 + p_2). \tag{2.65}$$

From the first-order condition to maximize (2.65) with respect to p_1, we obtain the equation of firm 1's price best response function (Figure 2.15):[12]

$$p_1 = 30 + \tfrac{1}{4}p_2. \tag{2.66}$$

---

[12] There are two additional segments of the price best response curves which, for simplicity, are not shown in Figure 2.15. When p_2 is sufficiently high, $q_2 = 0$ and firm 1's price best response curve is constrained to move along the $q_2 = 0$ line. At even higher levels of p_2, firm 1 is able to charge the unconstrained monopoly price, and firm 1's price best response curve becomes vertical.

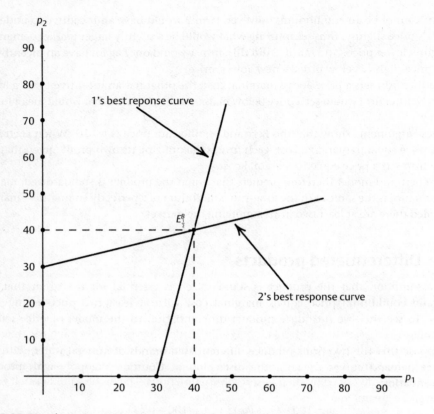

Fig. 2.15 Price best response curves, Bertrand duopoly with product differentiation

When firms set prices, best response curves slope upward: if firm 2 sets a higher price, firm 1's profit-maximizing price is higher.[13]

Bertrand equilibrium prices can be found (for this example) by symmetry: the two firms are identical, and in equilibrium they will charge the same price, $p_{\frac{1}{2}}^B$. Setting $p_1 = p_2 = p_{\frac{1}{2}}^B$ in (2.66) and rearranging terms gives

$$p_{\frac{1}{2}}^B = 40. \tag{2.67}$$

For general values of the product differentiation parameter θ, the equation of firm 1's best response curve is

$$p_1 = \tfrac{1}{2}(110 - 100\theta + \theta p_2) \tag{2.68}$$

(this corresponds to (2.66)).

If $\theta = 0$, the two products are independent in demand, and (2.68) reduces to

[13] At a deeper level, with linear demand and constant marginal cost, quantity best response curves slope downward because if one firm produces more output, the marginal profitability of the other firm falls; outputs are then said to be strategic substitutes. With linear demand for differentiated products and constant marginal cost, price best response curves slope upward because if one firm raises its price, the marginal profitability of the other firm increases; prices are then said to be strategic complements. See Bulow et al. (1985).

$$p_1 = 55, \qquad\qquad (2.69)$$

which is the monopoly price for a firm that faces no substitute products.

If $\theta = 1$, the two products are perfect substitutes, and (2.68) reduces to

$$p_1 = 5 + \tfrac{1}{2}p_2. \qquad\qquad (2.70)$$

This is the homogeneous-product Bertrand case, and in equilibrium (set $p_1 = p_2 = p_1^B$ in (2.70)) price equals marginal cost:

$$p_1^B = 10. \qquad\qquad (2.71)$$

With price-setting firms, the greater the degree of product differentiation (the lower is θ), the greater the equilibrium price-cost margin. As long as products are differentiated to some extent, equilibrium price-cost margins fall as the number of firms rises, when firms set price as when they set quantities (Problem 1–3).

2.4 **Summary**

A common characteristic of the oligopoly models developed in this chapter is that it is possible to understand the impact of a change in market characteristics on equilibrium market performance by working out how the change affects the strategic choices of individual firms, as described by their best response functions. The models predict that firms will exercise greater market power, all else equal,

- if market shares are large;
- if seller concentration is high;
- if products are differentiated;
- if there are consumer switching costs;
- if firms set outputs in ways that have the effect of cooperating to reduce total output.

Study points

- basic assumptions of the Cournot model (pages 23–4)
- Cournot equilibrium (page 24, 26)
- residual demand curve (page 24)
- best response function (page 25)
- economic rent (page 34)
- conjectural variations (pages 34–7)
- switching costs (pages 37–9)

- basic assumptions of the Bertrand model with a standardized product (page 43)
- product differentiation and market performance (pages 37 and 45–7)

Problems

2-1 For quantity-setting duopoly with inverse demand curve

$$p = 100 - (q_1 + q_2) \tag{2.72}$$

and constant marginal cost 10 per unit, find equilibrium prices and profits if each firm maximizes a weighted average of profit and sales,

$$g_i = (1 - \sigma)\pi_i + \sigma p_i q_i. \tag{2.73}$$

Illustrate noncooperative equilibrium on a best response curve diagram.

2-2 For a price-setting duopoly with product differentiation, let the equations of the inverse demand curves be

$$p_1 = 100 - (q_1 + \tfrac{1}{2}q_2) \qquad p_2 = 100 - (\tfrac{1}{2}q_1 + q_1), \tag{2.74}$$

with corresponding demand functions

$$q_1 = \tfrac{2}{3}(100 - 2p_1 + p_2) \qquad q_2 = \tfrac{2}{3}(100 + p_1 - 2p_2). \tag{2.75}$$

Let marginal cost be constant at 10 per unit.

Find equilibrium prices and profits if firm 2 maximizes profit while firm 1 maximizes a weighted average of profit and sales

$$g_1 = (1 - \sigma)\pi_1 + \sigma p_1 q_1. \tag{2.76}$$

2-3 For a price-setting oligopoly with product differentiation, let the equations of the inverse demand curves be

$$p_i = 100 - (q_i + \theta Q_{-i}), \tag{2.77}$$

for $i = 1, 2, \ldots, n$ and $Q_{-i} = \Sigma_{j \neq i}^{n} q_j$.

The equations of the corresponding demand curves are

$$q_i = \frac{90(1 - \theta) - [1 + (n - 2)\theta](p_i - 10) + \theta \Sigma_{j \neq i}^{n}(p_j - 10)}{(1 - \theta)[1 + (n - 1)\theta]}. \tag{2.78}$$

If marginal cost is constant at 10 per unit, show that when firms set prices to maximize own profit, equilibrium prices are

$$p_B = 10 + (1 - \theta)\frac{90}{2 + (n - 3)\theta}, \tag{2.79}$$

so that for all $\theta < 1$, equilibrium prices fall as the number of firms rises.

Chapter 3

Collusion and tacit collusion

It was possible to effect an arrangement with a few of the outside firms as to selling prices with the object of stopping the rot, but the agreements entered into to this end were not enforceable . . . gentlemanly agreements—the passing of the "word of honour", were all that we had to rely upon and they were observed until the manufacturer saw his way to "making a bit" by ignoring them.

O'Hagen (1926, Volume II, p. 73), quoted in Cook (1958, p. 46).

3.1 Introduction

In Chapter 2 we examined the Cournot and Bertrand oligopoly models. These models are static, in the sense that they do not explicitly consider the passage of time; they are one-period models. In these and most other one-period models of noncooperative oligopoly, equilibrium output exceeds the monopoly level, with the result that firms can increase their profit if they are able to restrict output and raise price.

There is sometimes a tendency to identify collusion with output restriction (below the equilibrium output level of a one-period model), but this is imprecise. Whether output is or is not restricted below its one-period equilibrium level is an objective question, but collusion is a legal concept. At an elementary level, one can say that collusion occurs when independent firms reach joint decisions about their market conduct. If firms make independent decisions that move output to or toward the monopoly level, they have not colluded. If firms make joint decisions that have the same effects, they have colluded. The standards that must be satisfied to justify a finding that firms' decisions have been jointly arrived at depend on the details of the legal regime that applies to business behaviour.[1]

In this chapter, we first look at one way to formalize the factors that influence firms' output decisions when firms compete repeatedly over time, not just for a single period.

---

[1] In much the same way, whether one person has killed another is a reasonably objective question. Killing is only murder (a legal concept) if the applicable legal standards are satisfied.

We also examine some practices (basing point pricing and publicity of prices and quantities in individual transactions) that may facilitate output restriction and look at the impact of collusion on market performance. Finally, we study EC competition policy toward collusion.

3.2 Noncooperative collusion

3.2.1 Trigger strategy

Collusion is prohibited by Article 81 of the EC Treaty, which means (among other things) that firms cannot sign legally enforceable contracts to bind themselves to collusive understandings. Thus collusion, if it occurs, must be *noncooperative*, in the sense that each firm that is party to a collusive agreement, a member of a cartel, will keep the collusive agreement only so long as it is in its own interest to do so.

The basic elements of the economics of noncooperative collusion are straightforward. When firms independently maximize their own short-run profit, their combined profit is generally less than monopoly profit. We have seen this for Cournot oligopoly, and it is true for most other models of imperfectly competitive markets as well. It follows that firms can increase their profit, compared with noncooperative oligopoly equilibrium, if they can cooperate and restrict output.

If all firms restrict output, then any one firm can earn an even greater profit in the short run by cheating on than by keeping to the restrictive agreement—by producing more than its share of collusive output. However, if other firms realize cheating is taking place, it is reasonable to expect that the collusive agreement will break down, and that other firms would expand output as well. Thus a firm that defects from a collusive agreement for the extra short-run profit that defection brings would earn less profit in the more distant future than it would by keeping the agreement. It follows that the critical factors affecting whether or not noncooperative collusion will be successful are how firms trade off higher profit in the near future from cheating against lower profit in the more distant future and how quickly rival firms would become aware of cheating, if it should occur.

One way to formalize the idea of a tradeoff between profit received at different times is in terms of a so-called *trigger strategy* for noncooperative collusion (Friedman, 1971) in a market where firms repeatedly play a single-period Cournot game:

- each firm produces its share of the monopoly output in the first period, and produces its share of the monopoly output in each following period if all other firms produced their shares of monopoly output in the previous period;

- if in any period price is different from the monopoly price, all firms produce their Cournot outputs forever after.[2]

---

[2] The idea that one firm would believe that other firms would give up the possibility of colluding forever in response to one episode of defection may seem unrealistic. However, the results of the trigger strategy model carry over to strategies that involve less severe punishments.

Suppose, for example, that a market has the linear inverse demand curve

$$p = 100 - Q \tag{3.1}$$

in every time period and that all firms have constant marginal and average variable cost 10 per unit of output,

$$C(q) = 10q + F. \tag{3.2}$$

As explained in Section 1.3.1, fixed cost F does not vary with output.

Profit-maximizing monopoly output is 45,[3] and monopoly price 55. Monopoly profit per time period is

$$\pi_m = (55 - 10)(45) - F = 2025 - F. \tag{3.4}$$

If the market is a Cournot duopoly, equilibrium output per firm is 30, Cournot duopoly price is 40, and equilibrium profit per firm per time period is

$$\pi_1 = \pi_2 = (40 - 10)(30) - F = 900 - F. \tag{3.4}$$

Monopoly profit in this industry, before allowing for fixed cost, is 2025. The additional profit to be gained in any one time period if the firms collude and produce only the monopoly output is

$$2025 - 2(900) = 225. \tag{3.5}$$

If the two firms could agree to shut down one plant, they would also save one set of fixed cost, F, per period. Stepping outside the model, a firm that agreed to shut down its plant would most likely find its bargaining power sharply reduced in future communications about behaviour, making such an agreement unlikely.

Suppose the two firms agree that each will produce half the monopoly output; then each firm earns a profit that gives it half of the extra profit from colluding:

$$(55 - 10)(22.5) - F = 1012.5 - F. \tag{3.6}$$

If firm 2 produces 22.5 units of output, firm 1's residual demand curve is

$$p = 100 - 22.5 - q_1 = 77.5 - q_1. \tag{3.7}$$

Picking the output that makes marginal revenue equal to marginal cost along this residual demand curve gives firm 1's one-period profit-maximizing output if firm 2 is producing 22.5 units of output,

$$MR = 77.5 - 2q_1 = 10 \Rightarrow q_1 = 33.75 > 22.5. \tag{3.8}$$

If firm 2 produces half the monopoly output, firm 1's profit-maximizing output is greater than half the monopoly output.

If firm 1 defects from the cartel agreement in this way, price is

$$p = 100 - 22.5 - 33.75 = 43.75 \tag{3.9}$$

and firm 1's profit is

---

[3] This is found by setting marginal revenue, $100 - 2Q$, equal to marginal cost, and solving for output.

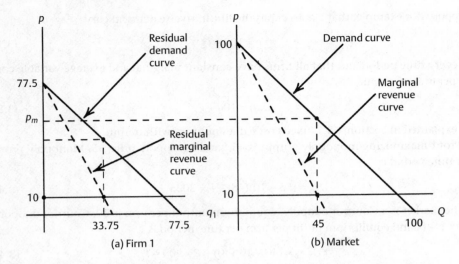

Fig. 3.1 Private profit maximization with a duopoly collusive agreement, $p = 100 - Q$, marginal cost = 10

$$(43.75 - 10)(33.75) - F = 1139.0625 - F, \tag{3.10}$$

which is greater than firm 1's share of the cartel profit (from (3.6), $1012.5 - F$).

The present-discounted value of the profit of a firm that follows the trigger strategy, assuming all other firms do so, is

$$V_{collude} = \frac{1}{1+r}\pi_{collude} + \frac{1}{(1+r)^2}\pi_{collude} + \ldots = \frac{1}{r}\pi_{collude}, \tag{3.11}$$

where r is the interest rate used to discount future income and $\pi_{collude}$ is the firm's collusive payoff in a single period.

The present-discounted value of the profit of a firm that defects from the trigger strategy, assuming all other firms follow the trigger strategy, is

$$V_{cheat} = \frac{1}{1+r}\pi_{cheat} + \frac{1}{(1+r)^2}\pi_{Cournot} + \frac{1}{(1+r)^3}\pi_{Cournot} + \ldots = \frac{1}{1+r}\pi_{cheat} + \frac{1}{1+r}\frac{1}{r}\pi_{Cournot}. \tag{3.12}$$

A firm would be willing to follow the trigger strategy if doing so gives it as least as great a value as cheating, that is, if

$$\frac{1}{r}\pi_{collude} \geq \frac{1}{1+r}\pi_{cheat} + \frac{1}{1+r}\frac{1}{r}\pi_{Cournot} \tag{3.13}$$

or (rearranging terms somewhat)

$$\frac{1}{r} \geq \frac{\pi_{cheat} - \pi_{collude}}{\pi_{collude} - \pi_{Cournot}}. \tag{3.14}$$

We know that $\pi_{cheat} > \pi_{collude}$; in a single period, a firm will earn a greater profit by cheating on a scheme to restrict output if no other firms cheat. We also know that $\pi_{collude} > \pi_{Cournot}$:

monopoly profit is greater than Cournot profit. Thus the right-hand side of (3.14) is positive. If the interest rate r that is used to discount future income is sufficiently small, each firm will have a greater present-discounted value if it does not cheat on the scheme to restrict output.

In the formulation presented here, if a firm cheats on a scheme to restrict output, the cheating is detected after one period of cheating, and other firms retaliate immediately. If it takes more than one period for retaliation to take place, then it is more profitable to cheat, and noncooperative collusion is less likely to be stable.[4] It follows that one way to increase the stability of noncooperative collusion is to put arrangements in place that make it easier for firms to detect and verify cheating, if it should occur.

Stepping back from the details of the trigger strategy, overall output restriction creates a tension between the profit that any single firm could gain by maximizing its short-run payoff and the future profit to be lost if all firms behave in the same way. Market characteristics that reduce the profit to be gained from short-run individualistic behaviour make output restriction more stable.

> *Noncooperative collusion*: if the present-discounted value of the income to be gained over the long run by restricting output and raising price to maximize joint profit is greater than the present-discounted value of the income to be gained by maximizing short-run own profit and accepting tougher future behaviour from rivals as a result, it will be in the self-interest of each firm to restrict output and raise price.

3.2.2 Basing point pricing

The basing point pricing system is one arrangement that reduces the profit a colluding firm might gain by short-run individualistic behaviour.[5] The basing point system has been used in many markets for which the product is of relatively low value in relation to weight or volume and transportation cost is a large part of the total cost of getting the product to the consumer—cement, oil, plywood, and steel are examples.[6]

Under a single basing point system, one location is the basing point and the price a consumer pays for delivery from any location is the price at the basing point plus the cost of transportation from the basing point, no matter what the location of the plant from which delivery is actually made. With a multiple basing point system, the delivered price

---

[4] If it takes m time periods for other firms to detect cheating and then revert to Cournot behaviour, the value of a firm that cheats, (3.12) becomes

$$\left[\frac{1}{1+r}+\frac{1}{(1+r)^2}+\ldots+\frac{1}{(1+r)^m}\right]\pi_{cheat}+\frac{1}{(1+r)^m}\frac{1}{r}\pi_{Cournot}.$$

This would be substituted on the right-hand side of (3.13) to give a generalized form of the stability condition for noncooperative collusion with a trigger strategy.

[5] See Loescher (1959), Phlips (1983, 1993).

[6] The early steel-sector pricing policies of the European Coal and Steel Community compelled ECSC steel firms to use basing pricing, in effect enforcing a collusive scheme for the steel industry; see Section 10.3.1.

to any location is the base price plus transportation cost from the basing point that offers the lowest delivered price, no matter what the location of the plant from which delivery is actually made.

Figure 3.2 (which follows Phlips, 1983) shows a stylized version of a market with two firms, one located at basing point *I* and one plant located at basing point *II*.[7] mc_1 is marginal production cost at location *I*, mc_2 is marginal production cost at location *II*. The lower curves rising from location *I* show the marginal cost of delivery from location *I*, the lower curves rising from location *II* show marginal cost of delivery from location *II*. p_1 is the price to a consumer located at *I*, and the upper curves rising from *I* show the delivered price from plant *I* to consumers at various distances from the plant at *I*. p_2 is the price to a consumer located at *II*, and the upper curves rising from *II* show the delivered price from plant *II* to consumers at various distances from the plant at *II*.

Over the interval from *I* to *a*, the lowest delivered price is from *I* and this price is below *II*'s marginal cost of delivery. Thus it would not be profitable for the plant located at *II* to make sales to consumers located between *I* and *a*. Between *a* and *b*, the delivered price from *I* is lower than the delivered price from *II*; it is the delivered price from *I* that is the basing point price. Between *b* and *c*, the delivered price from *II* is lower than the delivered price from *I*; it is the delivered price from *II* that is the basing point price. Between *a* and *c*,

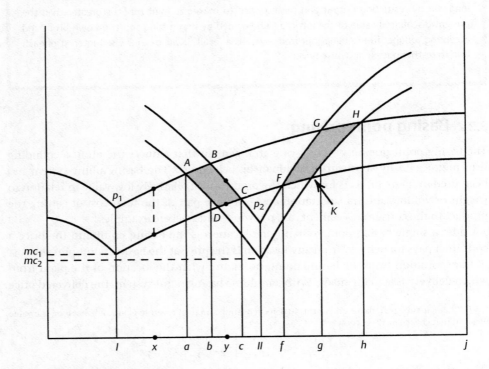

Fig. 3.2 Multiple basing point pricing

[7] More generally, there might be plants not located at a basing point: the delivered price from such a plant would be the delivered price from the basing point that offers the lowest delivered price.

the basing point price is greater than marginal delivery cost for both firms, so both firms would find it profitable to sell to consumers located between a and c.

Between c and f, the delivered price from II is lower than the delivered price from I; it is the delivered price from II that is the basing point price. This price is less than the marginal cost of delivery from I, so the plant located at I would not find it profitable to make sales to consumers located between c and f. By similar arguments, both firms would find it profitable to sell to consumers located between f and h, and only the plant located at I would find it profitable to sell to consumers located to the right of h.

Basing point pricing creates an appearance of rivalry, in the sense that there are some regions (a to c, f to h) where customers have a choice of more than one supplier. Basing point pricing also helps firms avoid tough price competition. With basing point pricing, it is easy for any firm to calculate what the delivered price to any location is supposed to be: since businesses make their price lists available to consumers, price lists will become available to rivals as well, without any need for direct communication between firms.[8] Transportation (for what are typically bulky, heavy products) will often be by rail or barge, and the rates for these modes of transportation will normally be publicly available. Since it is easy to compute the basing point price, if any firm were to charge a lower price, the act of price discounting would be obvious to any rival that learned of it, and in regions where both firms would be willing to make sales, consumers seeking similar discounts could be counted on to pass along information about discount prices offered to themselves or to other customers. Thus any one firm considering the possibility of cutting price (possibly only to a few select customers) would expect other firms to quickly detect and match the price cuts, reducing the extra profit that might be gained by cutting price.

With basing point pricing, all firms offer the same price for delivery to any point, but firms discriminate between consumers in terms of net price—price minus marginal cost. In Figure 3.2, for example, firm I's marginal profit supplying a customer located at x is $p_1 - mc_1$, while its marginal profit supplying a customer located at y is something less than that: the difference between the delivered price from II, p_2 plus the cost of shipment from II, and mc_1 plus the cost of shipment from I. Sales at x and y are both profitable for firm I, but firm I makes a greater net profit on sales to customers located at x than to customers located at y. When firms have different costs of supplying different locations, identical delivered prices mean discriminatory net prices.

3.2.3 Publicity

The theory of noncooperative collusion highlights the rapid detection of price cuts as a factor reducing the expected profitability of price cuts and, therefore, making it more likely that noncooperative collusion will be stable. It may seem surprising, therefore, that an early approach to fighting collusion was to rely on a policy of price transparency price (Interparliamentary Union, 1930):

cartels, trusts and other analogous combines are natural phenomena of economic life towards which it is impossible to adopt an entirely negative attitude. Seeing, however, that those combines

---

[8] In modern times, price lists might very well be posted on the internet.

may have a harmful effect both as regards public interests and those of the State, it is necessary that they should be controlled. This control . . . should simply seek to establish a supervision over possible abuses and to prevent those abuses.

An efficacious means of fighting such abuses and a basic condition for eventual control is to be found in publicity, which implies an obligation for cartels and similar combines to announce their existence and to register in the books of the state.

One rationale for the belief that publicity would bring better market performance seems to have been the idea that publicity would shame managers of collusive firms and lead them to alter their behaviour (Marshall, 1923, p. 442):

upright men are often half-way converted towards removing such just grounds as there may be for complaint against their conduct, by reading a well-informed and well-balanced statement of those grounds; and knowing that an impartial public is forming its judgment on them. In this and many other ways a careful authoritative inquiry, with publication of the evidence taken, goes a long way towards removing sources of social harm . . .

This would not now be found to be a convincing argument.

A rationale for a publicity policy against collusion rooted in a less optimistic but perhaps more realistic view of human nature can be found in the idea that publicity would alert rivals to profit possibilities, inducing entry and improved market performance (Jenks, 1900, pp. 223–4):

publicity . . . which should show with a reasonable degree of detail the profits of the larger combinations would, in the case of the abuse of their power, so stimulate competition against them, either actually or potentially, that consumers would to a great degree be protected against excessive increase in prices.

A publicity policy was practiced in many European nations in the early and middle 20th century, and gradually abandoned.[9] It survived in the Danish Competition Act of 1990 (since amended), which provided that:

The purpose of this Act is to promote competition and, thus, strengthen the efficiency of production and distribution of goods, services, etc., through the largest possible transparency of competitive conditions and through measures against restraints on the freedom of trade and other harmful aspects of anti-competitive practices.

In 1993, the Danish Competition Council suspected that collusion was taking place in the market for ready-mixed concrete, a product that is heavy in relation to value and which is normally shipped no more than 20 to 30 kilometres from the plant.[10] At this time, there were 115 production sites in Denmark. The largest firm had a national market share in 1987 of 37 per cent; the second largest firm had a national market share of 11 per cent. Since geographic markets were local, many local markets were very close to being monopolized.

Implementing a transparency policy against the suspected anticompetitive practices, the Danish Competition Council began to collect price data—transaction prices, taken

---

[9] A publicity policy was also pursued in the US, before passage of the 1914 Federal Trade Commission Act; see Scherer (1990), Martin (1998a).

[10] This discussion is based on Albæk et al. (1997).

from invoices—and publish them on a quarterly basis. Prices rose 15 per cent to 20 per cent in the first year after publication of the transaction prices, and the variability in prices over time fell.

During this period, there was no particular boom in the construction industry, the major user of ready-mix concrete. Thus it does not seem possible to explain the price increase in terms of demand factors. Average concrete prices increased more, in percentage terms, than the price of cement, a major ingredient of concrete. The most likely explanation for the price increase is that by publishing actual transaction prices, the Danish Competition Council reduced incentives for firms to secretly cut prices. With published transaction prices, price cuts would quickly be revealed, inviting retaliation. In effect, the Danish Competition Council made it easier for the ready-mix concrete industry to avoid price competition. In a perfectly competitive market, no transparency policy is needed. In an imperfectly competitive market, the effects of a transparency policy are perverse: it makes noncooperative collusion easier, because it makes it easier for firms to detect rivals' output expansion.

Price transparency and market performance: in imperfectly competitive markets, business or government policies that make it easier for firms to detect sporadic price cuts make such price cuts less profitable and facilitate tacit collusion.

3.3 Welfare consequences of collusion

If firms collude on the monopoly price and the number of firms supplying the market is held constant, collusion means that market performance changes from that of oligopoly to that of monopoly: the price rises, output falls, and deadweight welfare loss increases. This follows from the fact that monopoly output is less than equilibrium oligopoly output.

Additional effects arise if colluding firms succeed in raising price but cannot prevent new firms from coming into the market. Suppose, for example, that in a market with inverse demand curve (3.1) and cost function (3.2), fixed cost F is 550.

Then Cournot duopoly profit per firm per period is positive:

$$\pi_1 = \pi_2 = (40 - 10)(30) - F = 900 - 550 = 350 > 0. \tag{3.15}$$

With three firms in the market, Cournot triopoly profit would be negative:

$$\left(100 - 3\,\frac{100 - 10}{4} - 10\right)\left(\frac{100 - 10}{4}\right) - 550 = -43.75 < 0. \tag{3.16}$$

With Cournot behaviour, the equilibrium number of firms is two.

If three firms collude on monopoly output, each firm produces 15 units. The monopoly price is 55; hence each of the three firms earns positive profit:

$$(55 - 10)(15) - 550 = 675 - 550 = 125 > 0. \qquad (3.17)$$

In this particular example, collusion on the monopoly output raises the equilibrium number of firms from two to three. More generally, if firms collude and raise the price, the higher price may make additional entry profitable, depending on the size of fixed costs.

In the example, if two incumbent firms collude on the monopoly price and as a result a third firm comes into the market, the first two firms earn less profit than they would as Cournot duopolists: monopoly profit split among three firms is 125 per period, Cournot duopoly profit per firm is 350. It might very well be, however, that firms could find ways to restrict output and raise price without violating anticollusion laws (we take up this topic in greater detail later) but that actively trying to keep a third firm out of the market would leave evidence of other kinds of anticompetitive behaviour (abuse of a dominant position) against which it would be more difficult to defend. It might simply be, in the oft-quoted words of Hicks (1935, p. 8), that "The best of all monopoly profits is a quiet life".

If raising price to the monopoly level would make entry profitable, incumbent firms might noncooperatively collude to raise price above the Cournot level, but not so high as the monopoly level. Noncooperative collusion would still worsen market performance, but not so much as if entry were not possible. Thus we have the possibility that potential entry—the threat of competition, rather than actual competition—might improve market performance.[11]

A kind of natural experiment generated by UK competition policy suggests that collusion may in fact result in excess entry (Symeonidis, 2000). Before 1956, agreements to restrain trade were not illegal under UK competition law, but they could not be enforced in court. Trade associations in a number of industries administered elaborate schemes to exchange information about prices and quantities sold, schemes which appear to have had the effect of making it easier for rivals to detect output expansion or price cutting.[12] As suggested by our discussion of noncooperative collusion, making it easier for rivals to detect cheating should discourage defection from a collusive scheme.

In 1956 the UK Restrictive Trade Practices Act, made restrictive agreements illegal, and required that existing restrictive agreements be registered with public authorities. The Act left open the possibility that a Restrictive Practices Court could permit an agreement if it found benefits that outweighed the negative effects of a restrictive agreement.

Immediately after the law went into effect, it was not known what approach the Restrictive Practices Court would take, and it appears that most existing restrictive agreements were in fact registered. As it developed, the Court took a tough approach to applying the law, and did not permit many restrictive agreements. Information exchange agreements ceased to function, and between 1958 and 1977 the combined market share

---

[11] We also have the possibility that one equilibrium oligopoly price is the highest price that will not induce entry, in contrast to the long-run equilibrium price of a perfectly competitive industry, which is the lowest price that will not induce exit.

[12] See Chandler (1990, Part III) for case studies documenting the inclination of British industrialists to avoid tough competition.

of the five largest firms in industries affected by the Restrictive Practices Act rose by an average of 15 percentage points. The most likely explanation is that in the UK, trade association activities supported noncooperative collusion but did not restrict entry, thus permitting the survival of relatively inefficient firms. When trade association activities were limited by a more vigorous competition policy, rivalry increased and less efficient firms went out of business.

Collusion or tacit collusion and market performance: successful tacit collusion or tacit collusion raises price, leaving consumers worse off than would otherwise be the case, and may allow excess entry and the continued operation of inefficient firms, leaving producers worse off as well.

3.4 Article 81

3.4.1 Provisions

It is Article 81 (see box, below) of the EC Treaty that deals with collusion and cooperative arrangements. Article 81, Paragraph 1 prohibits agreements and decisions by firms or associations of firms and concerted practices that affect trade between the Member States and have the object or effect of distorting competition, on the ground that they are incompatible with the common market.[13] Paragraph 2 declares that such agreements are void. Paragraph 3 allows the European Commission to permit restrictive agreements, if the agreements have certain types of specified beneficial effects (improving static efficiency or technological progress) and if a fair share of those benefits are passed along to consumers. Under Article 81(3), the Commission has, for example, sometimes permitted agreements of rival firms to specialize in the production of different varieties of a product, to set up joint marketing arrangements, or to cooperate in research and development.

3.4.2 Applications[14]

As we have noted above, Article 81 refers to "agreements and decisions by firms or associations of firms and concerted practices". Vital practical questions are:

---

[13] To be precise, Article 81 refers to undertakings rather than firms; "undertaking" is a classification that includes private firms but also other organizations that supply goods and services to markets (for example, public enterprise). A completely different meaning of the word "undertaking" in the context of EC competition policy is an agreement made by firms to close an investigation before a negative decision is formalized.

[14] See, generally, Neven et al. (1998).

Article 81 of the EC Treaty (ex Article 85)

1. The following shall be prohibited as incompatible with the common market: all agreements between undertakings, decisions by associations of undertakings and concerted practices which may affect trade between Member States and which have as their object or effect the prevention, restriction or distortion of competition within the common market, and in particular those which:

(a) directly or indirectly fix purchase or selling prices or any other trading conditions;

(b) limit or control production, markets, technical development, or investment;

(c) share markets or sources of supply;

(d) apply dissimilar conditions to equivalent transactions with other trading parties, thereby placing them at a competitive disadvantage;

(e) make the conclusion of contracts subject to acceptance by the other parties of supplementary obligations which, by their nature or according to commercial usage, have no connection with the subject of such contracts.

2. Any agreements or decisions prohibited pursuant to this Article shall be automatically void.

3. The provisions of paragraph 1 may, however, be declared inapplicable in the case of:

— any agreement or category of agreements between undertakings;

— any decision or category of decisions by associations of undertakings;

— any concerted practice or category of concerted practices, which contributes to improving the production or distribution of goods or to promoting technical or economic progress, while allowing consumers a fair share of the resulting benefit, and which does not:

(a) impose on the undertakings concerned restrictions which are not indispensable to the attainment of these objectives;

(b) afford such undertakings the possibility of eliminating competition in respect of a substantial part of the products in question.

- what sort of evidence must be produced to establish, in a legal sense, the existence of an agreement, decision, or concerted practice?;[15] and

- what is the distinction, in terms of standards of proof required, between an agreement and a concerted practice?

Franco-Japanese ball-bearings

Given the historically charitable attitude of EC Member States to collusion, it is not surprising that the most clear-cut examples of collusion are found early in the history

---

[15] To find a violation of Article 81, it must also be shown that the behaviour complained of "may affect trade between Member States" and has the object or effect of preventing, restricting, or distorting competition within the common market.

of EC competition policy.[16] One such example is the Franco-Japanese ball-bearings case.[17] Representatives of Japanese and French trade associations and ball-bearing producers met in Paris in 1972 and agreed that Japanese firms would raise their prices in Europe from 15 per cent below the prices of European firms to not more than 10 per cent below, with a later increase to only 5 per cent to 8 per cent below the prices of European firms. The French participants in the meetings prepared careful minutes, which were obtained by the European Commission during the course of its investigation. Based on this and other evidence, the Commission concluded that the agreements violated Article 81(1) of the EC Treaty.

Suiker Unie

Experience quickly teaches business executives that it is not wise to leave such unambiguous evidence of cartel meetings.[18] The difficulty this creates for competition policy is that in oligopoly industries, the kinds of market performance that might be obtained by naked collusion can also be obtained by genuinely independent behaviour. If prudent managers learn not to engage in obvious collusion, but the standards of proof required to find existence of a concerted practice are not as strict as those required to find existence of collusion, one might think that the Article 81(1) prohibition of concerted practices would make it possible to effectively promote independent market behaviour. Thus the question of the distinction between the evidence needed to show that firms have reached an agreement and the evidence needed to show that firms have engaged in a concerted practice moves to the fore.

The Suiker Unie case,[19] which involved business conduct that had the effect of splitting the EC sugar market along national lines, sheds light on the concepts of agreement and concerted practice. The decision records ample evidence of meetings and direct communications among the firms involved, so that it most likely would have been possible to find a violation of Article 81 on the basis of a restrictive agreement alone. But the case also found the presence of concerted practices, which the Court defined as ([1975] ECR 1663 at 1696) "a form of coordination which knowingly substitutes practical cooperation for the risks of competition". The Court also said that the notion of a concerted practice ([1975] ECR 1663 at 1942; emphasis added):

must be understood in the light of the concept inherent in the provisions of the Treaty relating to competition that *each economic operator must determine independently the policy which he intends to adopt on the common market* including the choice of the persons and undertakings to which he makes offers or sells.

Although it is correct to say that this requirement of independence does not deprive economic

[16] During the interwar and indeed early post-World War II periods, as well as in the initial phases of the European Coal and Steel Community, cartels were seen as an effective way to organize sectors of the economy which (it was believed) would otherwise have been subject to politically unacceptable fluctuations. See Gillingham (1995), Morelli (1997).

[17] OJ L 343 21 September 1974, p. 19.

[18] Such episodes nonetheless continue to surface from time to time (the Archer Daniels Midland case under US antitrust law being one example), suggesting (as if evidence were needed) that greed and stupidity are not mutually exclusive human characteristics.

[19] *Suiker Unie and others* v. *Commission*, Joined Cases 40–48/73, 50/73, 54–56/73, 111/73, 113–114/73 Judgment of 16 December 1975 [1975] ECR 1663; [1976] 1 CMLR 295.

operators of the right to adapt themselves intelligently to the existing and anticipated conduct of their competitors, *it does however strictly preclude any direct or indirect contact between such operators, the object or effect whereof is either to influence the conduct on the market of an actual or potential competitor or to disclose to such a competitor the course of conduct which they themselves have decided to adopt or contemplate adopting on the market.*

The first part of this discussion affirms that independent behaviour does not violate Article 81. The second emphasizes the importance of direct or indirect contacts that alter the incentives a competitor faces when it makes its own decisions. Such contacts are critical to a finding that there is a concerted practice. They might also, however, be thought to justify a finding that firms had acted in agreement, raising the question of the distinction between an agreement and a concerted practice.

Italian flat glass

Early decisions of the European Commission suggested that the distinction between the two concepts lay in the nature of the proof required to establish a violation of Article 81. In the Italian flat glass decision,[20] for example, the Commission relied heavily on evidence that Italian producers of flat glass (used in the windows of buildings and automobiles) set essentially identical price schedules, changed those price schedules at essentially the same times, and granted discounts from price schedules in essentially the same way to justify its finding that there was a concerted practice (OJ L33, p. 61):

the fact remains that the publication of identical price lists over a long period, the existence of the same discount scales and the application of uniform terms of sale to the same customers could only be the result of concerted practices either directly between the three producers or through the intermediary of the spokesman for the wholesalers.

It must be said that viewed through the lens of economic theory, this analysis is exactly wrong. In theory, firms that operate in the same market over long periods of time could all independently decide to engage in the kind of parallel behaviour that is described (sustained by the kinds of independent reactions modelled by a trigger strategy). On a more practical level, it is precisely over long periods of time—during which firms have an opportunity to study rivals and acquire experience that allows them to anticipate rivals' conduct—that parallel patterns of behaviour might be expected to emerge in oligopolistic markets as a result of entirely independent decisions.

Woodpulp and the oligopoly problem

In its Woodpulp decision,[21] the European Court of Justice moved away from accepting parallel conduct as sufficient evidence of a concerted practice. Wood pulp is an input in the production of paper. During the period involved in this case, the European Community was supplied with wood pulp by firms located in North America and Northern Europe. The European Commission relied on several factors to justify its conclusion that the firms involved in the case had engaged in a concerted practice in violation of Article

---

[20] Commission Decision of 7 December 1988 OJ L 33 4 February 1989, p. 44.
[21] *A. Ahlström OY and others* v. *EC Commission* [1988] 4 CMLR 901; [1993] 4 CMLR 407; see also Commission Decision of 19 December 1984 OJ L 85 26 March 1985, p. 1.

81(1). Some US producers were members of an export cartel.[22] Some firms were members of a trade association, based in Switzerland, that hosted regular meetings at which firms exchanged information about prices and formulated price policies. The Commission also relied on evidence of parallel behaviour: the prices set by different firms changed by more or less the same amount at more or less the same time, even though the firms involved were based in many different countries and kept their accounts in many different currencies.[23]

The Advocate General's arguments when the case was appealed, later accepted by the European Court of Justice, rejected the parallel pricing approach ([1993] 4 CMLR 407 at 470):

Each company is entitled to align itself independently on the conduct of its competitors, if knowledge of such conduct is obtained solely by monitoring the market.

and ([1993] 4 CMLR 407 at 478):

In any event, if there is a plausible explanation for the conduct found to exist which is consistent with an independent choice by the undertakings concerned, concertation remains unproven.

The European Court of Justice found that while parallel price movements might have been the result of collusion, they might also have been the result of a combination of a high degree of price transparency—prices widely known and news of price changes circulating rapidly—and the oligopoly structure of the market. For the Court, evidence of parallel pricing in combination with other factors might justify a finding of concertation, but in this instance the other evidence assembled by the Commission was not sufficient.

This is the heart of the problem that oligopoly presents for the enforcement of competition law: if the number of firms is small, independent action can lead to results that closely approximate those of collusion. But competition law in free-market economies does not condemn the results of decisions that are independently arrived at, and long experience suggests that neither regulation nor public ownership are likely to result in improved (or even good) market performance. Thus even if firms in an oligopolistic market really are colluding in a legal sense, it may be difficult to obtain legally acceptable evidence of that collusion.

There is also the problem of remedy. If firms are colluding, they can be ordered not to collude, and they may be subject to large enough fines so that they decide it is in their own best interest not to collude. But firms in oligopolistic industries will often be able to avoid tough competition without colluding; equilibrium market performance in oligopoly may be much the same with or without collusion. But if such an outcome is produced by independent business decisions, there is not much competition authorities can do about it, taking market structure as given.

A clear implication of the oligopoly problem for competition policy is that if there are

---

[22] The US Sherman Act of 1890 prohibits collusion with respect to the US market (and thus corresponds, in a general way, to Article 81). But the 1918 Webb-Pomerene Act makes it legal for US firms to collude with respect to export markets (see Section 9.2.2). The EC Treaty does not cover export cartels that do not affect trade between the Member States. However, the European Commission has been sceptical toward the possibility that firms could collude on export markets without some spillover effect on the EC internal market.

[23] OJ L 85 26 March 1985, p. 16.

practical difficulties in influencing business conduct in oligopoly markets, competition authorities should take great care administering policy toward market structure. Proposed mergers should be carefully evaluated to determine if they are privately profitable because they increase efficiency or because they increase market power.

Trade association activities

Trade associations may serve legitimate purposes (development of guidelines for product standardization, for example, or dissemination of aggregate information about demand trends, which helps firms make effective investment decisions) but they frequently serve as a forum for activities that restrict competition. When they do, they will run foul of Article 81.

One example is found in the Commission's FEG/TU decision.[24] FEG was an association of Dutch wholesale distributors of electrotechnical equipment (cables, plugs, switches, sockets) used in construction. FEG members supplied 96 per cent of the Dutch market for electrotechnical equipment. TU was the largest single member of FEG.

FEG administered informal exclusive dealing arrangements between manufacturers, its members, and the construction firms that were the main direct customers for the products distributed by FEG members. Dutch and foreign manufacturers for the most part agreed to distribute only through FEG members; construction firms for the most part agreed to obtain supplies only through FEG members. This informal agreement was the successor to a formal agreement that had been in place from 1928 to 1959.

Given the large share of the market covered by FEG members, the exclusive dealing arrangements made it difficult for firms based outside the Netherlands to make significant sales in the Netherlands. Combined with the fact that one requirement for FEG membership was annual sales revenue in the Netherlands of 5 million NLG for three years in a row, the effect of the exclusive dealing arrangements was to create artificial barriers to entry around the Dutch wholesale market for electrotechnical equipment.

FEG subgroups, organized along product lines, carried out regular meetings at which information about price lists, discounts, and prices actually paid by customers. Some of the product subgroups took active measures to keep supplies out of the hands of price-cutting wholesalers based in the EC but outside the Netherlands. The result was that the wholesale price level for the products in question in the Netherlands tended to be higher than elsewhere in the EC.

In its decision under Article 81, the European Commission concluded that FEG and TU had violated Article 81, ordered them to end the restrictive behaviour, and fined FEG €4.4 million and fined TU €2.15 million.

---

[24] OJ L 39 14 February 2000, p. 1. FEG is an acronym for Nederlandse Federatieve Vereniging voor de Groothandel op Elektrotechnisch Gebied; TU is an acronym for Technische Unie. See Ferdinandusse (2000).

3.5 **Enforcement**

3.5.1 **Leniency**

The Commission's *Leniency Notice*[25] creates incentives for members of collusive agreements to repent and return to the path of righteousness. A participant in a cartel may benefit from a reduction of from 10 per cent to 100 per cent of the fine that would otherwise be imposed, depending on the nature of its cooperation and the extent to which its evidence contributes to Commission handling of the matter.

3.5.2 **Cooperation**

The European Commission's *Draft Guidelines* (27 April 2000b)[26] take an economic approach to the analysis of inter-firm cooperation. Leaving naked collusion to restrict output and raise price aside, inter-firm cooperation may have some efficiency effects that improve market performance and some anticompetitive effects that worsen market performance. The Commission's view is that if the combined market share of cooperating firms is relatively small (less than 20 per cent for specialization agreements, less than 25 per cent for R&D cooperation), beneficial effects of cooperation are likely to outweigh anticompetitive effects, since effective competition from other suppliers will restrict the exercise of market power by cooperating firms. In such cases, the cooperation qualifies for an automatic block exemption[27] under Article 81(3).

If the cooperating firms have a combined market share that is greater than the threshold for a block exemption, the Commission may nonetheless grant an exemption under Article 81(3). In this case, factors to be considered in evaluating the likely impact of the proposed cooperation on market performance, in addition to the market shares of the firms involved, include the degree of seller concentration, the nature of entry conditions, whether suppliers or buyers are likely to exercise countervailing power, and other elements of market structure. If the conclusion of the analysis is that the net effect of the cooperative agreement is positive and that a fair share of the benefit will go to consumers, the Commission will grant an exemption. In evaluating the tradeoff between increased efficiency and market performance, priority is given to market performance: even great efficiency gains do not justify the complete elimination of effective competition (Draft Guidelines, p. 37).

3.5.3 **Direct applicability**

The Commission (1999a, 2000c) has also proposed a fundamental change in the way Article 81(3) is enforced. At the beginning of the European Community, the Commission

---

[25] Commission Notice on the non-imposition or reduction of fines in cartel cases OJ C 207/4 18 July 1996. Peña Castellot (2001) reviews early applications of the Leniency Notice.

[26] See also Lücking (2000), Lücking and Woods (2001).

[27] Under Regulation 19/65.

had to introduce a prohibition-based competition policy to a Community of six Member States, only one of which (West Germany) had a similar national competition policy. The other Member States either had no explicit competition policy or followed an abuse control approach that viewed collusion as a natural and inevitable outcome of market processes.[28] The theory of an abuse control policy was that cartels would register with the government, which would keep tabs on their behaviour and take steps to prevent excesses. In practice, abuse control often turned into "industry capture'', with cartels using government policy to promote collusive outcomes.

Faced with the need to introduce a culture of competition in the fledgling European Community, the Commission established a system under which cooperating businesses were required to notify the Commission of their agreement, and only the Commission could decide whether or not an exemption would be granted.[29]

Particularly in the early years of EC competition policy, some agreements were not notified to the Commission, and these were condemned if and when the Commission discovered their existence. But the Commission was faced with a flood of notifications that required some response and overwhelmed the Commission's resources. One reaction of the Commission was to develop the block exemption system. Block exemptions are formal policy statements outlining broad classes of agreements, typically based on market share thresholds and other conditions, that automatically qualify for an Article 81(3) exemption. Another response was to issue so-called comfort letters to notifying firms. A comfort letter is a statement that on the basis of the information before the Commission, the notified arrangement either does or does not appear to meet the conditions for an exemption under Article 81(3). The Commission issued comfort letters on an informal basis, and the European Court of Justice held that they did not constitute legally binding decisions.

Today the foundations of a culture of competition in the EC seem firmly established, and a good deal of the supporting superstructure as well. All EC Member States have national competition authorities; most have adopted national competition policies with provisions that parallel those of the EC Treaty (Martin, 1998). The number of Member States is expected to double in the foreseeable future. The advent of the euro and monetary integration is likely to broaden and deepen integration and market integration. The increase in the number of Member States and progress in market integration will both increase the workload of EC competition authorities.

The Commission has therefore proposed to eliminate the requirement that it be notified of cooperative arrangements. Article 81(3) would be enforced by national authorities and before national courts, as is now the case for Article 81(1).[30] The Commission would then be able to concentrate its attention and resources on the most serious competition policy matters, leaving routine enforcement to national authorities.

A necessary condition for the success of this reform is that Article 81(3) be enforced in a

[28] Historically, the predominant European approach to market behaviour has what Gillingham (1995, p. 163) calls "organized capitalism. Its characteristic features are the cartel, the producer association, and close ties to the state." See Lister (1960, pp. 126–9), and also Chamberlin (1954).
[29] Regulation No. 17/62 JO 13/204 21 September 1962 [1959–62] OJ spec. Ed. 57.
[30] In some Member States, national law would need to be amended to implement this approach. The Commission would have the power to intervene in matters decided at the Member State level if it feels that such intervention is appropriate.

consistent and vigorous way in the different Member States. Competition policy continues to be an essential force in the ongoing process of EC integration, and it will not fulfil its role if weak enforcement in some Member States undermines overall confidence in its effectiveness.

3.6 Market definition for the application of competition policy

If cooperating firms have a combined market share that falls below the limits specified in the Draft Guidelines, they will be able to go forward with their cooperation without having to seek and obtain explicit permission. This approach reduces compliance costs for business and enforcement costs for the Commission. It also brings the process of deciding what the market is to centre stage: businesses need to know how the Commission thinks markets should be defined, for the purposes of competition policy, to decide if they need to seek explicit exemption for a cooperation agreement. As we shall see, the process of market definition is central to the application of almost all elements of competition policy.

For the Commission (1997b, p. 1):

The main purpose of market definition is to identify ... the competitive constraints that the undertakings involved face. The objective of defining a market in both its product and geographic dimension is to identify those actual competitors of the undertakings involved that are capable of constraining their behaviour and of preventing them from behaving independently of an effective competitive pressure.

In principle, the Commission emphasizes the demand side when it defines markets (1997b, p. 2): "A relevant product market comprises all those products and/or services which are regarded as interchangeable or substitutable by the consumer" and (p. 3) "the exercise of market definition consists in identifying the effective alternative sources of supply for customers of the undertakings involved, both in terms of products/services and geographic location of suppliers". The primary theoretical test that the Commission applies is one based upon how consumers would respond to price changes (1997b, p. 4):

The question to be answered is whether the parties' customers would switch to readily available substitutes or to suppliers located elsewhere in response to an hypothetical small (in the range 5%–10%), permanent relative price increase in the products and areas being considered. If substitution would be enough to make the price increase unprofitable because of the resulting loss of sales, additional substitutes and areas are included in the relevant market. This would be done until the set of products and geographic areas is such that small, permanent increases in relative prices would be profitable.

Implicitly, this methodology takes it for granted that products are differentiated; otherwise, there would be only one price, and it would not make sense to speak of "relative prices" or "prices in products and areas being considered". In the real world, of course, most markets do involve differentiated products. The existence of product differentiation has implications for how market share should be measured for the purpose of assessing market power; see Problem 3–1. If products are differentiated but market size and market shares are calculated as if products were standardized, the result will be to underestimate market shares.

Although the Commission clearly gives priority to demand-side substitutability in the principles for defining markets, it also indicates that it will take supply-side substitutability into account if suppliers are (1997b, p. 4) "able to switch production to the relevant products and market them in the short term without incurring significant additional costs or risks in response to small and permanent changes in relative prices". In such cases, for the Commission (1997b, p. 5) "the relevant product market will encompass all products that are substitutable in demand and supply, and the current sales of those products will be summed to calculate the total value or volume of the market".

To the extent that it is motivated by economic models of oligopoly, such a procedure is incorrect. Economic models clearly indicate that the total value of the market (adjusted for product differentiation, if it is present) is the sum of sales of products that are sold in the market, and does not include the sales of products that could be sold in the market if the firms producing those products found it profitable to switch their activities from one market to another (Problem 3–1). It is demand-side substitutability that determines where market boundaries are. Supply-side substitutability (entry conditions) determines the extent to which a firm with a large market share will find it profitable to exercise market power.[31]

It is possible to carry out sophisticated econometric analyses of demand patterns to reach conclusions about the nature of the market. The time and data requirements of such tests often mean that they cannot be applied by the Commission when it defines a market. The Commission often looks at practical information about the nature of demand for a class of products (1997b, pp. 8–10): historical substitution patterns, the views of customers and competitors, evidence of costs of switching from one brand or supplier to another, whether there are distinctive national preferences or national (for example, tax or environmental) policies.

3.7 Summary

Equilibrium output in an imperfectly competitive market generally exceeds the monopoly level, which gives firms in such markets an incentive (the potential for increased profit) to restrict output. It is possible (depending on the tradeoff between long-term

[31] Consider the following stylized example: a single local firm supplies a standardized product in a national area. The firm's average cost is €10 per unit of output, and if there were no possibility of entry, the monopoly price would be €12. But if price is higher than €11 per unit of output, foreign suppliers with capacity sufficient to supply the entire local area would find it profitable to enter the national market. If the local firm sets a price of €11 or less, it is the only supplier and has a 100 per cent share of the national market: but the threat of entry makes holding price below the unconstrained monopoly price the most profitable option. For a price of €11 or less, including the sales that foreign suppliers could make at higher prices would give a misleadingly lower evaluation of the local firm's market share. See Gaskins (1971) for a formal model.

gains from output restriction and short-term gains from own-profit maximization) that it will be a noncooperative equilibrium for individual firms to restrict output. If firms reach such an equilibrium as a result of meetings or of exchanges of information, trade association activities, and some types of contracts with distributors, they can be found to have agreed or engaged in a concerted practice in violation of Article 81 of the EC Treaty. But if firms reach such an equilibrium in a genuinely noncooperative way, as a result of independent decisions independently arrived at, then they will not have colluded (made agreements in restraint of trade) in the sense of EC competition law.

Study points

- trigger strategy (page 50)
- basing point pricing (pages 53–5)
- price transparency and market performance in imperfectly competitive markets (pages 55–7)
- collusion or tacit collusion and the survival of inefficient firms (page 58)
- EC Treaty, Article 81 (page 59)
- competition policy and tacit collusion in oligopoly (page 63)
- enforcement of Article 81 (pages 65–7)
- market definition in applications of competition policy (pages 67–8)

Problem

3-1 (Measuring market share with differentiated products) Show that if (for example, for duopoly) inverse demand curves have equations (2.41) and (2.42),

$$p_1 = 100 - (q_1 + \theta q_2), \tag{3.18}$$

$$p_2 = 100 - (\theta q_2 + q_1), \tag{3.19}$$

the expression for the Lerner index of market power that corresponds to (2.34) is

$$\frac{p_1 - c'(q_1)}{p_1} = \frac{s_1}{\varepsilon_{Q_1 p_1}}, \tag{3.20}$$

where

$$s_1 = \frac{q_1}{q_1 + \theta q_2} \equiv \frac{q_1}{Q_1} \tag{3.21}$$

is firm 1's market share, taking account of the imperfect substitutability of variety 2 for variety 1, and

$$\varepsilon_{Q_1 p_1} \equiv -\frac{Q_1}{p_1}\frac{dp_1}{dQ_1}. \tag{3.22}$$

Chapter 4

Dominance

Upon what meat doth this our Caesar feed, that he is grown so great?

Julius Caesar, Act I, scene ii.

4.1 Introduction

Few if any real-world markets are either perfectly competitive or true monopolies. Unless a single supplier is granted a legal monopoly, it faces the threat of entry, and potential competition may reduce profit below the monopoly level. If so, it is profitable for a dominant incumbent to employ strategies that raise entry costs. Such strategies are one of the topics of this chapter. This kind of strategic behaviour by dominant firms may impede the process of market integration as well as worsen market performance, and we also examine EC competition policy toward dominant behaviour.

4.2 Quantity leadership

One of the earliest models of dominant firm behaviour is obtained by considering a situation in which one firm has an informational advantage over the other. Following von Stackelberg (1934), keep all but one of the assumptions of the basic Cournot duopoly model. Instead of supposing that both firms have the same knowledge about the market, suppose that

• firm 2 behaves as in the basic Cournot model; and that

• firm 1 knows this.

Firm 1 has an informational advantage over firm 2 and is able to use that advantage to act as a leader and increase its own profit.[1]

If the inverse demand curve is

$$p = 100 - (q_1 + q_2) \qquad (4.1)$$

and both firms have cost function

$$c(q) = 10q, \qquad (4.2)$$

then in the usual way the equation of firm 2's best response function is

$$q_2 = 45 - \tfrac{1}{2}q_1. \qquad (4.3)$$

The equation of firm 1's residual demand curve is

$$p = (100 - q_2) - q_1. \qquad (4.4)$$

Substituting (4.3) on the right in (4.3) to eliminate q_2 and rearranging terms gives the equation of firm 1's residual demand curve,

$$p = 55 - \tfrac{1}{2}q_1. \qquad (4.5)$$

(4.5) shows the market-clearing price for any quantity sold by firm 1, taking into account firm 2's profit-maximizing output choice.

Firm 1, with superior information, maximizes profit by setting marginal revenue along the residual demand curve (4.5) equal to its marginal cost,

$$MR_1 = 55 - 2(\tfrac{1}{2}q_1) = 10. \qquad (4.6)$$

$$q_{SL} = 55 - 10 = 45. \qquad (4.7)$$

The Stackelberg quantity leader maximizes profit by producing more than the Cournot duopoly equilibrium output (in fact, the Stackelberg leader produces the same output that would be produced by a monopolist in an otherwise identical market).

In the Cournot model, best response functions are downward sloping: since the Stackelberg leader produces more than the Cournot duopoly equilibrium output, the Stackelberg follower produces less than the Cournot duopoly equilibrium output:

$$q_{SF} = 45 - \tfrac{1}{2}(45) = 22.5. \qquad (4.8)$$

Total output under Stackelberg leadership exceeds Cournot duopoly output:

$$45 + 22.5 = 67.5 > 60. \qquad (4.9)$$

It follows that equilibrium price under Stackelberg leadership is less than Cournot duopoly price:

$$100 - 67.5 = 32.5 < 40. \qquad (4.10)$$

The Stackelberg quantity leader earns greater profit than it would in Cournot duopoly equilibrium, and the Stackelberg quantity follower less:

---

[1] Like von Stackelberg, we consider the case in which the identity of the leader is given by assumption. See Dowrick (1986), Hamilton and Slutsky (1990) for models that make the choice of leader, follower roles endogenous.

$$(32.5 - 10)(45) = 1012.5 > (40 - 10)(30) = 900 \qquad (4.11)$$

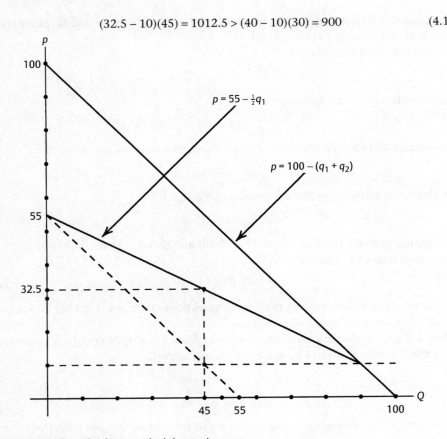

Fig. 4.1 Stackelberg leader's residual demand curve

$$(32.5 - 10)(22.5) = 506.25 < 900. \qquad (4.12)$$

This relationship is reversed if firms set prices rather than quantities (Problem 4–1). If firms set prices, the Stackelberg price leader and the Stackelberg price follower both set prices that are higher than equilibrium prices in the basic Bertrand model (Section 2.3.2); the leader's price is higher than the follower's price. The payoffs of both firms rise compared with the basic model, but the follower's equilibrium payoff is greater than that of the leader.

4.3 Limit pricing

4.3.1 Entry deterrence with output commitment

One definition of *strategic behaviour* is business conduct that is profitable because of the effect that it has on the incentives facing rivals.[2] The Stackelberg quantity leadership model can be modified to become a model of entry deterrence that is strategic in this sense.

Although the resulting model is one in which firms set quantities, it is most usefully thought of as a formal descendent of an earlier informal model, due to Bain (1949), in which firms set prices, and for that reason is often referred to as a model of *limit pricing*. What it is that is being limited in the limit price model is entry: an incumbent firm makes choices that alter the incentives of potential entrants to come into the market.

To develop the quantity-setting version of the entry deterrence model, reinterpret the inverse demand curve (4.1) so that firm 1 is an incumbent, already in the market, and firm 2 is a potential entrant, a firm that will come into the market if it expects it to be profitable to do so.

Suppose that entry involves a fixed and sunk entry cost e, an investment that must be made if the firm is to produce at all and which cannot be recovered by resale of any assets if the firm should decide to leave the market. Suppose also that if the entrant comes into the market, it operates with constant marginal and average variable cost 10 per unit (as does the incumbent, which is already in the market).

If the entrant comes into the market, its single-period profit depends on the incumbent's output after entry:

$$\pi_2 = (p - 10)q_2 = (90 - q_1 - q_2)q_2. \tag{4.13}$$

The post-entry market will be a noncooperative quantity-setting duopoly: if the entrant comes into the market at all, it will maximize profit by producing the output that makes its residual marginal revenue equal to its marginal cost,

$$q_2 = 45 - \tfrac{1}{2}q_1. \tag{4.14}$$

From the equation of the entrant's residual demand curve,

$$p - 10 = 90 - q_1 - (45 - \tfrac{1}{2}q_1) = 45 - \tfrac{1}{2}q_1, \tag{4.15}$$

and the entrant's present-discounted value if it comes into the market is[3]

$$V_2 = \frac{1}{r}\left(45 - \frac{1}{2}q_1\right)^2 - e. \tag{4.16}$$

---

[2] Williamson (1985, p. 373), for example, defines strategic behaviour as "efforts by established firms to take up advance positions in relation to actual or potential rivals and/or to respond punitively to new rivalry".

[3] That is, the entrant has a profit $(45 - \tfrac{1}{2}q_1)^2$ at the end of the first period, of the second period, and so on, with present discounted value

$$\left(45 - \frac{1}{2}q_1\right)^2 \left[\frac{1}{1+r} + \frac{1}{(1+r)^2} + \dots\right] = \frac{1}{r}\left(45 - \frac{1}{2}q_1\right)^2.$$

Suppose now that the incumbent can commit in advance to the output it will produce. Such a commitment might be possible, for example, if the incumbent can sign long-term contracts. Stepping outside the specific assumptions of the model, effective commitment might be possible if the incumbent can choose a technology that makes most cost fixed and marginal cost near zero up to some capacity level. Then if it is profitable for the incumbent to produce at all, it will be profitable for the incumbent to produce at the full capacity level.

If the incumbent commits to an output level that makes the best value the potential entrant could have after entry equal to zero, the potential entrant would be indifferent between entering and staying out of the market. By producing just a little bit above the output level that makes the entrant's value zero, the incumbent would make entry unprofitable.

The entry-deterring or limit level of output is the one that makes the potential entrant's post-entry value equal to zero:

$$V_2 = \frac{1}{r}\left(45 - \frac{1}{2}q_1\right)^2 - e = 0 \rightarrow q_1 = q_L = 90 - 2\sqrt{re}.$$ (4.17)

Whether or not entry deterrence is the most profitable choice for the incumbent depends on the size of entry cost. We can distinguish two extreme cases.

The first is the case in which entry is *blocked* (reaching ahead to Chapter 6, we could also describe this as a case in which the industry is a natural monopoly). If the entry-deterring output is less than the monopoly output,

$$q_L = 90 - 2\sqrt{re} \leq 45 \text{ or } e \geq \frac{1}{r}(22.5)^2 = \frac{506.25}{r},$$ (4.18)

the entrant will not find it profitable to come into the market even if the incumbent produces the monopoly output.

At the other extreme, suppose entry is costless, $e = 0$ (so that the market is said to be *contestable*)[4]. Then to deter entry, the incumbent would need to commit to producing the output that would be produced in long-run equilibrium of a perfectly competitive industry,

$$q_L = 90$$ (4.19)

(this follows from (4.17) if $e = 0$). If price is already at the level that would make price equal to marginal cost, then if the second firm were to sell anything at all, price would be below marginal cost and both firms would lose money.

Between these two extreme cases, if the incumbent commits to producing slightly more than the limit output, the entrant will stay out of the market; price will be slightly less than

$$p_L = 100 - q_L = 100 - (90 - 2\sqrt{re}) = 10 + 2\sqrt{re}.$$ (4.20)

The limit price p_L is higher, the greater are entry costs.

---

[4] Chadwick (1859), Baumol et al. (1982).

If the market is neither contestable nor a natural monopoly, but somewhere in between, the incumbent's limit profit if it commits to the entry-deterring output level is

$$\pi_L = (p_L - 10)q_L = 2\sqrt{re}(90 - 2\sqrt{re}).$$ (4.21)

and the incumbent's present discounted value if it deters entry is

$$V_L = \frac{2\sqrt{re}(90 - 2\sqrt{re})}{r} = 2\sqrt{\frac{e}{r}}(90 - 2\sqrt{re}) = 180\sqrt{\frac{e}{r}} - 4e.$$ (4.22)

We now need to ask whether or not the incumbent would find it profitable to block entry. The answer to this question depends on the size of entry costs and on the interest rate used to discount future income.

Suppose first that if the entrant comes into the market, the two firms compete as Cournot duopolists. Then we know that the incumbent's profit per period would be 900. If $r = \frac{1}{10}$, the incumbent's Cournot duopoly value is 9000.

If entry cost is 350 and $r = \frac{1}{10}$, the entry-deterring output level is

$$q_L = 90 - 2\sqrt{35} = 78.168$$ (4.23)

and the incumbent's value if it pursues an entry-deterrence strategy is

$$\frac{2\sqrt{35}(90 - 2\sqrt{35})}{\frac{1}{10}} = 9248.9,$$ (4.24)

which is greater than the incumbent's Cournot value.

On the other hand, if entry cost is 300, the entry-deterring output level is greater,

$$q_L = 90 - 2\sqrt{30} = 79.046,$$ (4.25)

and the incumbent's value as an entry-deterring monopolist is less than it would earn as a Cournot duopolist:

$$\frac{2\sqrt{30}(90 - 2\sqrt{30})}{\frac{1}{10}} = 8659.$$ (4.26)

If entry cost is sufficiently great, the incumbent will find it profitable to expand output and deter entry.

In general, the incumbent would have a greater value by committing to output q_L and deterring output if

$$\frac{2\sqrt{re}(90 - 2\sqrt{re})}{r} \geq \frac{900}{r} \text{ or if } e \geq \frac{32.827}{r}.$$ (4.27)

Entry deterrence requires that the incumbent be able to commit in advance to a given output level, and that it has the information and calculating ability to compute the output level that will deter entry. It may be more reasonable, therefore, to suppose that if entry occurs, the incumbent is a Stackelberg leader and the entrant is a Stackelberg follower, not that the post-entry market is a Cournot duopoly.

From (4.11), if the incumbent acts as a Stackelberg leader, its profit is 1012.5. The incumbent will earn a greater profit deterring entry if

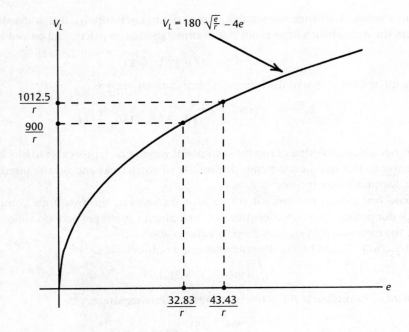

Fig. 4.2 Incumbent's value at limit output

$$\frac{2\sqrt{re}(90-2\sqrt{re})}{r} \geq 1012.5, \text{ or if } e \geq \frac{43.429}{r}. \tag{4.28}$$

The greater is entry cost e, the less output the incumbent must commit to producing to deter entry (equation (4.17)), the greater the incumbent's profit if it deters entry (Figure 4.2), and the more likely that the incumbent will find entry deterrence to be a value-maximizing strategy.

4.3.2 Entry deterrence with imperfectly informed entrants

If the incumbent firm cannot commit in advance to producing a specific output level, there must be some sort of uncertainty in the mind of the entrant for entry-deterring behaviour to work (Bain, 1949, pp. 452–3):

At the extreme, it could even be argued that a potential entrant to an oligopoly should pay little regard to price or profit received by established firms, especially if he thought price was being held down in order to "bluff" him away from the industry. He should look at the industry demand, the current competitive or collusive conditions in the industry, the prospects for rivalry or collusion after his entry, the share of the market he expects to capture, and his projected costs of production. Paramount in his considerations, provided the industry demand under some conceivable arrangement could provide profits to an entrant, should be his appraisal of the sort of rivalry and the type of price policies he will encounter from the previously established seller(s) after he enters. In judging these determinants of his decision, current price or profit need play no *direct* role, since the anticipated industry price *after entry* and the entrant's anticipated market share are the strategic considerations. And if he knows the industry demand with reasonable certainty and makes calculations concerning the conditions of rivalry after his entry . . . he might look entirely past any current price set by the established firm(s). He would then be immune to bluffing, and the established firm(s) could never discourage entry by lowering price and earning moderate profits.

To illustrate how uncertainty in the mind of the entrant can permit entry deterrence, suppose entry cost is 8000, the interest rate $r = \frac{1}{10}$, that the entrant's marginal cost is 10 per unit, and that there are two possibilities for the incumbent's unit cost.

The first possibility is that the incumbent's unit cost is also 10 per unit. Then if the entrant comes into the market, the post-entry market is a Cournot duopoly in which the two firms have identical marginal cost of 10 per unit. We know from previous discussions of this example that each firm's equilibrium output is 30 units, that equilibrium price is 30, and that the entrant's present discounted value if it comes into the market is

$$V_2(10, 10) = \frac{1}{r} \pi_2(10, 10) - e = 10(900) - 8000 = 1000. \tag{4.29}$$

If the entrant knows with certainty that the incumbent's unit cost is 10, it would come into the market, because it would know that it would make an economic profit by doing so.

The second possibility is that the incumbent's unit cost is 1 per unit. The post-entry market is a Cournot duopoly with unequal unit costs. Equilibrium outputs and price are[5]

$$q_1 = 36 \qquad q_2 = 27 \qquad p = 100 - (36 + 27) = 37. \tag{4.30}$$

Firm 2's value if it enters would be negative:

$$V_2(1, 10) = \frac{1}{r} \pi_2(1, 10) - e = 10(37-10)(27) - 8000 = 7290 - 8000 = -710. \tag{4.31}$$

If the entrant knows with certainty that the incumbent's unit cost is 1, it would stay out of the market.

Now suppose that the incumbent has marginal cost 10 per unit, but the entrant does not know this. The entrant only knows that the incumbent's marginal cost could be 1 or could be 10.

The incumbent is a monopolist in the pre-entry period. If it produces the monopoly output of a firm with constant marginal cost 10 per unit,

$$q_m(10) = 45, \tag{4.32}$$

price is

$$p_m(10) = 55 \tag{4.33}$$

and its profit is the profit of a monopolist that has a marginal cost 10 per unit and acts as if it has a marginal cost 10 per unit,

$$\pi_m(10, 10) = (55 - 10)(45) = 2025. \tag{4.34}$$

---

[5] The equations of the best response functions are (incumbent) $2q_1 + q_2 = 99$ and (entrant) $q_1 + 2q_2 = 90$; these may be solved to find equilibrium outputs. Equilibrium price can then be found from the equation of the inverse demand curve.

Acting in this way, the incumbent would reveal its marginal cost to the potential entrant, which would then come in to the market. After entry, the incumbent would earn Cournot duopoly profit 900 per period.

The present discounted value of the incumbent's income stream if it reveals its cost and entry occurs in the next period is[6]

$$V_1(10, 10) = \frac{1}{1+r}(2025) + \frac{1}{(1+r)^2}(900) + \frac{1}{(1+r)^3}(900) + \dots$$

$$= \frac{1}{1+r}(2025 - 900) + 900\left[\frac{1}{1+r} + \frac{1}{(1+r)^2} + \frac{1}{(1+r)^3} + \dots\right]$$

$$= \frac{1125}{1+r} + \frac{900}{r}. \tag{4.35}$$

Suppose now that instead of producing 45 units of output in the first period, thus revealing the nature of its marginal cost, the incumbent produces the monopoly output of a firm that has marginal cost 1 per unit:

$$q_m(1) = \tfrac{1}{2}(100 - 1) = 49.5. \tag{4.36}$$

The incumbent gives up some profit if it has high cost but acts as if it has low cost:

$$\pi_m(10, 1) = (50.5 - 10)(49.5) = 2004.75 < 2025 = \pi_m(10, 10). \tag{4.37}$$

Acting in this way, the incumbent reveals nothing about its unit cost: it might have low cost, it might have high cost—the potential entrant cannot tell which by observing pre-entry output.

Whether or not the potential entrant would stay out of the market depends on its beliefs about the cost level of the incumbent.[7] If the potential entrant does stay out of the market and the incumbent continues to masquerade as a low-cost firm, the incumbent's present discounted value can be greater than its value if it reveals its unit cost (4.35), depending on the potential entrant's beliefs and on the interest rate used to discount

---

Entry deterrence with entrant uncertainty: if potential entrants are uncertain about an incumbent firm's costs, and entry cost is sufficiently high, an incumbent with high marginal cost may be able to discourage entry by acting as if it has low unit costs. Depending on the entrant's beliefs, a high-cost incumbent may maximize its value by discouraging entry in this way.

---

[6] For $r = \frac{1}{10}$, $V_1(10, 10) = 10022\frac{8}{11}$.

[7] Let λ, a number between 0 and one, be the entrant's prior (before observing the incumbent's output) probability that the incumbent has low unit cost. Then $1 - \lambda$ is the entrant's prior probability that the incumbent has high unit cost, and if the entrant learns nothing by observing the incumbent's output, the entrant's expected post-entry value is

$$\lambda(-710) + (1 - \lambda)(1000) = 1000 - 1710\lambda.$$

The entrant's expected profit is positive for $\lambda < 1000/1710 = 0.59$. If the entrant maximizes expected profit, it would come into the market for $\lambda < 0.59$. .

future income.[8] It may be profitable for the incumbent to expand output and deter entry.

If the incumbent does expand output and deter entry, market performance is better—greater output, lower price, less deadweight welfare loss—than it would be if entry were blocked. In general, market performance will be worse than it would be with entry.

4.4 Predation and the chain store paradox

A dominant firm that follows a predatory pricing strategy cuts price below rivals' average cost, even if this means short-run losses for itself as well, to drive rivals from the market. Once rivals go out of business (possibly by selling out to the dominant firm), the predator raises price and collects enough economic profit to more than balance out any short-term losses.

One of the early documented incidents of predation resulted in the *Mogul Steamship* case, which involved a group of firms that colluded to jointly engage in predation against a firm outside the group.[9] The predatory group was a conference of merchant shippers operating in and around southeast Asia in the 1880s (Taft, 1914, p. 19):

The facts were that a number of shipowners who were regular carriers of tea entered into a combination to drive out of business an outsider who was in the habit of coming into the harbour of Hankow and lowering prices. The combiners agreed to conduct a year's steady and persistent campaign of underbidding against his ships and thus end his competition.

Selten's (1978) *chain-store paradox* model shows that predation (like limit pricing) does not work if there is complete and perfect information and the dominant firm cannot commit to an aggressive strategy. In the chain store model, a dominant firm—the incumbent—operates a chain of stores in 20 separate local markets. In each market, one

---

[8] Continuing footnote 7, if the incumbent produces 49.5 units of output, the entrant stays out with probability λ (the entrant's probability that the incumbent has low cost), and then the incumbent's value is $2004.75/r$; the entrant comes in to the market with probability $1 - \lambda$, and then the incumbent's value is

$$\frac{1}{1+r}(2004.75) + \frac{1}{(1+r)^2}(900) + \frac{1}{(1+r)^3}(900) + \ldots = \frac{1104.75}{1+r} + \frac{900}{r}.$$

The high-cost incumbent's expected value from masquerading as a low-cost incumbent is

$$\lambda\frac{2004.75}{r} + (1-\lambda)\left(\frac{1104.75}{1+r} + \frac{900}{r}\right) = \lambda\frac{4419}{4r(1+r)} + \frac{4419}{4(1+r)} + \frac{900}{r}.$$

The high-cost incumbent's value if it reveals its costs to be high is (4.35), and the difference between the two values is

$$\lambda\frac{4419}{4r(1+r)} + \frac{4419}{4(1+r)} + \frac{900}{r} - \left(\frac{1125}{1+r} + \frac{900}{r}\right) = \frac{4419}{4r(1+r)}\left(\lambda - \frac{81r}{4419}\right)$$

and this rises with λ. The more likely the potential entrant thinks it is that the incumbent has low cost, the greater the payoff to a high-cost incumbent from acting as if it has low cost. If $\lambda = 0$, so that the potential entrant is certain the incumbent has high cost, then the entrant will come in to the market anyway, and there is no possible gain to the incumbent from pretending that it has high cost.

[9] *Mogul Steamship Co. v. McGregor, Gow & Co. et. al.* (1884/1885) 54 LJQB 540; (1887/1888) 57 LJKB 541; 23 (1889) QBD 598 (CA); [1992] AC 25.

after another, it faces the prospect of entry by a single rival. A game tree and payoff matrix for one such stage game are shown in Figure 4.3. Each entrant earns a payoff that is determined in the single market in which it operates. The incumbent's overall payoff is the sum of its payoffs in the 20 markets.

In each market, the entrant's choices are to enter or to stay out of the market. If the entrant stays out, it earns €1 (the return from the best alternative investment); the incumbent earns €5. If the entrant comes in, then the incumbent must decide whether to cooperate with the entrant (both earn a return of €2) or to fight entry (both earn a zero return). A cooperative incumbent restricts output and shares the market; an aggressive incumbent expands output, even at the cost of lost profit.

If the dominant firm follows a deterrence strategy, it announces its intention to react aggressively to entry. If an entrant believes this, then the entrant is better off staying out of the market. If entry occurs, it is likely to be early on, and the incumbent will have to give up some short-run profit by carrying out the threat to deter entry. But it seems reasonable to suppose that later potential entrants will learn of the incumbent's aggressive behaviour and become convinced that the incumbent will react aggressively to entry. The incumbent will earn more than enough profit in later markets to make up for losses in early markets.

But deterrence will not work in the final market. If predation is attractive at all for the incumbent, it is because predation generates future benefits. What the incumbent does in the final period cannot generate future benefits, since after the final period there is no future. An aggressive reaction in the final period would mean a loss for the incumbent without the prospect of any later gain; thus the threat of an aggressive reaction in the final market would be an empty one. If the potential entrant to the final market believes the incumbent acts to maximize its own payoff, then the potential entrant to the final market would not believe a threat by the incumbent to react aggressively to entry.

But if a threat to react aggressively to entry in the final period would not be credible, then neither would a threat to react aggressively to entry in the next-to-last period. If

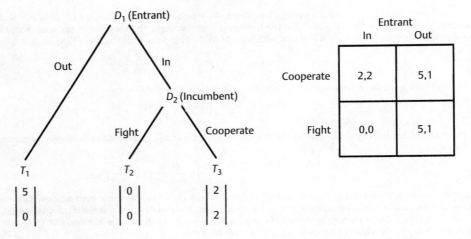

Fig. 4.3 Game tree and payoff matrix for one stage of the chain store game

aggressive behaviour in the next-to-last period is attractive to the incumbent, it is because of the benefits the incumbent will get in the final period. Since the potential entrant in the final period would not believe a threat to react aggressively to entry, there is no last-period payoff to acting aggressively in the next-to-last period.

The *backward induction argument* pushes the reasoning that the incumbent could not credibly threaten to react aggressively to entry in the final period to its logical conclusion. If the incumbent could not credibly threaten to deter entry in the final period, then it would have nothing to gain from reacting aggressively to entry in the next-to-last period. But in this case, it would have nothing to gain from reacting aggressively to entry in period 18, and so on back to period 1. No entrant would ever believe a threat to react aggressively; the only equilibrium has each entrant enter in each stage and the incumbent accommodate entry in each stage: the incumbent's payoff is €40.[10]

Why does Selten call this result a *paradox*? Because the logical result is not believable (Selten, 1978/88, pp. 38–9):

If I had to play the game in the role of [the incumbent], I would follow the deterrence theory. I would be very surprised if it failed to work. From my discussions with friends and colleagues, I get the impression that most people share this inclination. . . . mathematically trained persons recognize the logical validity of the induction argument, but they refuse to accept it as a guide to practical behaviour. . . .

The fact that the logical inescapability of the induction theory fails to destroy the plausibility of the deterrence theory is a serious phenomenon which merits the name of a paradox.

The conclusion that predation would not be a credible strategy depends on the assumptions that there is complete and perfect information and that all the entrants have sufficient calculating ability to work out the subgame perfect equilibrium of the game. Kreps and Wilson (1982) show that if there is imperfect information, deterrence may be an equilibrium strategy.

Game trees for a single stage of the Kreps and Wilson extension of the chain store game are shown in Figure 4.4. The entrant earns zero if it stays out, loses money if it comes in and the incumbent fights ($b - 1 < 0$), makes a profit ($b > 0$) if it comes in and the incumbent cooperates. If the potential entrant stays out, the incumbent's payoff is $a > 1$.

But the entrant is uncertain about the incumbent's payoffs in the event of entry. There are two possibilities. If the incumbent is weak, it earns more by cooperating than by fighting entry. Payoffs for the weak incumbent are shown in Figure 4.4(a). If this game tree held for every stage of the game, and entrants knew that it held for every stage of the game, the backward induction argument would apply, and equilibrium would require the incumbent to cooperate with entry in every period.

A weak incumbent will always cooperate in the last period. Depending on beliefs, it may be a value-maximizing strategy for a weak incumbent to pretend to be strong in early periods, creating a reputation for being strong that will keep entrants out of the market in the middle and toward the end of the game. If information is imperfect, predation may be an equilibrium strategy.

---

[10] The outcome in which each entrant comes in and the incumbent accommodates entry is a *subgame perfect equilibrium*, which in the context of this model means that it is an equilibrium if the game starts in period 1, or in period 2, or in period 20.

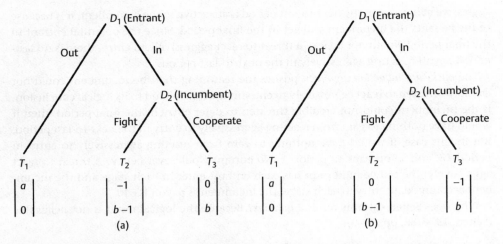

Fig. 4.4 Possible game trees for one stage of the Kreps and Wilson entry game: (a) weak incumbent; (b) strong incumbent ($a > 0$; $0 < b < 1$)

4.5 Article 82

It is Article 82 of the EC Treaty, which prohibits abuse of a dominant position, that applies to the behaviour of dominant firms. The Article gives as examples of abuse the setting of unfair prices, limiting production "to the prejudice of consumers", price discrimination to other firms when that discrimination puts some firms at a competitive disadvantage, and the use of restrictive clauses in contracts.

These examples combine economic and noneconomic goals. There is no clear definition in economics of an unfair price.[11] "Limiting production" must harm consumers, in the sense that it reduces consumers' surplus. Price discrimination is said to be an abuse if it places other firms at a competitive disadvantage, and what this targets is the impact of dominant firm pricing on the process of market integration, not the impact of price discrimination on consumer welfare or net social welfare.[12] The kinds of restrictive

[11] In a market economy, managers are expected to set prices to maximize stockholder value, and may well have a legal obligation to do so. There are economic reasons for the usual competition policy positions that value-maximizing prices should be set independently (without collusion) and without strategic purposes (that is, specifically to make it more difficult for rivals to compete). These conditions being met, price differences across markets are an essential part of a market economy, a signal for resource reallocation that leads to an efficient allocation of resources across markets; there is no basis in economics for labelling prices as unfair if net prices differ to different consumers or if prices are different from long-run competitive equilibrium prices.

[12] If a manufacturer charges distributors in France a lower net price than it charges distributors in Germany, the German distributors are disadvantaged with respect to the French distributors, and this could be expected to undermine political support for market integration in the German business community. It does not obviously harm German consumers, who might have an opportunity to buy at lower prices from French distributors.

clauses that have been targeted under Article 82 are those that have the effect of raising entry barriers, particularly entry barriers around national markets. Prohibiting such restrictions will improve market performance and promote market integration.

Article 82 of the EC Treaty (ex Article 86)

Any abuse by one or more undertakings of a dominant position within the common market or in a substantial part of it shall be prohibited as incompatible with the common market insofar as it may affect trade between Member States.

Such abuse may, in particular, consist in:

(a) directly or indirectly imposing unfair purchase or selling prices or other unfair trading conditions;

(b) limiting production, markets or technical development to the prejudice of consumers;

(c) applying dissimilar conditions to equivalent transactions with other trading parties, thereby placing them at a competitive disadvantage;

(d) making the conclusion of contracts subject to acceptance by the other parties of supplementary obligations which, by their nature or according to commercial usage, have no connection with the subject of such contracts.

4.5.1 Price discrimination

The *United Brands* decision[13] is an early application of Article 82. In the early 1970s the United Brands Company (UBC) was the leading banana producer in the world and in particular in the European Community, where it had a market share of about 40 per cent. It was vertically integrated from banana plantations in equatorial regions to ocean shipping to distribution networks in final markets, where its contracts with banana ripeners and distributors included a variety of vertical restraints. Ripeners could not resell green bananas, keeping them out of competition with UBC or with other importers. UBC cut off supplies to a Danish distributor that dealt in bananas from more than one supplier. The effect of these vertical restraints was to divide the EC into national submarkets.

Product market definition was critical to the outcome of the United Brands case. The European Commission defined bananas as the relevant product market, on the ground that bananas have distinctive characteristics that distinguish the demand for bananas from the demands for other kinds of fruit. As part of its defence, United Brands argued that the relevant product market was fresh fruit. Using this larger definition, UBC's market share would have been too small to justify a finding that it had a dominant position. The European Court of Justice (ECJ) rejected UBC's arguments and accepted bananas as the relevant product market.

[13] *United Brands Company and United Brands Continental BV v. EC Commission* [1978] ECR 207.

This decision was one of the first in which the European Court of Justice interpreted the concept of dominance for purposes of EC competition policy ([1978] ECR 207 at 277):

The dominant position referred to in [Article 82] refers to a position of economic strength enjoyed by an undertaking which enables it to prevent effective competition being maintained on the relevant market by giving it the power to behave to an appreciable extent independently of its competitors, customers, and ultimately of its consumers.

This language has been repeated in many later Article 82 decisions. The distinction between customers and consumers arises in wholesale and retail markets, in which (as in this case) a manufacturer sells its product directly to distributors (its customers), who in turn sell to final consumers.

From an economic point of view, without effective competition, a firm has a dominant position whether or not it takes specific steps to prevent competition.[14] Barriers to entry may permit a firm to act independently of its competitors. The ability of a firm to act independently of distributors or final consumers is limited by the price elasticity of demand (final consumers) or derived demand (distributors), as summarized by the Lerner index of market power (see equations (1.18), (2.34)) (la Cour and Møllgaard, 2000).

The Commission argued, based mainly on UBC's market share and vertically integrated operations, that UBC had a dominant position, and the European Court agreed with the Commission.

UBC charged distributors located in different Member States substantially different prices, although the costs of supplying the different markets were similar. For the European Commission, these price differences were themselves an abuse of a dominant position. UBC's reaction was that ([1978] ECR 207 at 249):

It is important to understand what is really involved in the Commission's argument that [United Brands] have committed an abuse in this respect. What it amounts to is that it is the duty of an undertaking in a dominant position to create a single market out of the existing national markets and that if it fails to act accordingly it is guilty of an abuse.

Essentially, United Brands argued that it was simply acting as a profit-maximizing firm in distinct local markets. The European Court of Justice agreed that it was not the responsibility of United Brands to establish a single market ([1978] ECR 207 at 298) but also said that the interplay of supply and demand should take place at each vertical level in the distribution chain: at a lower level between United Brands and distributors, at a higher level between distributors and final consumers. As a dominant firm, UBC committed an abuse if it imposed terms that gave it, rather than distributors, most of the available profit.

Of course, in the interplay of demand and supply between UBC and distributors, the behaviour of distributors reflects a demand that is derived from the demand of final consumers. Despite the protests of the European Commission and of the Court, it is difficult to escape the conclusion that there is an element of truth in UBC's argument: a

---

[14] A firm may have a dominant position because the market is a natural monopoly (Chapter 6). A firm may have a dominant position because it holds a patent granting it a legal monopoly (Chapter 5) or because it is granted a legal monopoly for some other purpose (Section 4.5.3).

firm with a dominant position in EC markets runs the risk of violating Article 82 if it fully exploits differences in regional demand characteristics. The underlying rationale may be that to sustain a system of different profit-maximizing prices in national submarkets, a dominant firm will have to put in place formal or informal restrictions that block the flow of goods across national boundaries: otherwise, consumer arbitrage will eventually erode national price differences. Such barriers to cross-border trade, however, undo the process of economic integration that is the core of the European Community. Indeed, the European Court of Justice found that UBC had abused its dominant position by its use of marketing practices that had the effect of dividing the EC into national submarkets.

The European Commission also found that United Brands had abused its dominant position by charging unfair prices. The Commission compared UBC's highest and lowest prices in different national markets, and argued that UBC's prices in the high-price areas must be unfair, if UBC could profitably supply other areas at lower prices. The Court ruled that the Commission should have made a direct investigation of UBC's costs and reached a conclusion about unfairness by comparing costs and prices. The Commission had not done this, and the Court set aside the Commission's conclusion that UBC had abused its dominant position by setting unfair prices.

4.5.2 Loyalty rebates

The *Hoffmann-La Roche* decision[15] is one of a number of decisions under EC competition law that revolve around restrictive marketing practices. In this case, the geographic market was the Common Market as a whole. There were six product markets in which the European Court of Justice found that Hoffmann-La Roche had a dominant position: one each for vitamins A, B_2, B_6, C, E, and H.[16]

The European Commission and the Court of Justice found that Hoffmann-La Roche had a dominant position in these markets, where it had the largest market share, and that market share was much larger than that of the next largest supplier. It had a more elaborate sales network than other suppliers, and did not face important potential competition.

Hoffmann-La Roche marketed its products using contracts that sometimes contained *exclusive dealing* contracts—customers agreed to buy only from Hoffmann-La Roche—and sometimes *fidelity rebates*—retroactive refunds based on total purchases. The ECJ condemned exclusive dealing contracts and fidelity rebates as an abuse within the meaning of Article 82 because they ([1978] ECR 461 at 540) "are designed to deprive the purchaser of or restrict his possible choices of sources of supply and to deny other producers access to the market". In more economic terms, such contracts raise barriers to entry.

In its decision, the ECJ upheld the bulk of the fine imposed by the Commission and the requirement that Hoffmann-La Roche put an end to the restrictive contracts.

In the late 1990s British Airways used incentive schemes that paid travel agents more, the greater the increases in bookings that they delivered to BA over the level of the

[15] *Hoffmann-La Roche & Co. AG* v. *EC Commission* [1979] ECR 461. See also Commission Decision of 9 June 1976 OJ L 223 16 August 1976; EC Commission (1977, pp. 88–9; 1980, pp. 27–30).
[16] The Commission urged upon the ECJ, without success, that Hoffmann-La Roche had a dominant position in the market for vitamin B_3, where Hoffmann-La Roche's market share in value terms was estimated at 34.9 per cent in 1973, 51 per cent in 1974, and there was a Japanese competitor with 30 per cent of the market in 1973.

previous year. These loyalty rebate schemes made it more profitable for travel agents to book travellers with British Airlines, and the payments received by agents were not directly related to any cost savings that might have resulted from the higher booking level.

Once again, market definition played a critical role in the decision.[17] The Commission took the relevant market to be air travel agency services for the UK. British Airways argued for a broader market definition, pointing out that some consumers purchase plane tickets directly from airlines over the internet. Using its narrower market definition, the Commission found that 39.7 per cent of 1998 UK airfare sales through travel agents were for travel on BA and therefore that BA had a dominant position as a customer of air travel agencies in the UK. This dominant position was derived from BA's position in the passenger air transport market and from its control of landing slots at UK airports. The Commission also found that BA's loyalty payment scheme was an abuse of a dominant position, ordered it to stop making loyalty payments, and fined it BA €6.8 million. The abuse of a dominant position was interference with the ability of rival airlines to compete for the services of travel agencies.

The impact of the loyalty rebates at issue in this British Airways decision is much the same as in the Hoffmann-La Roche case, with the difference that Hoffman-La Roche was a seller in its markets, while British Airways was a buyer. Under Article 82, a dominant seller commits an abuse if it offers lower prices only for consumer loyalty, because such loyalty schemes interfere with the ability of equally efficient rivals to compete. The BA decision extends this rule to the situation of a dominant buyer.

4.5.3 Public monopolies

EC competition policy does not aim to limit the ability of dominant firms to compete on the merits, but it does insist that rivalry be based on efficiency, not on strategic anticompetitive behaviour (European Commission, 1999b, p. 38). To this end, the European Commission has applied Article 82 to firms that have a dominant position as a result of Member State legislation.[18]

For example, the *Frankfurt Airport* decision[19] involved the market for the provision of airport facilities—services like baggage handling that must be performed for aircraft to land and take off—at the Frankfurt airport. Under German law, the company (FAG) managing the airport had a legal monopoly, hence a dominant position, in the supply of airport facilities at the airport. The Commission determined that the market for the provision of ground-handling services constituted a distinct product market and found that FAG had abused its monopoly position in the market for airport facilities by

---

[17] OJ L 030 4 February 2000, pp. 1–24. See also Finnegan (1999). British Airways announced its intention to appeal the Commission's decision to the Court of First Instance.

[18] We may also mention the Commission's *AAMS* decision (Commission Decision 98/523/EC of 17 June 1998 OJ L 252 12 September 1998), finding that an enterprise with a legal monopoly on the wholesale distribution of cigarettes in Italy had committed an abuse by using contracts that restricted competition from suppliers outside Italy; and the *Football World Cup* decision (Commission Decision of 20 July 1999 OJ L 005 8 January 2000), in which the Commission imposed a symbolic fine of €1000 on the French organization that distributed tickets for the 1998 World Cup tournament (CFO, Comité français d'organisation de la Coupe du monde de football) for employing sales conditions that discriminated against consumers living outside France.

[19] OJ L 72 11 March 1998.

reserving the right to supply ground-handling services to itself. The Commission ordered FAG to allow independent firms to supply ground-handling services.[20]

4.6 **Summary**

A monopolist has a 100 per cent share of its market and does not face the possibility of entry. A dominant firm may have a near-monopoly share of its market, but actual or potential competition may make performance in dominant-firm markets different from monopoly. A Stackelberg quantity leader increases its own profit, industry output, and consumers' surplus, compared with noncooperative oligopoly. Depending on entry costs, a quantity leader may find it profitable to expand output, lower price, and preserve a dominant market position. The result is improved market performance, although an incumbent's reaction to potential competition does not generally bring as much of an improvement in market performance as would entry and an increase in the number of independent rivals.

Strategic behaviour may allow a firm to obtain or maintain a dominant position. At one extreme, predation in selected product or geographic markets could allow a firm to establish a reputation that would cause potential rivals to back off from other markets. Less extreme forms of strategic behaviour include contracts and marketing arrangements that raise the cost to rivals of getting their products in front of consumers. Models of limit pricing suggest that when entry costs are greater, incumbents will be able to exercise greater market power without inducing entry.

Article 82 of the EC Treaty condemns abuses of a dominant position. The behaviour that has been prohibited under Article 82 has the effect of raising entry costs, and thus makes it possible for a dominant firm to exercise greater market power. The application of Article 82 thus serves to improve market performance, although it seems fair to say that the underlying goal of Article 82 is to safeguard the process of EC market integration, not to improve market performance.

Study points

- Stackelberg leadership model (pages 70–2)
- strategic behaviour, limit pricing (pages 73–6)
- uncertainty and entry deterrence (pages 76–8)
- the chain store paradox (pages 79–81)

---

[20] See also the *Aéroports de Paris* (ADP) decision, in which the Commission found that the firm operating two Paris airports had abused its dominant position by charging discriminatory fees to airlines that provided their own ground-handling services.

- Article 82 (page 82)
  - price discrimination (pages 83–5)
  - loyalty rebates (pages 85–6)
  - public monopolies (page 86)

Problems

4–1 (Price leadership with product differentiation) For a price-setting duopoly with product differentiation, let the equations of the inverse demand curves be

$$p_1 = 100 - (q_1 + \tfrac{1}{2}q_2) \qquad p_2 = 100 - (\tfrac{1}{2}q_1 + q_1), \tag{4.38}$$

with corresponding demand functions

$$q_1 = \tfrac{2}{3}(100 - 2p_1 + p_2) \qquad q_2 = \tfrac{2}{3}(100 + p_1 - 2p_2). \tag{4.39}$$

Let marginal cost be constant at 10 per unit.

Find equilibrium prices and profits if firm 2 sets its price p_2 noncooperatively to maximize its own profit, if firm 1 knows this, and if firm 1 maximizes its own profit, taking firm 2's behaviour into account.

4–2 (Limit pricing) For the price-setting market of Problem 4–1, let firm 1 be an incumbent and firm 2 a potential entrant that must pay a fixed and sunk entry cost e if it comes into the market. If firm 1 can commit to a post-entry price, what price must it set to make entry unprofitable? Under what circumstances (for what values of re, where r is the interest rate used to discount income) would firm 1 prefer to deter entry (a) if the post-entry market would be a Bertrand (noncooperative) duopoly; and (b) if firm 1 would be a Stackelberg price leader in the post-entry market?

Chapter 5

Innovation

Grace is given of God, but knowledge is bought in the market.
   Clough

5.1 Introduction[1]

New products and processes do not fall like manna from heaven. In a market system, innovation is most often the result of investment by private, profit-seeking firms. But investment in innovation is different from other types of business investments. Investment in innovation is riskier than other kinds of investments. It is difficult for a business to control the use of its R&D efforts or of its discoveries, because the knowledge that results from innovation has some aspects of a public good. It can be put to productive use by the firm that paid for it, but it can also be put to productive use by other firms as well.

In a market system, resources are allocated efficiently if risk-adjusted social rates of return are the same in all activities. Thus one question economists ask when they study innovation is how the rate of return on investment in innovation compares with the rates of return on other kinds of innovation. Also, just as we ask what kind of market structure is likely to yield good static market performance—price near marginal cost, average cost near its theoretically efficient level—so we can ask what kind of market structure is likely to yield good dynamic market performance, and whether or not there is a tradeoff between static and dynamic market performance. More generally, we examine the kinds of policy tools that might be available to improve dynamic market performance, and how those tools might be used to best advantage.

---

[1] This chapter draws on Martin and Scott (2000) and Martin (2001a).

5.2 **Innovation in a market system**

5.2.1 **Spillovers**

Investment in innovation is characterized by input spillovers and output spillovers, both of which reduce the private payoff to R&D.

R&D input spillovers occur when the R&D efforts of one firm help rivals reach their own research goals. For example, Henderson and Cockburn (1996, pp. 35–6) say of the pharmaceutical industry that it

is characterized by high rates of publication in the open scientific literature, and many of the scientists . . . stressed the importance of keeping in touch with the science conducted both within the public sector and by their competitors. Nearly all of them had a quite accurate idea of the nature of the research being conducted by their competitors, and they often described the ways in which their rivals' discoveries had been instrumental in shaping their own research.

Effective R&D effort in high science-content sectors like pharmaceuticals requires that researchers keep abreast of the knowledge frontier in their field, and the interactions this requires reveal what they are doing to researchers working in other places just as they learn what other researchers are doing.

R&D output spillovers occur when first-discoverers are not able to collect all of the economic profit generated by their innovation. For 48 US new product innovations, Mansfield et al. (1981) report that 60 per cent of successful patented innovations were imitated within four years of introduction. For a sample of 100 US manufacturing firms, Mansfield (1985) reports survey evidence indicating that rivals have information about R&D decisions in 12–18 months, and information about new products or processes in 12 months or less. Such leakages occur (Mansfield, 1985, p. 221) because

input suppliers and customers are important channels (since they pass on a great deal of relevant information), patent applications are scrutinized very carefully, and reverse engineering is carried out. In still other industries, the diffusion process is accelerated by the fact that firms do not go to great lengths to keep such information secret, partly because they believe it would be futile in any event.

"Copycat" innovation may involve simply replicating another firm's invention, but need not be so crude. Simply knowing that some lines of research work, while others do not, will allow follow-on firms to carry their own independent work forward more rapidly and at a lower cost than first innovators.

Neither R&D input spillovers nor R&D output spillovers are unambiguously bad, from a social point of view. R&D input spillovers increase the productivity of such R&D efforts as do take place, and make it more likely that some firm will make a discovery (which is what is important from a social point of view). R&D output spillovers improve static product market performance after discovery takes place. But both types of spillovers reduce the incentives of firms to invest in innovation.

5.2.2 **Uncertainty**

The creative process is inherently uncertain. Even in sectors where there is a strong link between scientific analysis and commercial applications, as in pharmaceuticals, exactly how a particular approach will turn out cannot be foreseen with certainty; in the words of one drug-industry researcher (quoted in Tapon and Cadsby, 1996, pp. 389–90):

I think that rational drug design is obviously very admirable. It's more than a great idea, it's a move in the right direction. It applies as much rationality to your programmes as possible. But, you're not going to be able to predict 100% . . . of the outcome. You're always going to have things that happen that nobody really foresaw and you look back in hindsight and say that there is no way that we could have predicted that outcome . . . There is a certain amount of good luck involved . . . you have to have the breaks; if you don't have the breaks in drug development you may have great difficulty in getting any compound.

Not only is it uncertain, *ex ante*, how a particular research project may turn out, but it may also be uncertain, *ex post*, whether results obtained have interesting commercial possibilities.[2]

Uncertainty is, of course, part of life and part of business: if a firm decides to locate a retail outlet in a particular place, it cannot know with certainty how population patterns will develop over the expected life of the store. In many sectors of the economy, however, uncertainty about the nature and timing of R&D activity is an order of magnitude greater than other types of uncertainty with which businesses must deal.[3] Uncertainty, too, reduces the incentives of firms to invest in R&D.

5.3 **The rates of return to R&D**

A large empirical literature suggests that private returns to research and development are much larger than typical rates of return to other types of investments, and that social rates of return to research and development are larger than private rates of return to research and development. Both findings indicate that from a social standpoint the private sector underinvests in R&D, making a case for government policy measures to promote private investment in innovation.

> *Innovation in a market system*: the incentives for profit-maximizing firms to invest in new products and processes are reduced by R&D input and output spillovers and by the inherent uncertainty of the innovative process. Private and social rates of return to investment in R&D are larger than rates of return to investments in other types of business assets.

[2] For example, the fundamental innovation embodied in the now ubiquitous post-it sticker was essentially an adhesive substance that was not terribly sticky, developed in 1968; the product was first introduced in 1980, 12 years later (http://www.3m.com/about3M/pioneers/fry.html).
[3] See also Scherer and Harhoff (2000), whose work suggests that R&D successes are substantially less likely than R&D failures.

Table 5.1 Social and private rates of return from investment in innovations.

	Rate of return (%)	
Innovation	**Social**	**Private**
New type of metal that reduced cost of appliances	17	18
Machine tool innovation—new computer controls	83	35
Component for control system	29	7
Construction material—reduce cost of building	96	9
Drilling material—reduce cost of drilling wells	54	16
Industrial equipment—new type of drafting	92	47
New paper product that cuts cost of users	82	42
New type of thread that cut costs of garment makers	307	27
New mechanism for doors	27	37
New device that reduced costs of certain video tape operations	negative	negative
Chemical product innovation—new product that reduced costs of users	71	9
Chemical process innovation—reduced costs of production	32	25
Chemical process innovation—reduced costs of certain aromatic chemicals	13	4
Major chemical process innovation	56	31
Household cleaning device—new product that reduced cost of cleaning floors	209	214
New stain remover	116	4
Dishwashing liquid—new product that cut costs of operating dishwashers	45	46
Median	56	25

Source: Mansfield et al. (1977)

Mansfield et al. (1977) report the results of case studies of 17 innovations—13 new product innovations, four new process innovations (Table 5.1). For each innovation, they estimated the present-discounted value of consumers' surplus, incremental firm profit, and the social return (from the time of discovery through 1973).[4] In about 30 per cent of the cases, they estimate a private rate of return so low that no profit-maximizing firm, with perfect foresight, would have invested in the innovation, although the social rate of return was so high that the investment was socially beneficial.

Griliches (1992) reports estimates of the rate of return to public R&D in agriculture that range from 28 to 67 per cent. Jones and Williams (1997, Table 1) survey the literature that examines the impact of R&D on productivity growth, and indicate that typical results are a rate of return of about 30 per cent if attention is limited to the returns to R&D within the industry carrying out the R&D, with the rate of return rising as high as 100 per cent if returns in other industries that use R&D are taken into account.

---

[4] In some cases, the main effect of innovations they studied was to increase profit (Mansfield et al., 1977, p. 231)

In the case of three of the four process innovations included in our sample, there was no apparent effect on product prices. By lowering the costs of the innovators, these process innovations increased the innovator's profits. Also, since they were imitated (or used at nominal cost) by other firms, they soon increased the profits of other firms as well.

The fourth process innovation in their sample led to a reduced price to consumers, which would mean an increase in consumers' surplus.

5.4 **Market structure and innovation**

5.4.1 **Schumpeter**

Joseph Schumpeter conceived of innovation in a broad sense, writing (1934, p. 66) of "the carrying out of new combinations" as including the introduction of new products or new varieties of existing products, the introduction of new production processes, opening new markets, development of new sources of supplies, and development of new organizational forms (for example, creation or destruction of a monopoly position).

At different times, he put forward fundamentally different views about the relation between market structure and dynamic market performance. For what has come to be called Schumpeter Mark I, the Schumpeter of *The Theory of Economic Development*, it was the new firm that carries out innovation (1934, p. 66):

it is not essential to the matter—though it may happen—that the new combinations should be carried out by the same people who control the productive or commercial process which is to be displaced by the new. On the contrary, new combinations are, as a rule, embodied, as it were, in new firms which generally do not arise out of the old ones but start producing beside them; in general it is not the owner of stage-coaches who builds railways.

If this vision of innovation in a market system is correct, to promote innovation means facilitating the establishment of new, and often relatively small, firms.

For a later Schumpeter, the Schumpeter Mark II of *Capitalism, Socialism, and Democracy*, it is the established firm that generates technological progress (1943, p. 82):

As soon as we go into details and inquire into the individual items in which progress was most conspicuous, the trail leads not to the doors of those firms that work under conditions of comparatively free competition but precisely to the doors of the large concerns . . . and a shocking suspicion dawns upon us that big business may have had more to do with creating that standard of life than with keeping it down.

This alternative vision of the innovative process leads to the idea that poor static market performance (large firms that are able to hold price above marginal cost for extended periods of time) may be a small price to pay for good dynamic market performance (a cornucopia of new products, produced ever more efficiently).

Four main reasons for expecting large firms to have advantages in carrying out R&D appear in the literature:[5]

- larger firms are able to spread fixed cost of research over a larger sales base;
- large firms may have advantages in financial markets;

---

[5] The first three are noted by Henderson and Cockburn (1996, p. 33); the first and third are cited by Galbraith (1952, p. 86):

Technical development has long since become the preserve of the scientist and the engineer. Most of the cheap and simple inventions have, to put it bluntly, been made. Not only is development now sophisticated and costly but it must be on a sufficient scale so that successes and failures will in some measure average out. Few can afford it if they must expect all projects to pay off.

- larger firms may be better able to exploit economies of scale and scope in research, if such economies exist;
- (the serendipity effect) a large, diversified firm is more likely to be able to exploit an unexpected discovery.

On the other hand large, established firms may become bureaucratic and resistant to change; familiarity with established products and processes may make management slow to see the advantages to be gained from new products or processes.

5.4.2 Arrow

Arrow (1962) provides a seminal formal analysis of the market structure-innovation relationship by comparing the profit to be gained from cost-reducing innovation under monopoly with the profit to be gained from an identical cost-reducing innovation under perfect competition.[6]

To illustrate Arrow's approach, consider a monopoly market with inverse demand curve

$$p = 100 - Q. \tag{5.1}$$

If marginal and average cost are $c_1 = 50$ per unit of output, the monopolist maximizes profit by producing 25 units of output,[7] and the monopoly profit is 625. If, on the other hand, marginal and average cost are $c_2 = 25$ per unit of output, the monopolist maximizes profit by producing 37.5 units of output, and monopoly profit is 1406.25. The profit a monopolist can gain by developing a new production process that reduces marginal and average cost from 50 to 25 is

$$\pi_2 - \pi_1 = 1406.25 - 625 = 781.25. \tag{5.2}$$

This is shown in Figure 5.1 as the difference between the area $(P_2 - c_2)(Q_2 - Q_1)$, profit on additional units of output sold if unit cost is lower, and the area $(P_1 - p_2)Q_1$, lost profit on units of output that would be sold at a higher price if unit cost were higher.

Now suppose that an otherwise identical industry is perfectly competitive. If marginal and average cost are 50 per unit, then in long-run equilibrium price is also 50 per unit, the quantity supplied is 50 units, and firms earn zero economic profit, $\pi_1 = 0$. If a single firm develops a cost-reducing innovation for which it receives a completely effective patent and is able to produce at constant marginal and average cost 25 per unit, it can supply the entire market—sell slightly more than 50 units of output at a price slightly less than 50, and earn an economic profit[8] $\pi_2 = (50 - 25)(50) = 1250$. This is shown in Figure 5.2 as the area $(p_1 - c_2)q_1$. The profit a firm in a competitive industry can gain by developing a new production process that reduces marginal and average cost from 50 to 25 is more than the payoff to a monopolist that develops the same innovation:

[6] There is a large theoretical literature on market structure-innovation relationships in oligopoly; see among others Loury (1979), Lee and Wilde (1980), Reinganum (1982), Beath et al. (1988), d'Aspremont and Jacquemin (1988), Kamien et al. (1992), Katsoulacos and Ulph (1998), and Amir (2000), Martin (2001a).
[7] See Section 1.3.2; this is the output that makes marginal revenue, $MR = 100 - 2Q$, equal to marginal cost when marginal cost is 50.
[8] Also an efficiency rent; see Figure 2.7 and the associated text.

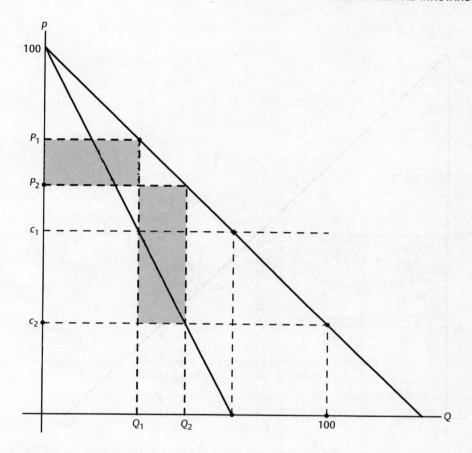

Fig. 5.1 Profit to be gained by innovation under monopoly; $p = 100 - Q$; $c_1 = 50$; $c_2 = 25$; $Q_1 = 25$, $P_1 = 100 - 25 = 75$, $Q_2 = 37.5$, $P_2 = 62.5$

$$\pi_2 - \pi_1 = 1250 - 0 = 1250 > 781.25. \qquad (5.3)$$

The result that innovation yields greater profit in a perfectly competitive industry than in an otherwise identical monopoly is a general one, and does not depend on the particular example that we have used here. For a monopolist, the payoff to innovation is the difference between the monopoly profit it will get with a new product or process and the monopoly profit it gets in any case with the existing technology. For an innovating firm in a competitive industry—a firm that innovates to escape the constraints of static product market competition—all of the profit that flows from successful innovation is a net gain.

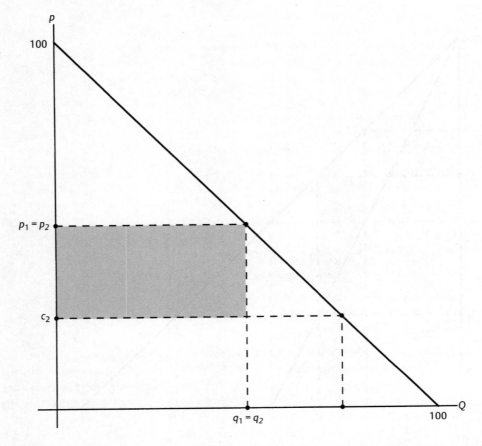

Fig. 5.2 Profit to be gained by innovation under perfect competition; $p = 100 - Q$; $p_1 = p_2 = c_1 = 50$; $c_2 = 25$; $q_1 = q_2 = 50$

5.5 **Appropriability and absorptive capacity**

It is often taken for granted that R&D output spillovers—the inability to completely appropriate the profit that flows from R&D—are an important source of underinvestment in R&D. This position is often supported by appealing to Arrow's (1962, p. 615) frequently quoted observation that[9,10]

[9] Note also that even if patents are completely effective, an innovator will not be able to appropriate the consumers' surplus generated by the new product or process unless the innovator can engage in first-degree price discrimination (charge each consumer his or her personal maximum price for each unit purchased).

[10] Nor should it be taken for granted that strong patent protection is desirable from a social point of view. In the US, a 1956 antitrust consent decree required AT&T to openly license patent-controlled technology at reasonable rates. This requirement is thought to have facilitated the development of the UNIX operating system (Salus, 1994, pp. 58–9). Operating under this constraint, AT&T required cross-licences of patents from firms to which it granted licences. This pattern of cross-licences contributed to rapid entry into and growth of the US semiconductor chip industry (Steinmueller, 1987, p. 13; 1988, p. 335).

no amount of legal protection can make a thoroughly appropriable commodity of something so intangible as information. The very use of the information in any productive way is bound to reveal it, at least in part. Mobility of personnel among firms provides a way of spreading information. Legally imposed property rights can provide only a partial barrier, since there are obviously enormous difficulties in defining in any sharp way an item of information and differentiating it from similar sounding items.

The view the information flows costlessly has been challenged on both theoretical and empirical grounds. Cohen and Levinthal (1989, pp. 569–70) emphasize that information often does not flow freely from an innovator to other users:[11]

we argue that while R&D obviously generates innovations, it also develops the firm's ability to identify, assimilate, and exploit knowledge from the environment—what we call a firm's "learning" or "absorptive" capacity. While encompassing a firm's ability to imitate new process or product innovations, absorptive capacity also includes the firm's ability to exploit outside knowledge of a more intermediate sort, such as basic research findings that provide the basis for subsequent applied research and development.

Vonortas emphasizes the tacit nature of some kinds of knowledge (1994, p. 415):[12]

technological knowledge involves a combination of poorly-defined, and often incomplete, know-how and a set of highly codified information which is hard to acquire and utilize effectively.

In sectors of the economy where knowledge has a tacit component, appropriability of the economic profit that flows from successful innovation will typically not be limited by the free flow of knowledge—where knowledge is tacit, firms need to maintain their own stock of knowledge and technical ability to absorb knowledge generated elsewhere in the economy.

In principle, it is patent rights that confer property rights in innovations.[13] It is not clear that patents rights are an important appropriability mechanism in practice, at least not for most industries.[14]

Pharmaceuticals are one of the sectors where it is generally thought that patents are important in ensuring property rights. But Caves et al. (1991) study 30 drugs that lost patent protection in the decade 1976–87 and find that after patent protection expires, the patented variety suffers only modest reductions in market share, even though generic substitutes sell at substantially lower prices. Marketing efforts aimed at prescribing physicians apparently create a product differentiation advantage that survives well after the introduction of generic substitutes and allows innovators to collect substantial economic profits.

---

[11] See also Kamien and Zang (2000) and Martin (2001a).

[12] See also Teece (1996).

[13] Issues in patent design include what can be patented (methods of doing business?), the length of the period for which a patent is valid, patent breadth (how wide a range of substitute products are covered by a patent?), patent height (how much of an improvement over an existing product or process must an innovation be before it can be patented?)

[14] Patents may serve other purposes. Mowery and Steinmueller (1990, p. 18) suggest that in the US semiconductor industry, patents historically served as bargaining chips that allow a firm to trade licenses for access to technology covered by patents held by other firms. In such cases, patents promote the diffusion of technology.

According to the results of Levin et al.'s (1988) survey of R&D executives in R&D-intensive industries, secrecy, lead time, learning-curve effects, and sales and service efforts all ranked ahead of patents as appropriability mechanisms. Jaffe (2000, p. 555) concludes that "patents are not central to appropriating the returns to R&D in most industries".

5.6 Promoting R&D

If (as seems to be the case) the private sector underinvests in innovation from a social point of view, then there is a case for government efforts to promote R&D. Government might, for example, promote extension services or university-industry enterprise zones, to facilitate the transmission of research knowledge from academic circles to the private sector. This kind of effort probably requires a relatively low level of expenditure at any one time, and may well yield important results, but only over the long run.[15]

Government might also subsidize private R&D, directly or by means of tax incentives. Tax incentives are unlikely to be effective in promoting R&D by high-technology start-up firms or small- and medium-sized enterprises: for an R&D tax credit to be effective, a firm must have tax obligations that the tax credit can be used to satisfy. Start-up firms will often have little or no profit, and therefore owe little or nothing in the way of taxes. Direct public subsidies for private R&D run the risk that government-funded R&D will simply pay for R&D that the private sector would have paid for in any case. The danger of such displacement is particularly important if government officials come under pressure to create a track record of success. Ideally, government should support the R&D projects that are too risky to attract private funding, or that promise large social benefits but small private benefits.[16]

5.6.1 R&D cooperation in practice

Public encouragement of R&D cooperation is much discussed as a means of improving dynamic market performance. Even without public encouragement, R&D cooperation is widespread in modern high-technology industries.

In the late 1970s a cooperative R&D effort in the Japanese semiconductor industry generated much attention for the idea that R&D cooperation might promote innovation. The VLSI (Very Large Scale Integrated Circuits) Project was an Engineering Research Association organized by the Japanese Ministry of International Trade and Industry (MITI). The VLSI project included five companies (Fujitsu, NEC, Hitachi, Mitsubishi, Toshiba) and over the four years of its existence (1976–79), it generated more than a thousand patents.

---

[15] See Burton and Hansen's description of Germany's Fraunhofer Gesellschaften, which (1993, p. 39) "conduct applied research for industry on a contract basis, using the facilities and personnel of regional polytechnics or technical universities".

[16] See Wallsten (2000), who examines the impact of R&D grants made under the US Small Business Innovation Research and finds that public grants replace private R&D spending but do not increase total R&D spending.

The VLSI project is rich in lessons for the public support of cooperative research, although those lessons are not necessarily those that are usually drawn. The VLSI project involved six joint labouratories. One of the six was a genuine joint laboratory, in the sense that it involved balanced participation of representatives from all the partner companies.[17] Each of the other laboratories was dominated by one or another of the specific companies. Of the patents generated by the project, 59 per cent were taken out by a single applicant; only 16 per cent were taken out by applicants from more than one of the VLSI partner firms (Sigurdson, 1986, p. 50).

The VLSI project, like most Japanese R&D joint ventures, seems really to have been a mechanism for administering government subsidies; Odagiri and Goto (1993, p. 88; see also Sigurdson, 1986, p. 110) write that for Japan's Ministry of International Trade and Industry (MITI), research associations

have been a convenient way to distribute its subsidies to promote the technology MITI (and participating firms) believed important, most notably semiconductors and computers, and have been used to avoid favouring particular firms and to minimize the cost of supervising the use of subsidies. Only two of the 87 associations had joint research facilities; in all other cases, each member firm simply took its share of research funds and carried out the research in its own laboratory. Therefore, how coordinated the research really was among participating firms within each [research association] is doubtful except for a few cases.

The VLSI budget was 60 million yen, half provided by the companies and half by MITI.

The VLSI project is often said to have established a leading Japanese presence in the world semiconductor market, but it is important to understand the nature of that presence. Duysters and Hagedoorn compare the performances of EU, Japanese, and US microelectronics firms in the 1980s and conclude that EU and US firms outperform the Japanese from a technological point of view (1995, p. 219):

Aggressive price competition and low cost production enabled Japanese firms to drive US competitors out of "commodity" markets such as DRAMs [Dynamic Random Access Memory chips]. The inability to compete with Japanese companies in price-sensitive mature markets induced European and US firms to upgrade their product line and move into high-end growth markets such as microprocessors and custom chips.

In the US, Sematech (Semiconductor Manufacturing Technology) was formed in 1987 as a joint industry-government sponsored research consortium intended to revitalize the US semiconductor industry, in no small measure as a strategic response to the rise of Japanese semiconductor manufacturers. Sematech was founded with 13 corporate members. A fourteenth joined in short order; three of the 14 later withdrew.

Sematech maintains its own research facility, in which it seeks to simulate manufacturing conditions. It signs contracts with outside laboratories to carry out research in specified areas. That Sematech has its own research facility makes it exceptional among US joint R&D projects (Peck, 1986, p. 219):

the most common pattern in . . . US R&D joint ventures has been for the research to be carried out

---

[17] Mowery (1995, p. 527) argues that the role of most cooperative Japanese joint ventures was not so much to generate new knowledge as to circulate and diffuse existing knowledge. The VLSI project was exceptional in having one genuinely joint research laboratory; for the most part, it followed the general pattern.

by participants in their own facilities or by contract with universities and independent organizations. . . .

Sematech is widely credited with enabling the US industry to regain world market share, reversing losses to Japanese suppliers. In 1994, it announced its intention to give up US government support at the end of the 1996 fiscal year, and wean itself from direct subsidies.

From a policy point of view, it is important not only to ask if Sematech was successful but also what results might have been obtained without cooperative R&D. Irwin and Klenow (1996) estimate that Sematech member firms reduced their overall R&D spending, inclusive of their contributions to the consortium, by $300 million per year. Sematech's research budget during this period was $200 million per year, of which the member firms contributed about half of the funds. If this result is accepted, the net effect of Sematech was to reduce industry spending on R&D. The member firms put about $100 million a year into the consortium and reduced their own R&D spending apart from their contributions to the consortium by four times that amount, yielding the net change in their overall R&D spending as a reduction of $300 million.

The European Union supports a range of basic research projects under (most recently) the Fifth Framework Programme. These projects emphasize basic research (this can be seen as seeking to avoid the kinds of conflicts that arose early in the VLSI project) and participation of small- and medium-sized enterprises. Diffusion is also sought: research results are owned jointly by the EU and the companies involved.

R&D that is closer to the marketplace is carried out under the aegis of EUREKA, an organization that dates from 1985 and now includes 24 countries and the European Union as members. EUREKA programmes emphasize commercialization rather than basic research; research results of a project are the property of the partners involved.

Among the EUREKA projects are JESSI (1988–96) and its successor MEDEA, which target the semiconductor industry. JESSI was in part a vehicle for public subsidy: half of its 3.8 million ECU budget was funded by participating companies, the other half by various government and public sources. JESSI is credited with upgrading EU technology with respect to both specialty chips and computer aided design manufacturing techniques. MEDEA, which anticipates a 2 billion ECU budget over the 1997–2000 period, will concentrate on six areas and aim to maintain a European presence in the semiconductor chip industry.

5.6.2 **R&D cooperation in theory**

There is good reason to think that R&D cooperation improves market performance, but not because it encourages innovation. In theoretical models of independent R&D in oligopoly, R&D by one firm stimulates R&D by other firms. When firms carry out joint R&D, this stimulus is removed, and equilibrium R&D levels fall.[18] This theoretical result is consistent with at least some evidence from the world semiconductor industry. Yet theoretical models predict that R&D cooperation improves market performance, because of its impact on static market performance in the post-innovation market. With R&D

---

[18] See, for example, d'Aspremont and Jacquemin (1988), or Martin (2001a).

cooperation, it is typically the case that all cooperating firms have access to discoveries on identical terms, meaning that they compete on equal terms after discovery. R&D cooperation means greater rivalry, and therefore improved market performance, after discovery.[19]

5.7 Innovation and EU competition policy

5.7.1 Cooperative R&D under Article 81

The prediction that R&D cooperation will improve market performance by diffusing information about new products and processes depends on the assumption that firms behave independently in the post-innovation market. In principle, R&D cooperation can promote tacit collusion (Martin, 1996).

The heart of the economic analysis of tacit collusion is that firms hold back from expanding output in the short run, even though it would be profitable to do so, because of the threat of future lost profit once rivals realize that some firm is cheating on output restriction (Section 3.2.1). In a market system, if firms form an R&D joint venture, it is because they expect it to be profitable. It follows that the threat to break up an R&D joint venture could be part of a punishment strategy used to create incentives for firms to restrict output.[20]

Leaving such spurious R&D cooperation aside, agreements that contribute to technological progress may be permitted under Article 81, Paragraph 3 of the EU Treaty. The European Commission's attitude toward such cooperation is generally favourable. There is a block exemption for R&D cooperation if the combined market shares of the cooperating firms are no greater than 25 per cent, provided the agreement does not include restrictions on the right of cooperating firms to carry out independent R&D or restrict the rights of the cooperating parties to use the knowledge that results from the cooperation (*Draft Guidelines*, 2000a, p. 17).

If a proposed R&D cooperation does not fall under the block exemption, it may nonetheless be permitted under Article 81(3). For example, a 14 September 1999 Commission

---

[19] R&D cooperation is sometimes justified on the ground that it eliminates "wasteful duplication". This justification is discredited both theoretically (Dasgupta and Maskin, 1987) and empirically (Nelson, 1982, pp. 455, reviewing case studies):

From a social point of view, effective pursuit of technological advance seems to call for the exploration of a wide variety of alternatives and the selective screening of these after their characteristics have been better revealed—a process that seems wasteful with the wonderful vision of hindsight.

When the outcome of R&D projects is uncertain, it is socially beneficial, and frequently privately beneficial as well, to pursue multiple research paths toward a common target.

[20] Kaiser (2002, footnote 1) gives references to a number of cases in which proposed R&D cooperations were challenged under German competition law. In the one US antitrust case involving R&D cooperation of which I am aware, the claim was that R&D cooperation by automobile manufacturers was a cover for collusion to delay the development of emissions control technology. The case was settled by a consent decree. *US v. Automobile Manufacturers Association* 1969 Trade Cases (CCH) Para 72,907 (S.D. Cal. 1969) (consent decree), modified 1982–3 Trade Cases (CCH) Para 65,088 (C.D. Cal. 1982).

decision permitted Pratt & Whitney and General Electric to create an equally-owned joint venture to develop a new jet engine to be sold to Airbus Industrie. At this time, Pratt & Whitney and General Electric were two of the three largest engine manufacturers in the world (the third being Rolls Royce), and each might have been able to develop such an engine alone. The benefit seen flowing from cooperation was that each firm would be able to concentrate its efforts on areas where it had specific technological expertise. The Commission also limited its permission for cooperation to this one specific project, taking the view that cooperation to provide engines for other aircraft (that is, for Boeing) would create incentives to restrict product-market competition.

5.7.2 Intellectual property rights and Article 82

We have seen (Section 6.8) that vertical restraints with the effect of dividing the single market along national boundaries violate Article 81(1). Under some circumstances, a firm that holds a patent may be able to divide markets along national lines without, by so doing, abusing a dominant position in violation of Article 82. Thus in the early Parke, Davis case,[21] the pharmaceutical company Parke, Davis held valid a Dutch patent on an antibiotic. Such products could not at that time be patented in Italy. Probel obtained the product from a firm in Italy, and marketed it in the Netherlands. The European Court of Justice held that Parke, Davis did not abuse a dominant position when it used its patent rights to block sale of the Italian version of the product in the Netherlands: a patent is a legal grant of monopoly and Parke, Davis was simply exercising its legal monopoly rights. The facts that Parke, Davis was not itself (directly or indirectly) the source by which the product was available in Italy, and that patent protection was not available in Italy, were central to the Court's decision.

In 1984 IBM made a formal commitment[22] to alter some business practices and so bring to a close a commission investigation under Article 82. The Commission had taken the view that IBM held a dominant position in the common market for its System-370 mainframe computer and was able to control the markets for products compatible with it. The Commission argued that IBM had abused this dominant position by

- withholding interface information essential for independent producers to supply compatible equipment;
- which also interfered with development of standard computer networking procedures;
- bundling CPUs and main memory; and by
- bundling CPUs and software.

The essence of these alleged abuses involves issues of product design, and thus goes to the heart of the innovative process. In taking steps to end the Commission proceeding, IBM agreed to unbundle CPUs and main memory and to make interface information available to independent hardware and software producers and network designers. The Commission felt that the agreement would improve market performance (EC Commission, 1985, pp. 79):

---

[21] *Parke, Davis* v. *Probel* [1968] ECR 55; [1968] CMLR 47.
[22] An undertaking, in Eurospeak. The settlement is discussed in EC Commission (1985, pp. 77–79).

The undertaking will have the effect of substantially improving the position of both users and competitors in the markets for System/370 products in the EEC. As a result, competition in the common market can be expected to be strengthened and made more effective. Users will now be given the possibility of a choice between different suppliers at an earlier time. They may also be free to choose from a wider selection of products because other manufacturers will now have the incentive to develop new products in the knowledge that the essential interface information will be made available.

A 1991 decision[23] of the Court of First Instance helped clarify the limits EU competition policy places on the exercise of patent rights. The product market in the *Hilti* decision—nail guns and associated products, used in building and construction—would not normally be thought of as "high tech", but the issues involved in the decision anticipate those present in much more prominent recent cases.

Hilti AG had its legal home in Liechtenstein, and manufacturing operations there and in other EU Member States. It held patents on its nail guns, on nails for its guns, and on cartridge strips by means of which nails could be inserted into its nail guns.[24] Hilti tied the sale of nails and cartridge strips to the sale of its nail guns; it obliged its dealers not to supply cartridge strips to independent nail producers. The European Commission found, and the Court of First Instance agreed, that Hilti's 55 per cent in the supply of nail guns in the Community as a whole gave it a dominant position.

Although Hilti argued that nail guns, nails, and cartridge strips were components of a single product, the Court found that nail guns, Hilti-compatible nails, and cartridge strips were three distinct product markets. One bit of supporting evidence for the conclusion that these were separate product markets was that there was a history of independent producers specializing in the production of nails specifically designed for Hilti tools. Despite the fact that Hilti held patents on the products it was distributing, the Court found that its marketing practices were abusive in the sense of Article 82, because they had the effect of raising entry costs ([1990] ECR II-1483):

The strategy employed by Hilti against its competitors and their customers is not a legitimate mode of competition on the part of an undertaking in a dominant position. A selective and discriminatory policy such as that operated by Hilti impairs competition inasmuch as it is liable to deter other undertakings from establishing themselves in the market.

This decision shows that when a firm has a dominant position in a market for a differentiated product, EU courts will treat products that are compatible with the product of the dominant firm as a distinct product. The IBM settlement and the *Hilti* decision together indicate that intellectual property rights—whether based on product design or on patent rights—will not, under EU competition law, permit a dominant firm to divide the common market or to raise rivals' entry costs.

More generally, it is an established principle in EU competition law that conduct permitted for a small firm is an abuse in violation of Article 82 if committed by a dominant firm. Thus the 1991 *Tetrapak* decision involved the leading EU manufacturer of sterile cartons and machines for filling such cartons (which are used, importantly, for packaging ultra-high temperature sterilized milk). In 1986, Tetrapak took over another firm,

---

[23] *Hilti AG* v. *EC Commission* Case T-30/89 [1990] ECR II-1439; [1990] 4 CMLR 16.

[24] The details of the patents held varied from product to product and from Member State to Member State.

Liquipak, and as a result gained control of an exclusive licence for use of a new technique for filling cartons with sterile milk. At the time Tetrapak got control of the licence, the new technique was not yet being commercially applied, and the parties in the case disagreed about how much additional work would be needed to make commercial use possible. When Tetrapak got control of the licence, firms that had been working with Liquipak to bring the new technology to the market stopped work on the project. The Commission investigated Tetrapak's acquisition of the exclusive licence, and as a result Tetrapak gave up its exclusive right to use the new technology. Nonetheless, to clarify the area of law concerned, the Commission reached a decision that the acquisition of such an exclusive patent licence by a dominant firm was an abuse of a dominant position under Article 82. Tetrapak appealed the Commission's decision to the Court of First Instance. Once again, the impact of an exclusive licence on the ability of rivals to compete was central when the Court of First Instance upheld the Commission ([1990] ECR II-357):

the Commission was right not to put in issue the exclusive licence as such, but rather to object specifically under Article [82] to the anti-competitive effect of its being acquired by [Tetrapak]. . . .
   The decisive factor in the finding that acquisition of the exclusive licence constitute an abuse lay . . . in particular . . . on the fact that at the material time the right to use the process protected by the . . . licence was alone capable of giving an undertaking the means of competing effectively with [Tetrapak].

Under EU competition policy, a dominant firm may exercise its intellectual property rights to earn economic profit, subject to the limitation that it may not specifically make it more difficult for rivals to try to compete such profit away.[25]

5.8 Summary

Private investment in knowledge is discouraged by R&D input and output spillovers. Yet such spillovers are not automatic: firms need to maintain the ability to absorb knowledge flows, and this in itself is a costly enterprise. Taking the level of R&D efforts as given, R&D input spillovers are socially beneficial, since they make R&D efforts more productive; R&D output spillovers are also socially beneficial, as they improve static market performance.

   Patents offer some property rights in innovations, and there are other ways for firms to profit from their R&D investments as well (product differentiation, for example). Patents are a legal grant for single firms to exercise market power, but competition law does not generally allow single patent holders to extend their legal market power beyond the

[25] The issues raised for competition policy in these intellectual property rights cases have also surfaced in several of the Microsoft Corporation's dealings with the European Commission. Some of these are described in EC Commission (1995, pp. 116–21) (marketing practices that had the effect of raising the cost to users of choosing rival operating systems for personal computers), EC Commission (1998, pp. 116–17) (contract requiring a software developer to use a Microsoft version of UNIX as the basis for its own product development); EC Commission (2000c, p. 162) (contractual restrictions on internet service providers concerning their use of rival internet browsers).

specific terms of the patent, nor does it allow different patent holders to combine their separately legal grants of market power.

Private and social rates of return to innovation are estimated to be large, and greater than rates of return to other types of investments. Governments have encouraged innovation by direct subsidy, by tax credits, by promoting infrastructure for the transmission of knowledge, and by encouraging R&D cooperation. The effect of R&D cooperation may well be to reduce the amount of R&D that takes place, but nonetheless to improve static market performance by ensuring that several firms have access to new products and processes on equal terms.

Study points

- R&D spillovers (page 90)
- high rates of return to R&D (pages 91–2)
- Schumpeter Mark I, Schumpeter Mark II (page 93)
- incremental profitability and the incentive to invest in innovation (pages 94–6)
- capacity to absorb R&D spillovers (pages 96–8)
- R&D cooperation (page 100)
- innovation and competition policy (pages 101–9)

Chapter 6

Organization

The economies of modern industrialized society can more appropriately be labeled organizational economies than market economies.

Simon (1991, p. 42).

6.1 **Introduction**

When it examined the organization of economic activity, the historical focus of industrial economics was supply-side market structure. What factors determine the equilibrium number of firms in a market? Why are some firms in a market large, others small? What can be said about factors influencing the survival rate of new entrants to a particular market? Why is multiplant operation common in some markets, not in others?

Despite a history going back to Adam Smith and *The Wealth of Nations*,[1] questions about the structure of firms never received the same kind of attention as did questions about the structure of markets. The two topics are, of course, inextricably linked: multiplant operation, for example, is as much an aspect of firm as of market structure; the same is true of direct foreign investment.

This imbalance is now on its way to being corrected. It is possible to examine the determinants of market structure using standard oligopoly models, and we will do that in Section 6.2. We will also discuss the determinants of market structure in certain types of high-technology markets (those characterized by network externalities, which we define below), and review empirical evidence on the size distribution of firms. In Section 6.6, we turn our attention to factors explaining the organization of economic activity within firms. This is an essential prelude to the discussion of mergers—which often place policymakers in the position between having to compare the impact of a change in market structure that seems likely to make market performance worse with the impact of a change in firm structure that may make firm performance better—and merger policy in the EC.

---

[1] We touch on Smith's pin factory example in Section 6.6.

6.2 **Market structure**

6.2.1 **Cournot oligopoly, single-plant firms**

A first model of market structure can be obtained by generalizing the Cournot model of homogeneous-product oligopoly presented in Section 4. Once again, let the equation of the inverse demand curve be

$$p = 100 - Q, \tag{6.1}$$

and now let the cost function be

$$c(q) = \begin{cases} F + 10q + dq^2 & q > 0 \\ \\ 0 & q = 0 \end{cases}. \tag{6.2}$$

For the moment interpret (6.2) as the cost function of a single firm. Some costs are fixed ($F > 0$), which is to say that they must be paid if the firm operates at all, and do not vary with output.

The equations of the average variable and marginal cost functions are

$$AVC(q) = 10 + dq \tag{6.3}$$

and

$$MC(q) = 10 + 2dq \tag{6.4}$$

respectively. We will assume that $d > 0$, and with this assumption it appears from (6.3) and (6.4) that d is a diseconomy of scale parameter: as output increases, marginal cost and average variable cost increase as well.

With a fixed stock of physical capital, the existence of diseconomies of scale can be explained as a result of larger and larger amounts of variable factors of production (labour, materials) "crowding" a fixed capital stock. Over the long run, when the stock of physical capital is considered variable, one might still regard "management" as a fixed factor of production and expect to observe diseconomies of large firm scale.[2]

The equation of the average cost curve is

$$AC(q) = \tfrac{F}{q} + 10 + dq. \tag{6.5}$$

A few average cost curves, for $d = 1$ and for different values of F, are shown in Figure 6.1.[3] Considering the first term on the right in (6.5), F/q, when output is small, fixed cost per unit of output is large. As output increases, fixed cost is spread over more units of output and fixed cost per unit of output falls. Considering the third term on the right in (6.5), as

---

[2] If in (6.2) we set $F = d = 0$ (the kind of cost function we generally considered in Chapter 2), we obtain a cost function for a technology with constant returns to scale, marginal cost being the same whether output is high or low. See also Section 6.2.3 for an extension to the case of multiplant firms, and Section 6.6.

[3] For an explanation of the particular values of F that are used in Figure 6.1, see Figure 6.2 and the associated text.

output increases, variable cost per unit of output rises. For low output levels, the spreading of fixed cost effect predominates, average cost falls as output rises, and the average cost curve exhibits economies of scale. For large output levels, diseconomies of scale predominate, average cost rises as output rises, and the average cost curve exhibits diseconomies of scale. Over the whole range of output, the result is a roughly ∪-shaped average cost curve of the kind shown in Figure 6.1.

The minimum point on the average cost curve occurs where the marginal cost curve and the average cost curve intersect.[4] Solving equations (6.4) and (6.5), we find the output level at which the average cost and marginal cost curves intersect, the *minimum efficient scale* output level, so called because it yields the lowest value of average cost:

$$q_{mes} = \sqrt{\tfrac{F}{d}}. \tag{6.6}$$

Minimum efficient scale output is determined by the technology, as described by the cost function. It rises as fixed cost F rises and as the diseconomies of scale parameter d falls.

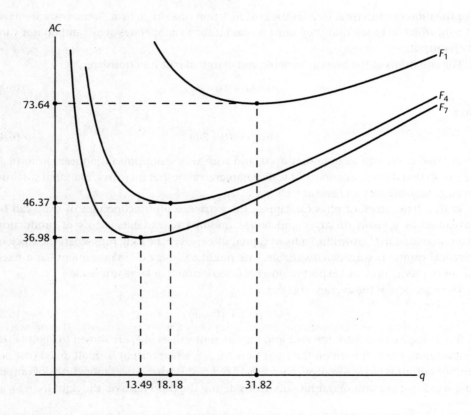

Fig. 6.1 Average cost, $c(q) = F + 10q + q^2$, alternative levels of fixed cost; $F_1 = 1012.5$; $F_4 = 330.61$; $F_7 = 182$

---

[4] See Figure 1.4 and the associated text.

Substituting (6.6) in either (6.4) or (6.5), the minimum value of average cost is

$$AC_{\min} = 10 + 2\sqrt{dF}. \tag{6.7}$$

The minimum value of average cost rises as F or d rises.

From this model of the costs of a single firm, we can obtain a basic model of market structure. Suppose that there are n firms, each with cost function of form (6.2), and that they behave as Cournot oligopolists. Then firm 1 (for example) maximizes profit along its residual demand curve by picking an output level that makes marginal revenue equal to marginal cost,

$$100 - (q_2 + q_3 + \ldots + q_n) - 2q_1 = 10 + 2dq_1, \tag{6.8}$$

leading to the expression

$$q_1 = \frac{1}{2(1+d)}[90 - (q_2 + q_3 + \ldots + q_n)] \tag{6.9}$$

for firm 1's best response output when the cost function implies that there are diseconomies of large scale.[5]

Because we have assumed that firms are identical, in equilibrium all firms will produce the same output.[6] Setting $q_1 = q_2 = \ldots = q_n = q_{Cour}$ in (6.8) and rearranging terms gives an expression for equilibrium output per firm,[7]

$$q_{Cour} = \frac{90}{n + 1 + 2d}. \tag{6.10}$$

Equilibrium profit per firm when there are n firms supplying the market is

$$\pi_{Cour} = (1+d)q_{Cour}^2 - F = (1+d)\left(\frac{90}{n+1+2d}\right) - F. \tag{6.11}$$

From a theoretical point of view, we can close the model by assuming that in the long run (and if incumbent firms do not engage in entry-deterring strategic behaviour), new firms enter the market if short-run equilibrium profit is positive, incumbent firms exit the market if short-run equilibrium profit is negative.[8] The long-run equilibrium number of firms n_{Cour} is the number that makes $\pi_{Cour} = 0$; from (6.11),

$$n_{Cour} = 90\sqrt{\frac{1+d}{F}} - (1+2d) = \frac{90}{q_{mes}}\sqrt{1+\tfrac{1}{d}} - (1+2d), \tag{6.12}$$

so that the long-run Cournot equilibrium number of firms n_{Cour} rises as the market is

---

[5] Strictly speaking, (6.9) is the equation of firm 1's best response function only if the resulting output means that firm 1 does not make losses that exceed its fixed cost. If firm 1 were to make losses that exceed its fixed cost, its profit-maximizing output would be zero (that is, its profit-maximizing choice would be to shut down).

[6] We make the assumption that firms have the same information, the same cost functions, and behave in the same way for expositional simplicity. Examining the case of different firms makes the algebra more complicated but does not change the qualitative nature of the results; see Section 2.2.5.

[7] Note that if $d = 0$ this reduces to (2.60), the (hopefully) familiar result when returns to scale are constant.

[8] In Section 6.3 we will argue that empirical evidence suggests that entry and exit do not in fact automatically drive economic profit to zero, even in the long run.

larger[9] and falls as either the minimum efficient scale output or diseconomies of scale rise.[10]

For concreteness, let $d = 1$. Then from the expression after the first equals sign in (6.12), the relation between fixed cost and the long-run equilibrium number of firms is

$$n_{Cour} = 90\sqrt{\tfrac{2}{F}} - 3, \tag{6.13}$$

which is shown in Figure 6.2.

If $F > 1,012.5$, the equilibrium number of firms is zero. If fixed cost is very high, relative to market size, it is not profitable even for a monopolist to supply the market. For lower values of fixed cost, $648 < F \le 1,012.5$, it is profitable for one firm to supply the market, but not two (the market is a natural monopoly). If $450 < F \le 648$, the Cournot equilibrium market structure is duopoly, and so on: the lower the value of fixed cost, the larger the equilibrium number of firms.[11]

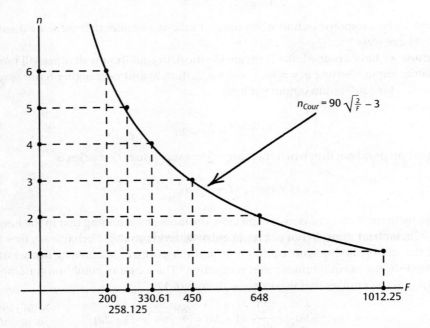

Fig. 6.2 Equilibrium number of firms—fixed cost relationship, Cournot oligopoly, $p = 100 - Q$, $c(q) = F + 10q + q^2$

---

[9] The impact of market size on the equilibrium number of firms is masked in (6.12) because we have used a specific numerical example. In a more general formulation, let the equation of the inverse demand curve be $p = a - Q$ and the equation of the cost function $c(q) = F + cq + dq^2$. Then in place of the number 90 in (6.12) we have $a - c$; as a, the price axis intercept of the demand curve, is larger, the demand curve is farther from the origin, the market is larger, and the long-run equilibrium number of plants is larger as well.

[10] For simplicity, we have ignored the fact that the number of firms must be an integer. To be precise, the equilibrium number of firms is the greatest integer less than the value of n_{Cour} given by (6.12). In the long-run, entry and exit will reduce profit to a level so low that if one additional firm were to come into the market, all firms would lose money.

[11] These figures are derived in the following way. Solve (6.13) for F to obtain $F = 16200/(n + 3)^2$. The value of F that makes $n = 1$ is $16200/16 = 1012.5$, the value of F that makes $n = 2$ is $16200/25 = 648$, and so on.

6.2.2 **Conjectural variations, single-plant firms**

Turning now to the conjectural variations generalization of the Cournot model outlined in Section 2.2.6, if each firm believes that rivals respond to a 1 per cent change in its own output by an a per cent change in their outputs, the equation (6.8) (marginal revenue equals marginal cost) becomes

$$100 - (1 + a)(q_2 + q_3 + \ldots + q_n) - 2q_1 = 10 + 2dq_1. \qquad (6.14)$$

Recall that $a > 0$ means a firm believes that rivals will change output in the same way that it does (matching conjectures), while $a < 0$ means a firm believes that rivals will change output in the opposite direction (contrarian conjectures). The smaller is a, the tougher is competition. $a = 0$ is the case of Cournot conjectures.

Setting $q_1 = q_2 = \ldots = q_n = q_a$ in (6.14) and rearranging terms gives an expression for equilibrium output per firm for the case of general conjectures,

$$q_a = \frac{90}{n + 1 + a(n - 1) + 2d}. \qquad (6.15)$$

The smaller is a, the smaller is the denominator on the right in (6.15) and the greater is short-run equilibrium output per firm, all else (and in particular, n, the number of firms), equal. Tougher rivalry, lower values of a, means a smaller number of firms and greater seller concentration, all else equal.[12]

> *Market equilibrium number of firms*: with single-plant firms, the Cournot equilibrium number of firms rises with market size, falls as minimum efficient scale output rises, and falls the more intense is rivalry.

6.2.3 **Cournot oligopoly, multiplant firms**

In theory

Up to this point, we have interpreted (6.2) as the equation of a cost function for a firm. If, instead, we take it to be the cost function of a single plant, then a firm with a high profit-maximizing output can avoid the effect of plant-level diseconomies of scale by operating more than one plant (Dewey, 1969, Chapter 3).

If a firm decides to produce all its output in a single plant, its cost function is (6). If all plants have the same cost function, and a firm opens a second plant, the efficient (cost-minimizing) allocation of output would be to produce the same amount in each plant.[13] Thus if a firm operates two identical plants, the firm-level cost function is

[12] In terms of the structure-conduct-performance paradigm, we have conduct feeding back and helping determine long-run structure.

[13] If plants are identical, and output is not the same in both plants, then since the firm will be operating plants on the upward-sloping segments of the average cost curves, marginal cost must be higher in the plant producing more output, and lower in the plant producing less output. But then the firm could reduce cost, keeping total output unchanged, by shifting some production from the high-marginal cost plant to the low-marginal cost plant. With identical plants, cost-minimization requires the same output level in all plants.

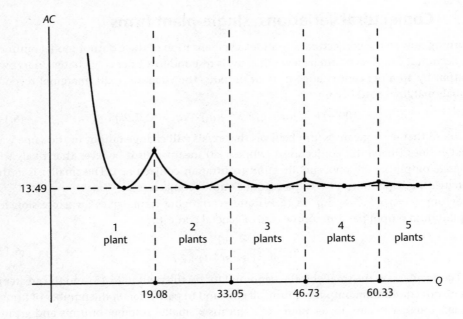

Fig. 6.3 Average cost, multiplant firm, plant cost function $c(q) = 182 + 10q + q^2$

$$2[F + 10(\tfrac{1}{2}Q) + d(\tfrac{1}{2}Q)^2].$$
(6.16)

The firm must pay a second set of fixed costs for the second plant, but as a result it is able to produce half its output in each plant, reducing the impact of diseconomies of scale. If output is large enough,[14] the firm will minimize its cost by opening a second plant. If output rises further still, the firm will minimize its cost by opening a third plant, producing one-third of its output in each plant. In this way, as shown in Figure 6.3, the firm-level average cost curve exhibits approximate constant returns to scale for output above q_{mes}. The firm's average cost never rises too much above the minimum value of average cost given by (6.7), because if firm output reaches a level that drives up average cost in existing plants, in the long run the firm can open an additional plant, redistribute output among plants, and bring average cost back toward the minimum level.

In practice

This theoretical story pictures multiplant operation as a way of organizing production that avoids diseconomies of scale at the plant level. Each plant produces an output that is not too different from the most efficient (cost-minimizing) output, and in the long run a firm expands output by opening up additional plants.

Empirical evidence (Scherer et al., 1975) suggests that multiplant firms frequently operate plants that appear to produce less than minimum efficient scale outputs. In some

---

[14] That is, if output reaches the level for which the cost of producing all output in one plant is the same as the cost of producing half of firm output in each of two plants, the value of Q for which

$$F + 10Q + dQ^2 = 2[F + 10(\tfrac{1}{2}Q) + d(\tfrac{1}{2}Q)^2].$$

cases, this may reflect the fact (left aside in neoclassical economic models) that markets have a spatial aspect. A firm may operate a plant that is of suboptimal size from the point of view of production cost alone at a location that allows the firm to save transportation costs to a particular group of consumers.[15]

Scherer et al. (1975, Chapter 2) emphasize that economies arising in the way the production of specific products is organized can be as important as economies of plant size.[16] An apparently suboptimal-scale plant may be one that is dedicated to production of a particular variety of a differentiated product. A larger plant might be more efficient from some points of view, but production of several different varieties of the product in a single plant would mean periodic down time (zero or reduced output) and fixed costs of switching from production of one variety to another. Concentrating production of large-output varieties can mean run-length economies. Concentrating production in a single plant can also reduce inventory carrying costs and be a source of technological progress, as workers whose attention is focused on a particular task develop more effective production methods over time.

Multiplant operation: allows firms to avoid the consequences of diseconomies of scale in a single plant, and may allow realization of efficiency advantages, such as run-length economies, particularly associated with multiplant operation.

6.3 Entry and exit[17]

The most basic theoretical story about entry and exit is the one we told on the way to equation (6.12): in the long run, the number of firms adjusts until equilibrium profit per firm is zero (keeping in mind that zero economic profit means a firm is earning neither more nor less than a normal rate of return on investment). Part of the story about moving the market to long-run equilibrium is that once a firm comes into the market, it is an incumbent and indistinguishable from other incumbents. If the rate of return on investment in the industry is below normal, some firms leave the market, but the model does not specify which firms will leave first.[18]

Real-world entry and exit is rather more complex than its theoretical counterpart. Table 6.1, taken from Schwalbach (1991), gives some descriptive statistics about entry and exit for a sample of 185 four-digit German manufacturing industries for the years 1983–1985.

---

[15] Models that take the spatial aspect of markets explicitly into account prove to be surprisingly subtle, and are beyond the scope of an introductory text. See Hotelling (1929) or Chapter 4 of Martin (2001b).

[16] This point anticipates the discussion of Section 6.6.

[17] See Acs and Audretsch (1990), Geroski (1991b), Geroski and Schwalbach (1991), Audretsch (1995), and Caves (1998), and particularly Geroski (1991a).

[18] For models of this question in the context of declining industries, see Ghemawat and Nalebuff (1985, 1990).

Table 6.1 Descriptive statistics on entry and exit, 183 German manufacturing industries, 1983–5.

	Minimum	Mean	Maximum	Standard Deviation
Number of entrants	0	20.923	231	34.707
Entry rate	0	0.115	0.778	0.099
Entrants' market share	0	0.049	0.256	0.040
Entrants' relative size (sales)	0.017	0.699	3.403	0.514
Number of exiters	0	24.716	187	35.695
Exit rate	0	0.138	0.500	0.072
Exiters' market share	0	0.083	0.341	0.062
Exiters' relative size	0.026	0.553	1.994	0.312

Source: Schwalbach (1991)

The nature of entry and exit flows that Schwalbach reports are typical of manufacturing sectors of developed countries.

The average number of entering firms per industry in this sample was almost 21, the average number of exiting firms almost 25. The average entry rate—number of entrants in relation to number of incumbents—was 11.5 per cent, the average exit rate 13.8 per cent. On average, entering and exiting firms were small, entrants being 69.9 per cent of the size of incumbents on average, exiters 55.3 per cent. Their combined market shares were also small, with entrants' combined market share being 4.9 per cent of industry sales on average, and the corresponding figure for exiting firms 8.3 per cent. Entry and exit rates were also positively correlated, meaning that entry and exit rates into any specific industry tended to be either both high or both low.[19]

These kinds of entry and exit flows are far from being the kind of straightforward adjustment mechanism that leads industries to an equilibrium in which all firms in all industries earn only a normal rate of return.[20] Entry seems instead to be a kind of selection mechanism, involving firms that explore their own abilities and test their own ideas about segments of a market that might be up for grabs. Most entrants, it appears, do not pass the test, and withdraw from the market after a relatively short period of time.

The standard story of entry and exit leads to a long-run equilibrium in which all firms earn only a normal rate of return on investment. The kind of entry and exit that is observed in the real world suggests a rather different kind of equilibrium, in which established incumbents compete oligopolistically among themselves, while an ever-changing group of small firms circle precariously on the edge of the market. The identities of the small firms change over time, but as far as established firms are concerned, the nature of

[19] If entry occurs automatically when profits are above normal, and exit occurs automatically when profits are below normal, then one would expect to see either entry or exit taking place at any point in time for a single industry, but not simultaneous entry and exit.

[20] They are also far from the story told in the model of Bertrand oligopoly (Section 2.3.1) with standardized products, according to which all consumers in a market will switch from one firm to another in response to a tiny price difference.

the fringe group as a whole does not change very often, and it is rare that a firm makes the leap from the fringe to the inner circle.

Empirically, there is evidence that the costs of moving from the fringe to the inner circle of established oligopolistic firms depends on *barriers to mobility* (Caves and Porter, 1977) that are higher the larger is minimum efficient scale output in relation to market size, the greater the fraction of operating investments that are sunk costs, and the more important is spending on advertising and on innovation.[21] These same factors influence the long-run size distribution of firms in an industry, a topic to which we now turn.

Entry and exit: empirical evidence suggests that entry is a risky proposition, most likely to result in exit, and that entry and exit act more as a screening mechanism selecting firms efficient enough to survive in an industry's oligopolistic core than an automatic adjustment mechanism that drives the economic profit of incumbent firms to zero.

6.4 Seller concentration and the size distribution of firms

6.4.1 Gibrat's Law

In most industries, there are substantial inequalities in firm size. We have seen this already in Table 1.2, which is the basis for Figures 6.4 and 6.5.

Figure 6.4 shows the individual market shares of the 22 firms identified by name in Table 1.2. Five firms have market shares of more than 11 per cent each, after which market share falls off sharply. The same size distribution is shown in a different way in the *Lorenz curve* of Figure 6.5, which shows the combined market shares of the largest 20 per cent of firms, the largest 40 per cent of firms, and so on. In the EC market for cars and light trucks, the largest 20 per cent of firms in 1997 had a combined market share of nearly 60 per cent, the largest 40 per cent of firms had a combined market share of nearly 90 per cent, while the smallest 60 per cent of firms divided up little more than 10 per cent of the market.[22,23]

Gibrat (1931) put forward the descriptive hypotheses, which he called the *law of*

---

[21] Audretsch (1995) distinguishes between an entrepreneurial technological regime, in which small firms have a comparative advantage in innovation, and a routinized technological regime, in which they do not. The need to invest in innovation would be a barrier to mobility in industries with a routinized technological regime.

[22] If all firms were of equal size, the largest 10 per cent of firms would have a combined market share of 10 per cent, the largest 20 per cent of firms would have a combined market share of 20 per cent, and so on: the Lorenz curve would coincide with the diagonal. The ratio of the area between the diagonal and the Lorenz curve to the area of the triangle below the diagonal is the *Gini coefficient*, an alternative measure of seller concentration.

[23] For an explanation of the solid curve in Figure 6.5, see Section 6.4.2.

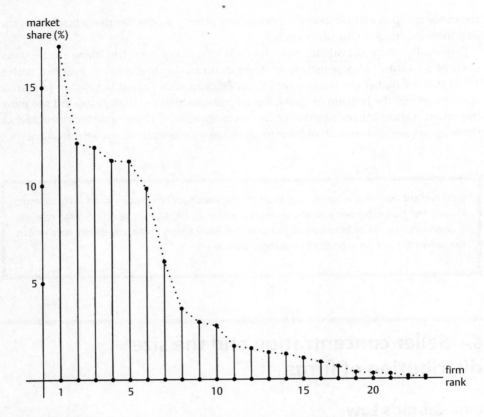

Fig. 6.4 Market shares, EU new car and light truck sales, 1997. Source: Table 1.2

proportionate growth (and which has come to be known as Gibrat's Law)[24] that the probability of a given percentage change in the size of a firm over a given time period for firms in an industry is independent of the firm's initial size. This type of firm growth has the attractive property that over time it produces highly skewed distributions of firm sizes, like those shown in Figure 6.4, which are commonly observed in a wide variety of industries.

Like many elegant propositions, it turns out that Gibrat's Law can be formulated in alternative ways when it is subjected to empirical tests: for any given time period, should it apply only to firms in the market at the beginning of the period, or should it include firms that enter during the period? Should it apply only to firms in the market at the end of the period? Should it apply only to firms at least as large as minimum efficient scale? Should it apply to firms or to individual plants?

The bulk of empirical evidence suggests that Gibrat's Law is a good approximation to the way firm sizes change over time for large, established firms. Entrants tend to exit more frequently than would be predicted by Gibrat's Law. Small, young firms that do not exit quickly tend to grow more rapidly than Gibrat's Law would predict.

[24] See Gibrat (1931), Hart and Prais (1956), Kumar (1985), Hall (1987), Sutton (1997), and Caves (1998).

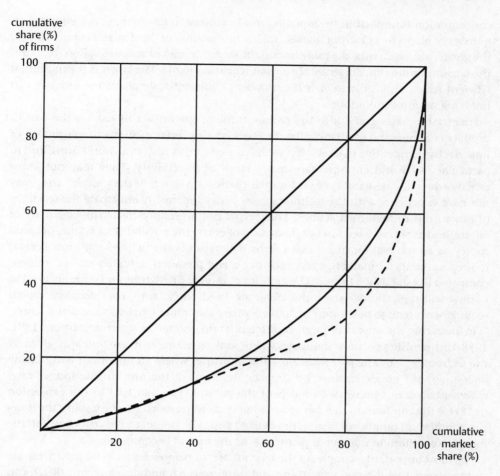

Fig. 6.5 Dashes: cumulative market shares, EU new car and light truck sales, 1997 (firms rank on vertical axis from largest to smallest): Source: Table 1.2.; solid line: Sutton lower bound

> *Gibrat's Law*: it appears to be an empirical regularity that for large, established firms, the probability of a given percentage increase in size over a specified time period is independent of size at the start of the period.

6.4.2 Seller concentration and endogenous sunk costs

The traditional analysis of market structure, beginning with Bain (1956), and to which we have referred at the end of Section 6.3, explained differences in industrial market structure in terms of differences across industries in the nature of economies of scale, in product differentiation, and also in the workings of financial capital markets.

The basic story behind the impact of scale economies on equilibrium seller concentration is implicit in the equation (6.12) expression for the long-run equilibrium number of plants in a Cournot market. Taking the location of the demand curve as given, the greater are fixed costs, the more important are economies of scale (equation (6.5)) and the larger is minimum efficient scale output (equation (6.6)). The larger is the minimum efficient scale output, the smaller the number of efficient-scale plants the industry can hold in long-run equilibrium.

Financial markets come into the picture through the impact of risk on the cost of capital of entrants and small incumbents. There is no uncertainty in the simple models of imperfectly competitive markets that we have used in this text. Real world firms, and in particular real world entrants, face many kinds of uncertainty. They may not know exactly where the demand curve is for their particular version of the product; they may not have experience with the technology; they may incorrectly anticipate the reactions of other firms to their own actions. These types of uncertainty create the possibility of failure, and as we have seen in our discussion of entry, the possibility of failure, of bankruptcy, is all too real for many small firms. The result is that when such firms borrow money on financial markets, they must pay a risk premium, a higher rate of interest, compared to established firms.[25] The amount of money small firms and entrants need to borrow will typically be larger, the larger are fixed entry costs. Thus absolute capital requirements tend to be greatest in markets where minimum efficient scale is also large.

In analyzing the impact of product differentiation on market structure, Sutton (1991, 1998) distinguishes between industries where sunk operating costs are primarily given by the technology—by the cost function—and industries where an important part of sunk operating costs are determined by strategic decisions of the firm. In the former case, *exogenous sunk cost* industries, models of the general type that lead to the expression (6.12) for the equilibrium number of firms apply: holding market size constant, the long-run equilibrium number of plants rises as fixed cost falls; holding fixed cost constant, the long-run equilibrium number of plants rises as the market becomes larger.

The most important examples of the second case, of *endogenous sunk cost* industries, are sectors where spending on advertising and/or on research and development (R&D) can increase a firm's profit by shifting the demand curve for its product.[26] Whatever level of spending on advertising and R&D a firm chooses, it will not vary with output, hence is a fixed cost. Such spending is also largely a sunk cost. If advertising is effective in shifting a firm's demand curve, it creates an intangible asset, goodwill. A firm that exits an industry might be able to sell its trademarks and brand names to a continuing firm, but most likely would recover only a small amount of its earlier spending on advertising. In the same way, spending on R&D creates an intangible asset, new product design and firm-specific production techniques, that may generate profit for an operating firm but could be sold for very little, if anything, upon exit.

Sutton (1998) shows that under reasonable conditions, the seller concentration ratio CRm (see Section 1.2.2) in endogenous sunk cost industries should not be less than a lower bound

$$CRm \geq \tfrac{m}{N}(1 - \ln\tfrac{m}{N}), \tag{6.17}$$

[25] See Martin (1988a, 1989) for formal models.
[26] R&D aimed at product development or improvement affects the firm's demand curve; R&D aimed at improving production processes alters the firm's cost function.

(where ln denotes the natural logarithm and the concentration ratio is measured for the largest m of a total of N firms), independent of industry size.[27] The prediction is that where firms can influence demand by endogenous sunk expenditures, firms in larger markets will spend more on advertising and/or research and development, increasing F endogenously so that the equilibrium concentration ratio remains above a minimum level. In terms of the kind of Lorenz curve shown in Figure 6.5, the prediction is that in industries where endogenous spending can promote product differentiation, the Lorenz curve will lie farther from the diagonal than the limit given by the right-hand side of inequality (6.17). The Sutton lower bound is shown as a solid line in Figure 6.5. The inequality is satisfied for all m/N (on the horizontal axis) above a low level, and very nearly satisfied throughout. Empirical tests suggest that Sutton's lower bound is an effective lower limit for endogenous sunk cost industries.[28]

Endogenous sunk cost industries: in industries where advertising, research and development, and other sunk investments are essential aspects of efficient operation, sunk costs rise with market size and equilibrium seller concentration is bounded above a minimum level, independently of market size.

6.5 Network externalities[29]

The examples of *network industries* that spring first to mind involve physical networks, either of consumers (telephone, telefax) or in a way that is inherent in the nature of the product itself (railways, passenger airlines). The distinctive economic aspects of such literal network industries have their origin in *network externalities*, which may arise even in markets that do not involve networks in a literal sense.

A product exhibits *direct* network externalities if the value of the product to any one consumer is greater, the greater the total number of consumers that uses the product. Thus if 100 homes are connected in a telephone system, each home can place a telephone call to any other and there are a total of 4950 possible calls that can be made in the system.[30] If one additional home is connected to the system, the number of possible calls

---

[27] See Bresnahan (1992), Schmalensee (1992), and Scherer (2000).

[28] Robinson and Chiang (1996); Walsh and Whelen (undated).

[29] See Katz and Shapiro (1985), the symposium on network externalities in the Spring 1994 issue of the *Journal of Economic Perspectives*, Economides (1996), and the October 1996 special issue of the *International Journal of Industrial Organization*.

[30] The first house can telephone 99 other houses; the second house can telephone 98 other houses, in addition to the first house, a call connecting the first and the second house already having been counted. The third house can call 97 other houses, in addition to the first and the second house, and so on. The total number of distinct connections is $99 + 98 + 97 + \ldots + 2 + 1 = 4950$. To obtain the total, note that $99 + 1 = 100$, $98 + 2 = 100$, $\ldots$, $51 + 49 = 100$, making 49 pairs of numbers that each add up to 100, plus the remaining 50. This calculation assumes that a call from house 1 to house 2 is the same "product" as a call from house 2 to house 1; for some purposes, one might wish to treat such connections as two distinct products.

rises to 5050 (each of the original 100 households can telephone the new home in the system). In the same way, a fax machine is useful only if it is connected to a network of fax machines, and the more fax machines that are connected to the same network, the greater the number of ways the owner of any one machine can use it to communicate.

Network externalities may also be *indirect*. If I own a VHS-format video cassette player, there is no direct relationship between the utility I get from using it and the number of other consumers who also own VHS-format video cassette players. But my VHS-format video cassette player will be more useful to me, the greater the number of prerecorded VHS-format programmes that are on the market and available for me to rent or buy. The larger the number of consumers who use VHS-format video cassette players, the larger the number of VHS-format video cassettes on the market will be, and the greater the value of VHS cassette players to consumers. Indirect network externalities arise when there are economies of scale in the production and distribution of compatible products (in this example, prerecorded cassettes).[31] More generally, the issues raised by network externalities for market structure and performance can carry over to markets that involve complementary goods—goods that must be used together to yield utility—rather than networks in a literal sense. Goods that are components of a system (such as a CD-player, an amplifier, and a set of speakers) are an example.

If a market involves indirect network externalities, a firm that is developing a system product may find it profitable to encourage competitors to come into the market. By ensuring that there are several independent producers of substitute components of a system (CD players; IBM-compatible personal computers), a system innovator can make an effective commitment to potential producers of compatible products (speakers; software, printers) that there will be a market for their goods, increasing the supply of compatible products and thus increasing the value of the innovator's product to consumers.

Compatibility, or the lack of it, raises issues of business strategy and market performance.[32] Suppose that any CD player can be used with any set of speakers and that consumers get utility only from a system composed of a CD player and a set of speakers. Then with m players and n speakers on the market, there are mn potential systems available to consumers. If m is small and n large, manufacturers of CD players could sharply reduce the number of combinations available to consumers by producing only integrated player-speaker sets, or by designing interfaces so that their player would connect only to speakers they produced.[33]

---

[31] There are both direct and indirect network externalities in the market for personal computers. The more people that use a personal computer operating system and software packages that are compatible with those I use, the easier it will be for me to exchange files with them and the more useful my personal computer/software combination will be to me. These are direct network externalities. At the same time, the more people that use a particular personal computer operating system, the greater the variety of compatible software packages that is likely to be available for use with that operating system. This is an indirect network externality.

[32] See Matutes and Regibeau (1988), the Symposium on Compatibility in the March 1992 issue of the *Journal of Industrial Economics*, and the 1996 special issue of the *European Journal of Political Economy* on the economics of standardization.

[33] In the latter case, an independent firm with sufficient information about the design of the interface might manufacture an adapter that would circumvent the manufacturer's intentions and make it possible to connect the manufacturer's stereo player to speakers produced by other firms.

6.5.1 **Market structure and market performance with network externalities**

Models of markets without network externalities[34] analyze the number of firms (or, at least, of plants) that will supply a market in long-run equilibrium in terms of fixed cost, market size, and the degree of product differentiation. Differences in firm size are explained in terms of differences in firms' costs,[35] and market performance is expected to be better,[36] all else equal, the greater the number of firms supplying the market.

Equilibrium market structure and market structure-performance relations are quite different in the presence of network externalities (Economides and Flyer, 1997). If there are direct network externalities, consumers value a product more, the greater the number of consumers that use the product. Equilibrium market structure will often involve a single firm, dominant in the sense that it supplies most consumers, but also (and for the same reason) delivering the product that consumers value most. A fringe of smaller firms may operate in the market as well, but they will not be able to compete away the economic profits of the leading firm: since their products have smaller networks, their products deliver less value to consumers. If network economies are important, market performance is best when a single leading firm supplies most of the market.

6.5.2 **Path dependence**[37]

There remains the question how, if network externalities are present, the market will select the firm that has the largest network. Whether we should expect markets to select a leading variety that is in any sense optimal is the subject of vigorous debate. The path dependence literature argues that when network externalities are present, chance historical events can have a critical impact on which amongst early products reaches a leading position.

David (1985), for example, suggests that the basic QWERTY keyboard layout, dominant in minor variations throughout the world, was developed by engineers for one of the early typewriter[38] manufacturers (Remington) to slow touch typists down and reduce the frequency of jamming in the physical mechanism of the typewriter keys. Once it became standard to teach touch typing according to the QWERTY layout, the dominant position of the QWERTY keyboard was secure.

In this instance, the compatible good that creates network externalities in the keyboard market is the training—the human capital—of those who use the keyboards.

The QWERTY keyboard, David suggests, became standard largely because it happened to accumulate a large pool of trained users before other keyboard layouts. Thus the QWERTY layout continues to be used, long after the problem of jamming typewriter keys (indeed, the keys themselves) has evaporated. Other keyboard layouts—David mentions

---

[34] The kind of standard oligopoly model that leads to expression (6.13).

[35] Firms with higher marginal cost being expected to have lower sales, in equilibrium; see Section 2.2.5.

[36] In the sense of yielding a greater equilibrium value of consumers' surplus plus firms' values.

[37] See David (1985), Farrell and Saloner (1985), Arthur (1989), Liebowitz and Margolis (1990).

[38] A device that has gone the way of the slide rule and the computer punch card (in the latter case, apparently, except in some types of voting machines).

the so-called Dvorak keyboard—might be more efficient in a time-and-motion study sense, but they are out of luck.[39]

Liebowitz and Margolis (1990) take aim at the claim that any evidence establishes the objective superiority of the Dvorak keyboard, raising doubts about the nature of the evidence that suggests it allows more efficient typing. They also make the more general point (1990, p. 4, footnote 4) that once a particular standard is in place as the largest network, the interesting question from an efficiency point of view is not "Would society have been better off if a different standard had been chosen from the beginning?", but rather "Given that the existing standard is now in place, will society be better off with a different standard, taking switching costs into account?". In the context of the keyboard example, switching costs would include retraining all the touch typists previously trained on the QWERTY layout.

Arthur (1989) suggests other examples of path dependent product development, including light-water nuclear reactors and petrol- rather than steam-engine automobiles. Liebowitz and Margolis are skeptical that any convincing claim of path dependent selection of an objectively inferior standard has been established.

It seems clear that chance historical events do influence, and sometimes in a critical way, which of a number of early varieties becomes the leader in an industry where network externalities play a role. It is less clear that such choices are often inferior, once the costs of making a transition to a different standard are taken into account.

Network externalities arise if the utility a single consumer receives from a product rises with the total number of consumers of the product. Equilibrium market structure often involves a single large firm with a fringe of smaller rivals; which of several possible products enjoys a dominant position may depend on chance events early in the history of the industry.

6.6 Firms and firm structure[40]

Once we think of (6.2) as representing the cost function of a single plant, we open the door to a whole set of questions about the way firms are organized, the way economic activity is divided between firms and markets, and the way the organization of activity within firms affects market performance.

It would go too far to say that economics has ignored these questions. Adam Smith

---

[39] Of course, it is not always the first format that becomes the standard: VHS video cassettes, which displaced the Betamax format, are a case in point. See Cusumano et al. (1992).

[40] See Williamson (1985), Chandler (1990), Williamson and Winter (1991), and Hart (1995). The evolutionary approach, which circles around the literature discussed here like a shark around a school of fish, is associated among others with Nelson and Winter (1982), and treats the firm as a repository of firm-specific knowledge. See Audretsch (1995, pp. 43–44) for discussion.

came very close to some of them in Book I, Chapter I of *The Wealth of Nations*, when (using the famous example of a pin factory) he discussed the tremendous increase in productivity that came with the division of labour and the specialization of productive activity. He attributed such increases in productivity to the increased skill of specialized workmen, to the saving of time that would otherwise be used shifting from one task to another, and to the development of specialized machinery.[41] Smith also touched on the impact of the nature of the market on the organization of the firm in Book I, Chapter III, where he noted that employments could be more finely subdivided, leading to greater increases in productivity, in larger markets.[42] In Book V, he discussed the implications of what has come to be called[43] the separation of ownership and control, writing about the executives of joint stock companies that (1776/1937, p. 700) "being the managers rather of other people's money than of their own, it cannot well be expected, that they should watch over it with the same anxious vigilance with which the partners in a private co-partnery frequently watch over their own".

But it is fair to say that the "theory of the firm" that is an important part of neoclassical microeconomics (and intermediate microeconomics courses) is not aptly named. The neoclassical theory of the firm is really a theory of the markets in which firms operate. The firms that appear in this theory are pale shadows of real-world firms: they purchase inputs and supply outputs, but the activity that goes on in between is subsumed in a cost or production function (as, by and large, it has been in this book). The neoclassical theory of the firm has little to say about the way activities are organized within firms, except to assume that operations are efficient in the sense of minimizing production cost.

6.6.1 Coase

Coase (1937) is the progenitor of the modern theory of the firm. He contrasted the neoclassical vision of resource allocation in markets by the invisible hand of the price mechanism[44] with the directed allocation of resources within firms. Coase traced the organization of productive activity within firms to the costs of using markets, particularly the costs of learning relevant prices (1937, p. 390) and the costs of negotiating contracts (1937, pp. 390–1). When these costs are sufficiently high, it becomes efficient to bring the associated transactions within a firm and carry them out under the authority of a manager rather than on a market by means of the price mechanism.

There are, of course, limits to firm size, among which is managerial loss of control. When a firm becomes sufficiently large (Coase, 1937, pp. 394) "the entrepreneur fails to place the factors of production in the uses where their value is greatest". In the basic Coasian story, firm size is determined by a balance between the marginal cost of using the

---

[41] Some of these factors were mentioned in our discussion of multiplant firms (Section 6.2.3). For a more recent discussion of pinmaking, see Williamson (1985, Chapter 9).

[42] This topic was taken up by Stigler (1951), who related the degree of vertical integration to market size. See also Williamson (1985, Chapter 9).

[43] Following Berle and Means (1932).

[44] Simon (1991, pp. 40–1) makes the point that real-world markets rely as much on quantity adjustment as on price adjustment as an equilibrating mechanism. Inventory changes are one example; delivery delays are another. It is also true that large modern corporations may use transfer prices to allocate resources within the firm. Thus the distinction between resource allocation by price within markets and by quantity within firms is not as clear-cut as it might at first appear.

market and the marginal cost of production within a firm (Coase, 1937, p. 395): "a firm will tend to expand until the costs of organizing an extra transaction within the firm become equal to the costs of carrying out the same transaction by means of an exchange on the open market or the costs of organising in another firm".[45]

6.6.2 **Transaction costs**

In a series of publications,[46] Oliver Williamson lays out a nonneoclassical framework for analyzing the division of activity between firms and markets in terms of relative transaction costs.[47] He assumes (in contrast to neoclassical economic theory) that the parties to transactions have only imperfect information and limited reasoning power: that, in the words of Simon (1947), economic agents are *boundedly rational*. He also assumes that the parties to transactions behave opportunistically: that they pursue their own self-interest, and that in so doing they will behave in a way that is devious if devious behaviour is privately optimal.

Given bounded rationality, Williamson expects that it will be relatively inefficient to use markets for types of transactions which occur frequently, under conditions of uncertainty, and which require investments in highly specific assets.

It is asset specificity, and the impact of asset specificity on the relative bargaining power of parties to a transaction, that is key to the transaction cost analysis of firm structure.[48] The concept of asset specificity is closely related to that of sunk cost. As we have noted in Chapter 1, footnote 20, the cost of investing in a tangible or intangible capital asset is sunk if the value of the asset cannot be recovered by resale upon exit from the market. If an asset is highly specific to a particular transaction, it may be quite valuable (the present discounted value of the income stream it generates will be large) if used in that transaction, but have relatively little value in other uses. In a world of uncertainty and bounded rationality, a firm that invests in assets that are highly specific to a particular transaction exposes itself to the possibility of devious, opportunistic behaviour by its partner in the transaction. The partner may try, after the specific investment is made, to engage in devious behaviour and revise the terms of an agreement in its own favour. As a practical matter, legal protection against such behaviour may not be available, or would be costly to obtain: bounded rationality will make it difficult for a court to determine if devious behaviour has taken place, or to devise appropriate remedies if it does so.

In circumstances of this kind, a firm may well conclude that it is optimal to bring the transaction within the firm, so that the potentially opportunistic independent trading partner becomes an employee, and, as an employee, with interests that are more likely to be allied with those of the firm.[49]

---

[45] For the X-efficiency approach to firm organization and performance, see Leibenstein (1966, 1987, among others).

[46] Williamson (1970, 1975, 1981, 1985), among others.

[47] Chandler (1990, p. 734, endnote 2), citing Herman Daems, distinguishes costs associated with transactions with customers, with suppliers, and with financial institutions.

[48] See, among others, Klein et al. (1978), Riordan and Williamson (1985), Joskow (1988), and Klein (1988), as well as discussions of the General Motors-Fisher Body merger in Williamson (1985, Chapter 5), Hart (1989).

[49] Of course, opportunistic behaviour may occur within firms as well as within markets. The principal-agent literature examines this topic; for references, see Sappington (1991).

Chandler (1990) places weight on uncertainty as a factor in bringing transactions within the firm. In industries where the technology permits cost reductions by means of continuous high-speed production, realizing those cost reductions depends on maintaining a steady stream of inputs from suppliers and delivering a steady stream of outputs to wholesale and retail distributors. In such industries, producers have powerful incentives to integrate vertically backward, bringing their input supplies within the firm, and vertically forward into distribution. Relying too much on markets for either input supplies or sales outlets places the low unit cost of production that comes with economies of scale at risk.

6.6.3 **Property rights**

The property rights approach[50] emphasizes the relationship of inputs in production as a factor determining which assets it is efficient for a single firm to own, and the incentives that combining assets under the ownership of a single firm creates for employee decisions. It is more likely for common ownership to be efficient if inputs are highly complementary, so that they are much more productive in combination, than otherwise. If the investment decisions of one party to a transaction are more important for efficient operation, then it is more likely to be efficient to make that party the owner of the firm: when unforeseen events occur, the owner's (more important) investment decisions will be taken in a way that is profit maximizing, since the owner's interests and those of the firm largely overlap.

6.6.4 **Chandler**

Chandler (1962, 1977, 1990) confronts the separation of ownership and control—the situation in which owners' and managers' interests may not overlap—and its implications for firm structure from the perspective of business history.

He documents the tendency of the first large industrial firms[51] to expand using the kind of *functional* (or *unitary*) organization illustrated in Figure 6.6.[52]

A small-scale firm that deals primarily in one product or one region has one purchasing department, one production department, one sales department, and so on. In very small firms, these "departments" may well all be the responsibility of a single owner-manager. As the size of the firm increases, by adding new products or extending operations to other regions, it is natural to scale up the functional operating divisions as well, at a certain point adding support staff and (in some industries) a formal R&D operation.

Bounded rationality, however, places limits on the size of firm for which the functional form is an effective form of business organization. Department managers naturally tend to pursue the interests of their functional divisions, rather than those of the firm as a whole, while corporate executives must deal with day-to-operating decisions as well as with long-term, strategic planning, even as the quantity of information reaching them from markets rises and the quality of information reaching them from markets declines.

---

[50] See Grossman and Hart (1986), Hart and Moore (1990), and Hart (1995).
[51] In many countries, these were railroads.
[52] Figures 6.6 and 6.7 are simplified versions of Figures 1 and 2, respectively, of Chandler (1990).

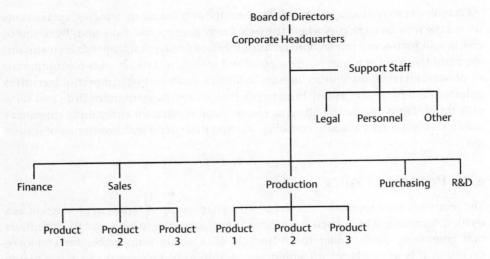

Fig. 6.6 Functional (Unitary or U-) form firm

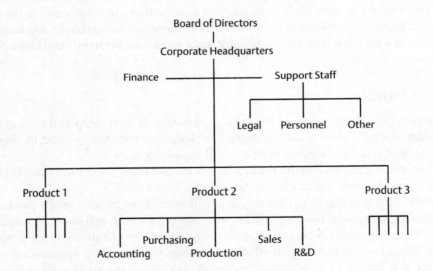

Fig. 6.7 Multidivisional (M-) form firm

To cope with managerial loss of control in large, functionally organized firms, innovative[53] entrepreneurs developed the *multidivisional* or M-form of business organization (Figure 6.7). In an M-form firm, the components of the firm are defined in terms of product groups or regions. Each such division has its own functional subdivisions, and is directed by a middle manager, an employee, who supervises division operations and reports to corporate headquarters. Corporate officers assess divisional performance and

---

[53] In the sense of Schumpeter; see Section 5.4.1.

formulate overall strategic plans for the firm. As emphasized by Williamson (1985, p. 288), the corporate headquarters of the M-form firm also operates as an internal capital market, allocating the funds generated by all the operations of the firm to the particular divisions that yield the highest rate of return.

Williamson (1985, p. 283) also points out that there is more to the M-form innovation than simply reorganizing the operations of the firm along product or regional rather than functional lines. In order to realize the efficiency advantages of the M-form, there must be a genuine redefinition of managerial responsibilities, so that corporate management withdraws from direct responsibility for operations and focuses on strategic planning.[54]

Where there are potential economies of large scale or broad product scope, business history suggests that the efficiency advantages of the M-form are substantial. Chandler (1962) documents the innovative development of the M-form of business organization at Du Pont and General Motors, firms that coped with the task of producing a wide range of products and supplying many different regional markets in what was the first continent-wide common market, that of the United States. In an exhaustive set of case studies, Chandler (1990) reviews the market characteristics that encouraged the adoption (or failure to adopt) of the M-form in the United States, Great Britain, and Germany.

From 1890 onward, tough as US antitrust laws exposed firms that divided markets or colluded on price to potentially harsh sanctions. Tough antitrust policy contributed to a climate of vigorous competition that encouraged firms to seek efficiency within their own operations, not through cooperation with independent rivals. In industries that offered economies of scale and/or scope, the result was high seller concentration, with large, low-cost M-form firms supplying mass markets and, perhaps, smaller firms supplying specialized market segments (Chandler, 1990, pp. 226–7):

the industries spearheading American economic growth were those dominated by a small number of large managerial enterprises. But these oligopolistic industries also included other types of business enterprises. Precisely because the leaders grew by exploiting the cost advantages of scale and scope, their standardized products often failed to meet the needs of specialized or regional markets.

In Britain, a strong preference for family-managed firms prevailed, along with the tendency to use trade associations as a vehicle to avoid tough competition that we have noted in Section 3.3, delayed development of M-form firms and the accompanying efficiency gains until well after they had spread to other countries. Britain, the leader of the First Industrial Revolution, was a follower in the Second (Chandler, 1990, p. 392):

the failure to consolidate industry-wide federations into modern industrial enterprises . . . meant the lack of effective enterprises to rationalize industries by investing in state-of-the-art facilities and developing the skills essential to exploit the economies of scale and scope.

Although there was some movement toward M-form organization in Germany (despite the economic disruption entailed by the First World War and the Great Depression), the absence of tough competition policy had a negative efficiency impact here as well (Chandler, 1990, p. 424):

---

[54] See also Chandler (1977, pp. 7–8).

Because cooperation was legal, there was less pressure for industry-wide mergers. Because industry-wide mergers were the prerequisite to industry-wide reorganization and rationalization, far fewer such rationalizations occurred before World War I in Germany than in the United States.

6.6.5 Reprise

There are interactions between firm structure and market structure. Where market size is sufficiently large and the technology implies that there are potential economies of scale or scope, efficiently organized firms can deliver lower unit costs, and earn for themselves larger market shares.[55] Smaller segments of such markets may be supplied by firms with smaller market shares that produce at higher unit cost than their larger colleagues.

There are also interactions between firm structure and market performance. In the kinds of markets described above, market performance is improved, all else equal, when large firms are able to reduce cost and enough rivalry remains to temper the extent to which such firms are able to extract monopoly rents.

Large firm size does not necessarily imply efficiency gains. Even in markets where the technology means that such gains are possible, a firm's internal organization must be efficient to permit it to operate efficiently at large scale. In markets where the technology does not imply economies of large scale or broad scope, large firm size carries the potential for exercise of market power without corresponding efficiency gains.

6.7 Merger policy

Although it is possible to examine mergers in a basic Cournot model (see Problem 6–6), the results are not satisfactory. When the product is homogeneous, the postmerger firm restricts output so that, in post-merger equilibrium, it produces the same output as firms outside the merger. Such models predict that unless a merger involves most firms in an industry, the post-merger firm will earn less profit than the combined profits of its parent in the pre-merger market (Salant et al., 1983).[56]

Basic oligopoly models predict that single-firm market power is greater, the greater is market share (equation (2.34)). Noncooperative collusion is also more likely to be the most profitable strategy for larger firms: the larger is a firm, the less profit it stands to gain by cutting price and stealing customers from smaller rivals. For their impact on market structure and firm conduct, therefore, mergers have the potential to worsen performance.

But a merger that leads to reorganization and more efficient use of the assets of parent firms can reduce costs, making the post-merger firm more efficient. This has the potential to improve market performance.

---

[55] In this sense, adoption of a multidivisional organizational form is like the impact of spending on advertising or R&D in endogenous sunk cost industries that is highlighted by Sutton (1991, 1998).

[56] There are, of course, other models of the impact of mergers on market performance. Deneckere and Davidson (1985) model mergers in markets where firms set price; Farrell and Shapiro (1990) take explicit account of asset ownership, so that a post-merger firm differs from rivals outside the merger because it controls the combined assets of its pre-merger parents.

The net effect of a merger, therefore, may be positive, increasing the efficiency of the firms that merge, or negative, allowing greater single-firm or joint noncooperative exercise of market power (Williamson, 1968). It is evaluation of the net effects of a merger, and the weight to be given to the positive and the negative effects of a merger, that is the task of competition authorities as they administer merger control policy.

6.7.1 **Merger control regulation**

Merger control was a relatively late addition to European Community competition policy. Control of collusion and of firms with dominant market positions dates to 1957 and the EC Treaty, merger control only to 1989.[57] The founding fathers of what has become the European Union were explicitly concerned with preventing collusion and price discrimination along national lines (and they may well have had some sympathy for the idea of promoting EC champions to operate in world markets). It was only 30 years into the process of EC market integration that political support allowed the European Commission's Directorate General for Competition to persuade Member State representatives to adopt the Merger Control Regulation.

In 1997, the Merger Control Regulation was amended to streamline merger control in the light of experience and in anticipation of an expected further wave of mergers thought likely to be triggered by the introduction of the euro and a hoped-for giant step forward in economic integration.

On a procedural level, the 1997 amendments allowed the Commission to accept early in the process a proposal (undertaking) from the parties concerned designed to make the nature of the post-merger firm acceptable to the Commission. Such adjustments (often involving divestitures) have been common in Commission enforcement of merger policy; the new rule makes it easier to put them into effect and economize on Commission resources.

Other changes to the Merger Control Regulation with an efficiency motive altered the conditions that must be met for a merger to fall under the authority of the Commission, targeting mergers with cross-border effects (European Commission, 1998, p. 60), thus reducing the number of cases that firms need to report to competition authorities in several Member States.

The focus of the Regulation is dominance (Article 2(3)):

A concentration which creates or strengthens a dominant position as a result of which effective competition would be significantly impeded in the common market or in a substantial part of it shall be declared incompatible with the common market.

Whether or not a concentration will create or strengthen a dominant position can be assessed only in the context of a relevant product and geographic market. The process of market definition thus assumes a central role in EC merger control, as it does in other areas of competition policy.

Factors the European Commission looks at to decide if merger would create a dominant position or strengthen an existing dominant position include:

[57] Council Regulation (EEC) No 4064/89 OJ L 395/1 30 December 1989, amended by Council Regulation (EC) No 1310/97, OJ L 180 9 July 1997. See Neven et al. (1993).

- the market shares of the firms involved;
- the market shares of firms in the same market but not involved in the merger (will firms in the market be able to compete effectively with the post-merger firm?);
- entry conditions (would new firms be able to compete effectively with the post-merger firm if it should become profitable to do so?):
  - is minimum efficient scale large relative to market size?
  - how large are the absolute capital requirements to set up a minimum efficient scale-sized plant?
  - are the investments that must be made to enter the industry *sunk* or not?;
  - what is the nature of distribution channels?;[58]
  - importance of product differentiation (must a successful firm invest heavily in advertising to be a commercial success?)

The *Aerospatiale-Alenia/de Havilland*[59] decision was the first in which the European Commission used its authority under the Merger Control Regulation to block a proposed merger.

The French firm Aerospatiale[60] and Alenia[61] were the parent firms of the French company Avions de Transport Régional (ATR), a producer of regional turbo-prop aircraft. The two firms proposed to acquire de Havilland,[62] a Canadian division of Boeing and also a producer of regional turbo-prop aircraft.

In order to assess the impact of the merger, the Commission needed to define the product and geographic market.[63] The nature of the geographic market (worldwide, excluding China and Eastern Europe) was not controversial.

Regarding the standard for product market definition, the Commission wrote (OJ No L 334/44):

A relevant product market comprises in particular all those products which are regarded as interchangeable or substitutable by the consumer, by reason of the products' characteristics, their prices and their intended use.

The Commission defined turbo-prop aircraft with 20 to 39 seats, 40 to 59 seats, and 60 or more seats as distinct product submarkets. It excluded jet aircraft as being more expensive and used on different kinds of routes; it excluded smaller turbo-prop aircraft as being subject to different certification procedures and often not specifically designed to carry passengers.

In the Commission's assessment of the information available to it, 30-seat and 60-seat

[58] See the discussion of the FEG/TU decision in Section 3.4.2.
[59] Commission Decision 91/619/EEC of 2 October 1991 OJ L 334/42 5 December 1991.
[60] Now part of EADS, the European Aeronautic Defense Space Company (http://www.eads-nv.com/eads/index_f.htm).
[61] Alenia-Aeritalia & Selenia SpA, a leading Italian aerospace firm.
[62] de Havilland began life as a subsidiary of British de Havilland Aircraft (http://collections.ic.gc.ca/canadair/dhcframes.htm). Its connection with the de Havilland Comet (http://www.geocities.com/CapeCanaveral/Lab/8803/comet.htm) is therefore only indirect.
[63] The Commission also needed to establish that the merger had what is called a Community dimension: that the sales of the firms involved were sufficiently large, and not concentrated in a particular Member State. These aspects of the decision were not controversial.

Table 6.2 EEC market share estimates, turbo-prop commuter aircraft. Avions de Transport Regional; DHC = de Havilland; BAe = British Aerospace.

20 to 39 seats		40 to 59 seats		60 to 70 seats		20 to 70 seats	
Embraer	41	ATR	51	ATR	74	ATR	49
Saab	31	DHC	21	BAe	26	DHC	16
DHC	21	Fokker	22			Fokker	12
BAe	6	Saab	7			BAe	8
Dornier	1	Casa	7			Embraer	6
						Saab	5
						Casa	3
						Dornier	1

Source: OJ No L334/.48–9

commuter aircraft were viewed differently by consumers, were used on different kinds of routes, and sold for significantly different prices.[64]

The firms involved in the merger argued for two submarkets, 20--50 seats and 51--70 seats. The Commission rejected this definition, noting that it would place one 48-seat plane in a different market from three 50-seat planes, although competitors and customers regarded these planes as competing one with another.

It is reasonable to expect the firms that hope to merge to put forward a market defin-ition that makes their market shares small. Equally, and particularly if the merger would have efficiency effects, one should expect competitors of the firms that propose to merge to advocate a market definition that makes the market shares of the firms involved in the merger large, particularly if the main effect of the merger would be to increase efficiency.

It is customers' views that are least likely to be self-serving: customers have an interest in trying to block mergers that increase market power, but not in trying to block a merger that leads to greater efficiency, since a more efficient firm will be able to sell at a lower cost.[65]

The Commission's market share estimates for the European Community for the three submarkets and overall are shown in Table 6.2.[66] The direct impact of the merger on single-firm exercise of market power would have been in the 40- to 59-seat submarket, in which the merger would have created a firm with a market share of 72 per cent. The merger would have had indirect effects on the other two submarkets: it would have eliminated ATR as a potential entrant into the 20- to 39-seat submarket, and it would have eliminated de Havilland as a potential entrant into the 60- to 70-seat submarket.

The Commission saw another anticompetitive effect in the fact that the post-merger firm would offer aircraft in all three submarkets. This is a market in which switching costs tend to tie consumers to their current supplier; broadening the range of products offered would also broaden the base of consumers linked to the post-merger firm.

---

[64] The Commission also discussed supply-side substitutability, the possibility that a producer of a turbo-prop aircraft of one size class could diversify into production of a turbo-prop aircraft of a different size. It viewed such diversification as possible, but only after a long transition period.

[65] See equation (2.35) and the associated text.

[66] The Commission also computed worldwide market share estimates.

The Commission's decision included a firm-by-firm analysis of the likely competitive strength of rival firms in the post-merger market. It concluded that there would be effective competition only in the 20- to 39-seat submarket. The Commission also discussed entry conditions, aspects of which included between two and three years marketing research to understand market needs and another four years to bring an aircraft to market, both parts of the entry process involving substantial fixed and sunk costs. It found that entry was not a realistic possibility.

The companies that proposed to merge put efficiency evidence on the record. By rationalizing procurement, marketing, and product support, they would save 5 million ECU per year. The Commission pointed out that this was $\frac{1}{2}$ of 1 per cent of the combined annual turnover of ATR and de Havilland, and noted that the reorganizations that generated the savings might to a large extent be undertaken by de Havilland alone, or by de Havilland and a partner in an alternative merger.

The Commission concluded that the merger, if allowed to go forward, would establish a dominant position in the 40- to 59-seat and 60- and over seat submarkets, and that this dominant position was not likely to be eroded by entry. It therefore declared the merger to be incompatible with the common market, and forbade it to go forward.

6.7.2 Joint ventures and joint dominance

The 1997 amendments to the Merger Control Regulation modified the treatment of certain types of joint ventures. So-called *full function cooperative joint ventures*—those (EC Commission, 1998, p. 68) "having all the necessary resources in terms of funding, staff and tangible and intangible assets" to operate as a stand-alone economic unit—are now treated under the Merger Control Regulation rather than under Article 81 of the EC Treaty, which deals with agreements among firms.

Partly in connection with the treatment of joint ventures, the Commission has sought to introduce the concept of joint (oligopoly) dominance to EC merger control. As we have seen in Section 3.4.2's discussion of the Woodpulp decision, the Commission has had limited success in applying Article 81 to situations in which existing market structures allow firms in oligopoly to jointly exercise market power. The European Court of Justice has held that parallel behaviour alone does not violate EC competition policy. Use of the concept of joint dominance in merger policy can be seen as a logical line of development of competition policy to attempt to prevent the emergence of market structures that would allow firms in the post-merger market to noncooperatively exercise market power.

The *Gencor/Lonrho* cases illustrate the issues involved in the concept of joint dominance.[67] Here the product market was platinum and the geographic market was the world, with various submarkets. The firms directly involved were Gencor, a South African firm controlling the leading South African platinum mining company, and Lonrho, a UK firm controlling two large South African platinum mines. These two firms proposed to merge. A third firm, Amplats (Anglo American Platinum Corporation), was not involved in the merger, but would have become the second largest supplier in the market if the merger had gone forward.

[67] See Christensen and Owen (1999).

The European Commission's theory of the case was that if the merger were permitted, Gencor/Lonrho and Amplats together would have a combined world market share of 60–70 per cent, a share that would grow to 80 per cent after Russian supplies were depleted.

As the European Commission (1999b, p. 66) interprets the rulings of the European Court of Justice, to justify a finding of collective dominance, the Commission needs to show that a merger would eliminate competition between the post-merger firm and some other firm or firms, allowing them to jointly act as a dominant firm. That is, a merger eliminates all competition between the firms that join together. If a merger creates a dominant position, it offends competition policy on that basis alone. If a merger does not create a dominant position, it may still run afoul of competition law if the post-merger firm is able to jointly dominate the market in conjunction with other leading firms, even though the behaviour by which such joint dominance would be made effective would not amount to collusion or a concerted practice under Article 81.

Market characteristics that might lead to a finding of joint dominance are high market concentration as well as (EC Commission, 1999b, p. 67) "homogeneous products, transport, high entry barriers, mature technology, static or falling demand, links between suppliers, absence of countervailing buyer power, etc". Such factors (EC Commission, 1999b, p. 66)

need not . . . include structural links, in the strict sense of cross-shareholdings, contracts, etc. between the alleged dominant firms, although where such links are cited, it is necessary to show how they would lead to the elimination of competition between the firms concerned.

Applying these standards, the European Commission blocked the merger. The firms appealed this decision to the Court of First Instance, which upheld the Commission.[68]

6.8 Cooperation

We have discussed the economics of horizontal cooperation in Sections 3.4.2 and 6.6.4. In contrast to horizontal cooperation, cooperation is said to be vertical if it is between firms that operate at different levels of the production chain—between a manufacturer and wholesalers, for example, or between a wholesaler and retailers.

Manufacturers and distributors often agree to contracts that embody vertical restraints, including but not limited to:

- exclusive territories (a manufacturer authorizes one and only one distributor for a certain area);
- exclusive purchasing (a distributor agrees to acquire all supplies of a certain product from a specified manufacturer);

---

[68] Another aspect of this case is that the Commission asserts jurisdiction over business actions that affect economic activity in the EU, no matter where that activity takes place. The US asserts the same right, although it is probably fair to say that the EU has been more active than the US in this area.

• resale price maintenance (the distributor agrees to sell at, or not below, the price designated by the manufacturer).[69]

A manufacturer may also administer a selective distribution system, specifying minimum standards of certain kinds that must be satisfied by a distributor and supplying all or a subset of qualifying distributors. Franchise agreements typically involve some vertical restraints.

Vertical restraints typically restrict competition among dealers of a single brand (intra-brand competition). If a manufacturer finds it profitable to restrict competition among dealers of his or her brand, it may be because the manufacturer feels that those restrictions will lead the dealers to behave in ways that promote competition between his or her brand and other brands (interbrand competition). In such cases, the vertical restraints have both pro- and anti-competitive effects, and the net impact on market performance is ambiguous.[70]

A fundamental purpose of EC competition policy is to promote market integration. The Commission has, therefore, consistently opposed vertical restraints that have the effect of splitting the Single Market along national boundaries. For example, national resale price maintenance systems do not come under the authority of EC competition law, since they do not affect trade between the Member States.[71] But the Commission has held that existence of a legal national resale price maintenance system cannot be used to block shipments of a manufacturer's product from one Member State to another. If a German record producer supplies a retail distributor in France, the French distributor must be allowed to sell in Germany if it is profitable to do so, even if such sales are at a price below the fixed German retail price.[72]

These cases illustrate the kinds of negative effects that may flow from vertical restraints: raising barriers to entry, foreclosing rivals from distribution channels, facilitating collusion, and impeding effective market integration. Possible efficiency effects include quality control and promoting distributor sales efforts in a way that increases interbrand competition.[73]

The 1999 vertical restraints regulation[74] adopts an economic effects approach to the treatment of vertical restraints. Minimum resale price maintenance is prohibited. So are airtight exclusive territories: if a dealer receives a request from a customer located outside the dealer's designated territory, the manufacturer must allow the dealer to fill the

---

[69] Infrequently, resale price maintenance imposes a maximum price rather than a minimum price.

[70] Vertical restraints may also be part of a collusive scheme, restricting competition among brands; see Section 3.4.2's discussion of the Commission's FEG decision.

[71] Thus the Commission challenged a resale price maintenance scheme that covered the retail book market in the UK and Ireland but not the separate application of such schemes within national boundaries. More recently, the Commission has challenged resale price maintenance in retail book distribution in Germany and Austria.

[72] *Deutsche Grammophon* v. *Metro* [1971] ECR 487. An earlier decision held, similarly, that legal trademarks could not justify exclusive distribution systems that divided the common market along national boundaries; see *Consten SA and Grundig-Verkaufs GmbH* v. *Commission* (Cases 56 & 58/64) [1966] ECR 299; [1966] CMLR 418.

[73] Vertical restraints may eliminate the *free rider* problem, which arises if some dealers underprovide sales efforts (from the manufacturer's point of view) and undersell other dealers who provide greater and therefore more costly sales efforts. If unchecked, free riding leads to market failure in the market for distribution services and prevents that manufacturer from obtaining the level of sales efforts it finds most profitable (from independent dealers).

[74] OJ L 336 29 December 1999; see also the *Green Paper on Vertical Restraints* (1997a) and Neven et al. (1998).

request. Other types of vertical restraints are permitted under a block exemption if the manufacturer's market share is less than 30 per cent. If a manufacturer's market share exceeds 30 per cent, an exemption under Article 81(3) is possible, taking into account the same general elements of market structure—seller concentration, entry conditions, among others—that come into play for a horizontal co-operative agreement.[75]

The motor vehicle sector has long benefited from exceptional treatment under EC competition policy. A specific regulation[76] permits car manufacturers to sell only through designated dealers, to assign dealers to specific territories, to require various quality standards (for example, showroom size and post-sales service facilities) and to impose other restrictions. This policy is said to be justified "because motor vehicles are consumer durables which at both regular and irregular intervals require expert maintenance and repair, not always in the same place". Importantly, the regulation also requires that car manufacturers allow a dealer to sell to customers or customers' designated representatives whether or not the customer is resident in the dealer's designated sales area.

Consumer groups have long challenged the idea that consumers benefit from the special car distribution regulation. It is seen as contributing to large and persistent car price differences among Member States.[77] Further, it appears that car manufacturers have not honoured the part of the regulation that requires them to allow dealers to supply customers resident outside the dealer's home territory. In 1995, the European Commission fined Volkswagen AG €102 million on the ground that VW discouraged its authorized dealers in Italy from supplying cars to customers from parts of Northern Europe. From 1993 to 1995, exchange rate movements made it attractive for customers in Germany and elsewhere to consider buying cars in Italy. VW structured its dealer programmes so that such sales did not count toward satisfying dealer quotas and did not help the dealer meet requirements for some bonus schemes. VW threatened to end the contracts of some Italian dealers if they sold to customers from outside their territories, and 12 dealerships were in fact cancelled. In July 2000, upon appeal by VW, the Court of First Instance allowed €90 million of the fine to stand.

In April 1999, the Commission suggested that DaimlerChrysler had sought to keep some of its dealers from selling outside their territories. In September 1999, VW was the subject of a second investigation by the Commission for restricting dealers in ways inconsistent with the car distribution regulation. In September 2000, the Commission fined General Motors' Dutch subsidiary €43 million for seeking to block sales by Dutch dealers to EC residents from outside the Netherlands (Krause-Heiber, 2001).

The car distribution regulation will expire on 30 September 2002. There seems to be a good chance that it will be renewed, if at all, only on substantially altered terms. If it is allowed to lapse, the car sector would be covered by the same vertical restraints rules that apply to other sectors of the EC.[78]

---

[75] See the *Guidelines on Vertical Restraints* (2000c) for examples.

[76] Most recently, Regulation 1475/95 OJ L 145, 29 June 1995.

[77] For a comprehensive review of auto price differences in the EU, see Degryse and Verboven (2000).

[78] As noted above, market structure is itself the product of market forces. If the car distribution regulation is allowed to lapse, one possibility is that car manufacturers will integrate forward into distribution and perform for themselves the function that is now carried out by independent dealers. Another possibility is that mergers or internal growth at the dealer level would lead to consolidation and the rise of "super dealers" able to effectively bargain with manufacturers.

6.9 **Summary**

Firms and markets are alternative frameworks for the organization of economic activity. Markets without network externalities work well if equilibrium firm size is small, relative to the market, if barriers to entry and mobility are small, if such sunk costs as are present tend to be exogenous rather than endogenous, and if the carrying out of transactions across markets does not involve too much investment in specific assets. Markets with network externalities work well when most consumers are connected to the network of a single firm, which then supplies them with the highest-value product.

If there are economies of scale and/or scope and if markets are large enough to allow such economies to be realized, firms work well if managed by a multidivisional form of organization.

Real-world entry is a hazardous process. Although entry does seem to respond to profit opportunities, this response is much less automatic than it is often taken to be in theoretical discussions. Entry and exit are more components of a screening mechanism than of an equilibrating mechanism.

Merger control requires competition authorities to trade off potential efficiency gains against potential increases in market power, including the possible creation of positions of collective dominance. Merger is itself the most extreme form of a range of less complete forms of horizontal and/or vertical cooperation. EC competition policy towards such cooperation relies on market-share based safe harbours that tend to permit cooperation by small firms (taking the view that remaining rivalry will block the exercise of market power) and analyzes the economic effects of such cooperation when the market shares of cooperating firms are large.

Study points

- minimum efficient scale output level (page 108)
- long-run equilibrium number of plants in a Cournot market (page 109)
- multiplant firms (pages 111–13)
- barriers to mobility (page 115)
- Gibrat's Law (pages 115–16)
- exogenous sunk cost industries v. endogenous sunk cost industries (pages 117–19)
- network externalities (pages 119–20)
- path dependence (pages 121–2)
- bounded rationality, asset specificity (page 124)
- functional v. multidivisional forms of firm organization (page 126)

- Merger Control Regulation (page 129), collective dominance (page 132)
- Article 81: vertical restraints (pages 133–5)

Problems

6–1 (fixed cost, sunk cost, market structure I) Let firms operate with production function

$$q = \min \left[\frac{K - 160}{1}, \frac{L - 20}{1} \right] \tag{6.18}$$

for $K \geq 160$, $L \geq 20$, and $q = 0$ otherwise, so that to produce at all requires hiring at least 180 units of capital and 20 units of labour, and that each unit of output requires one additional unit of capital and one additional unit of labour over these minimum amounts. Thus if production is efficient in the sense of minimizing cost, so that a firm employs no excess capital or labour,

$$q = \frac{K - 160}{1} = \frac{L - 20}{1} \tag{6.19}$$

and input levels are

$$K = 160 + q \qquad L = 20 + q. \tag{6.20}$$

Firms hire labour at wage rate $w = 5$ per period and purchase physical capital at price $p^k = 50$; for simplicity, assume both input prices are constant over time, and assume also that physical capital does not depreciate. The rental rate of the services of one unit of physical capital is then rp^k, where $r = \frac{1}{10}$ is the rate of return on a safe asset (the opportunity cost of investing financial capital in the firm). If the firm wishes to resell a unit of physical capital, it can do so at price αp^k, where the degree of sunk cost parameter α is a number that lies between 0 and 1. If $\alpha = 0$, investments in the industry are completely sunk, in the sense that if the firm should wish to exit the industry, it would not be able to recover any of its investment in physical capital. If $\alpha = 1$, investments in the industry are not sunk at all.

(a) Find the cost function of a firm. Identify fixed cost, variable cost, marginal cost, and sunk cost.

(b) In a market with inverse demand curve

$$p = 100 - Q, \tag{6.21}$$

what is the long-run equilibrium number of firms in Cournot oligopoly if firms produce efficiently? How does the level of fixed cost affect the long-run equilibrium number of firms? How does the level of sunk cost affect the long-run equilibrium number of firms?

(c) Now suppose that the rental cost of capital services rises, the more are investments in the industry sunk, that is, that the rental cost of capital services is

$$\rho = \rho(\alpha), \text{ with } \rho(1) = r, \rho' < 0. \tag{6.22}$$

The opportunity cost to a firm of investing in an industry is the amount it must pay to borrow financial capital. The resale value of physical capital is collateral that secures the value of loans (or that reverts to bondholders, if a firm should go bankrupt). The more are costs sunk (the lower is a), the lower the value of this collateral, all else equal, and the greater the interest rate that financial markets will require to finance investments in the industry.

How do changes in the extent to which an industry's costs are sunk affect the equilibrium long-run number of firms?

6-2 (sunk cost and market structure II) Continuing Problem 6–1, let $a = \frac{1}{2}$, so that half of a firm's investment in physical assets is sunk. Suppose the firm is supplied by one firm that produces the monopoly output.

(a) What is the firm's monopoly profit?

(b) If a second firm comes into the market, what is the first firm's marginal cost? (Hint: calculate the present-discounted value of the first firm's cost if it sells its excess capital at the start of the period in which entry occurs).

(c) if the post-entry market is a Cournot duopoly, what is the second firm's equilibrium profit? How do changes in the extent to which costs are sunk affect the second firm's post-entry profit?

6-3 Consider a market with linear inverse demand function

$$p(Q) = a - bQ, \tag{6.23}$$

where Q is total output. Let the firm-level cost function be cubic,

$$C(q) = F + cq - dq^2 + eq^3. \tag{6.24}$$

Here $F, a, b, c, d, e \geq 0$. Assume also that $a - c > 0$ and $d > b$.
Find the long-run equilibrium number of firms if the market is a Cournot oligopoly and entry occurs until profit per firm is zero.

6-4 (Equilibrium number of firms, Cournot oligopoly, differentiated products) For a price-setting oligopoly with product differentiation, let the equations of the inverse demand curves be

$$p_i = 100 - (q_i + \theta Q_{-i}), \tag{6.25}$$

for $i = 1, 2, \ldots, n$ and $Q_{-i} = \sum_{j \neq i}^{n} q_j$, with the equation of the firm-level cost function

$$c(q) = F + 10q. \tag{6.26}$$

Find the equilibrium number of firms if the long-run equilibrium number of firms adjusts until Cournot equilibrium profit per firm is zero. How does the equilibrium number of firms change as θ changes?

6-5 (Equilibrium number of firms, Bertrand oligopoly, differentiated products)

For a price-setting oligopoly with product differentiation, let the equations of the demand curves be

$$q_i = \frac{90(1 - \theta) - [1 + (n - 2)\theta](p_i - 10) + \theta \sum_{j \neq i}^{n}(p_j - 10)}{(1 - \theta)[1 + (n - 1)\theta]}, \tag{6.27}$$

with the equation of the firm-level cost function

$$c(q) = F + 10q.$$

Find the equilibrium number of firms if the long-run equilibrium number of firms adjusts until Bertrand equilibrium profit per firm is zero. How does the equilibrium number of firms change as θ changes? As F changes?

6-6 (Merger in a linear Cournot model) Let the market demand curve of a market initially supplied by three firms be

$$p = 100 - Q. \tag{6.28}$$

Let all firms have the cost function

$$c(q) = 10q. \tag{6.29}$$

(a) Find equilibrium price, outputs, and profits if the three firms act as Cournot oligopolists.

(b) Find the same results if firms 1 and 2 merge and the combined firm competes with firm 3, all firms in the post-merger market acting as Cournot oligopolists.

Chapter 7

Imperfect competition and international trade: I

Free trade, one of the greatest blessings which a government can confer on a people, is in almost every country unpopular.

   Thomas Babington, Lord Macaulay

7.1 Introduction

Questions of trade policy lie at the very roots of modern economics. At the dawn of the industrial age, Mercantilist thought held that the road to national prosperity lay in export promotion and import restriction. The Mercantilist argument was that building up wealth meant accumulating gold and silver, and that export surpluses would cause gold and silver to flow into a country as foreign countries paid with precious metals the bills that they could not pay with what they earned from their own exports.

Adam Smith's view of trade was quite different, and a primary purpose of *The Wealth of Nations* was to expound that view. For Smith, wealth was productive capacity, not the accumulation of precious metals.[1] Smith saw trade as being beneficial to all parties involved, allowing countries to specialize in the production of particular goods and to exchange the surpluses of domestic production over domestic consumption in international markets. Specialization in production would allow overall output to increase; exchange would allow all countries to share in the gains. It is not by accident that it is in his discussion of foreign trade that Smith introduces the notion of the *invisible hand*, guiding individuals who blindly pursue their own self-interest to promote society's best interest as well (Smith, 1937, p. 423).

Economists' traditional advocacy of free trade as desirable public policy stems from Smith's analysis and elaborations of it. Classical arguments in favour of free trade began

---

[1] The Mercantilist identification of wealth with money is a fallacy of composition: money is a store of wealth for an individual, but not for a society.

with the assumption that product markets are perfectly competitive, or at least are so close to being perfectly competitive that they can be treated as such for policy purposes. New theories of international trade abandon this assumption. They start from the premise that product differentiation and economies of scale make the typical international market imperfectly competitive, and they reach the neo-Mercantilist conclusion that trade restrictions might in some cases improve national welfare.

In this chapter we begin our consideration of the implications of imperfect competition for international market performance and, reciprocally, the implications of international competition for the performance of imperfectly competitive domestic markets. We start with a discussion of the classical comparative advantage theory of international trade, and of its not entirely happy confrontation with empirical tests. Then we turn to new models of intraindustry trade, tests of such theories, and of the impact of intraindustry trade on domestic market performance. In Chapter 8 we take up the question of strategic trade policy, the modern incarnation of the Mercantilist arguments of two centuries ago. Strategic trade arguments notwithstanding, most economists continue to advocate free trade as desirable public policy, and we discuss why this is so. In Chapter 8, we also examine the determinants of international firm and market structure, including the impact of domestic policy decisions on direct foreign investment flows, which arise when firms set up production operations outside their home market. In Chapter 9, we look at the interaction of trade policy and competition policy, first from a strictly national point of view and then from the perspective of international coordination of trade and competition policy.

Adam Smith on Mercantilism

Money in common language ... frequently signifies wealth; and this ambiguity of expression has rendered this popular notion so familiar to us, that even they, who are convinced of its absurdity, are very apt to forget their own principles, and in the course of their reasonings to take it for granted as a certain and undeniable truth. Some of the best English writers upon commerce set out with observing, that the wealth of a country consists, not in its gold and silver only, but in its lands, houses, and consumable goods of all different kinds. In the course of their reasonings, however, the lands, houses, and consumable goods seem to slip out of their memory, and the strain of their argument frequently supposes that all wealth consists in gold and silver, and that to multiply those metals is the great object of national industry and commerce.

The two principles being established, however, that wealth consisted in gold and silver, and that those metals could be brought into a country which had no mines only by the balance of trade, or by exporting to a greater value than it imported; it necessarily became the great object of political œconomy to diminish as much as possible the importation of foreign goods for home consumption, and to increase as much as possible the exportation of the produce of domestic industry. Its two great engines for enriching the country, therefore, were restraints upon importation, and encouragement to exportation.

(*The Wealth of Nations*. Edwin Cannan, editor. New York: The Modern Library, 1937, p. 418.)

7.2 **Interindustry trade**

7.2.1 **Comparative advantage**

Although Adam Smith argued in 1776 that countries would find trade mutually beneficial, it is to David Ricardo's 1817 *Principles of Political Economy* that we owe the theory of
comparative advantage and its explanation of trade flows as a response to relative rather
than absolute cost differences.

Ricardo's famous example was of trade in wine and cloth between England and Portugal. Ricardo discussed production by means of both labour and physical capital, but it is
easiest to interpret his example as a discussion of production by means of labour alone, as
we do in Table 7.1.

Suppose it takes 100 hours of labour input to make a certain amount of cloth in England, but only 90 hours to make the same amount of cloth in Portugal. Suppose also that
it takes 120 hours of labour input to produce a certain amount of wine in England, but
only 80 hours to produce the same amount of wine in Portugal. Portugal is thus more
efficient than England in the production of both cloth and wine.

If there is no trade between England and Portugal and if product markets are perfectly
competitive, then in each country wine and cloth will exchange in ratios determined by
the relative amount of labour needed to produce the two goods. In England, the price of a
unit of wine will be the wages of the labour needed to produce the wine, 120 hours. The
price of a unit of cloth will be the wages of the labour needed to produce the cloth, 100
hours. Wine and cloth will exchange in proportion to the wages of their labour inputs,
meaning that the ratio of the price of wine to the price of cloth in England will be 120/
100 or 6/5. Without foreign trade, the price of wine in England will be 120 per cent of the
price of cloth, which is to say that 1.2 units of cloth will exchange for 1 unit of wine.

Similarly, without trade wine will be relatively less expensive than cloth in Portugal:
the wages of 80 hours of labour must be paid to get a unit of wine, the wages of 90 hours
of labour must be paid to get a unit of cloth. Without foreign trade, the price of wine in
Portugal will be 80/90th or 89 per cent of the price of cloth, which is to say that 0.89 units
of cloth will exchange for 1 unit of wine.

As a result, any exchange of Portuguese wine for English cloth that gives Portugal more
than 0.89 units of cloth per unit of wine leaves Portugal better off, in the sense that with
trade, Portugal can have just as much wine and more cloth than without trade. Any

Table 7.1 David Ricardo's interindustry trade example

	Cloth	Wine	P_w/P_c
England	100	120	1.20
Portugal	90	80	0.89

Columns show the number of hours of labour needed to produce one unit of
cloth and wine, respectively in England (row 1) and Portugal (row 2)

exchange of Portuguese wine for English cloth that requires England to pay less than 1.2 units of cloth for a unit of wine leaves England better off, in the sense that England can have just as much cloth and more wine with trade than without trade. If England trades cloth for Portuguese wine at any ratio between 0.89 and 1.2 units of cloth per unit of wine, trade leaves both countries better off.[2] Even though Portugal is *absolutely* more efficient than England in the production of both wine and cloth, there is scope for mutually beneficial trade because England is *relatively* more efficient than Portugal in the production of cloth.

It should be emphasized that comparative advantage trade theory is a theory of *interindustry trade*. Interindustry trade means that different countries specialize in the production of different goods, each concentrating on the industries where it is relatively most efficient. The products of these different industries are exchanged in international markets, leaving all countries better off.

> *Comparative advantage*: *relative* differences in the cost of different goods in different countries create opportunities for beneficial *interindustry trade*.

7.2.2 **Factor mobility and immobility**

Comparative advantage trade theory is a theory of competitive *international* markets. What distinguishes it from the theory of competitive *domestic* markets is the idea that factors of production are mobile within a country but immobile between countries (Ricardo, 1951, p. 134):

If the profits of capital employed in Yorkshire, should exceed those of capital employed in London, capital would speedily move from London to Yorkshire, and an equality of profits would be effected; but if in consequence of the diminished rate of production in the lands of England, from the increase of capital and population, wages should rise, and profits fall, it would not follow that capital and population would necessarily move from England to Holland, or Spain, or Russia, where profits might be higher.

In the cloth–wine example, real wages would be higher in Portugal than England, since labour is absolutely more productive in both industries in Portugal than in England. This would create an incentive for workers to move from England (driving English wages up) to Portugal (driving Portuguese wages down). But today, as in Ricardo's time, labour is much less mobile across national boundaries than within them. Physical capital is similarly immobile.[3] Factors of production do not move easily across national boundaries in response to wage/price differentials. The *invisible hand* of resource allocation in competitive markets leads to specialization within a country based on absolute efficiency

---

[2] In other words, such trade results in a Pareto improvement in welfare for both countries.

[3] Financial capital, on the other hand, flows freely around the world in search of the highest rate of return, with important implications for microeconomic performance and macroeconomic policy. Discussion of the latter is not without interest or importance, but would take us far afield.

differences and to specialization between countries based on relative efficiency differences.

7.2.3 **Factor endowments and the Leontief paradox**

It is differences in relative national factor endowments that create national differences in relative costs. If the production of wine is labour-intensive—if it requires relatively more labour and relatively less machinery to produce wine than to produce textiles—the cost of producing wine will be lower, relative to the cost of producing textiles, in countries that are relatively rich in labour and relatively poor in machinery. If the production of textiles is capital intensive—if it requires relatively more machinery and relatively less labour to produce textiles than wine—the cost of producing textiles will be lower, relative to the cost of producing wine, in countries that are relatively rich in machinery and relatively poor in labour. Comparative advantage theory thus predicts that machinery-rich countries will export capital-intensive goods to labour-rich countries in return for labour-intensive goods.

This was indeed the case for Britain during the industrial revolution. Table 7.2 shows that the exports of capital-rich Britain in the first half of the nineteenth century were made up overwhelmingly of manufactured goods. Comparative advantage trade theory, which was developed in the nineteenth century, does a good job explaining the nature of nineteenth century trade among industrialized countries.

Comparative advantage theory predicts that exports from the capital-rich US would be mainly capital-intensive goods, while imports to the US would be mainly labour-intensive goods. It was something of a shock, therefore, when the first statistical investigation of the factor content of US trade flows suggested the contrary.

Measuring the factor content of trade flows is far from straightforward. An automobile is produced by workers and machinery from metal, plastic, glass, and other material inputs. Each of these inputs is itself produced by workers and machinery from other sets of inputs that are manufactured further back along the production chain (as indeed is machinery itself). To accurately measure the factors employed to produce an exported automobile requires disentangling this chain of production relationships to take account of indirect factor usage—the labour and capital used to produce inputs—as well as direct factor usage. In a pioneering use of *input-output tables* to measure direct and indirect factor requirements, Leontief (1953) estimated that to produce a representative bundle of

Table 7.2 Share of manufacturing exports in UK exports during the Industrial Revolution (per cent).

1794–1796	86
1814–1816	82
1834–1836	91
1854–1856	81

Source: Temin (1997, p. 74), based on Davis (1979).

Table 7.3 Domestic capital and labour requirements of a representative million dollar bundle of US exports and of competitive import replacements (1947).

	Exports	Imports
Capital	2,550,780	3,091,339
Labour	182.313	170.004
K/L	13,991	18,184

Capital measured in 1947 dollars, labour in person-years.

Source: Leontief (1953).

$1 million worth of US imports in 1947 required more capital and less labour than a similarly representative bundle of US exports (Table 7.3).

Leontief himself thought that this finding, which has come to be known as the *Leontief paradox*, was a result of the greater productivity of US than foreign labour.

Within the framework of comparative advantage trade theory, others have suggested that the Leontief paradox could be explained by allowing for more than two broad categories of inputs: land (natural resources), labour, and capital, for instance, instead of simply labour and capital.[4] This explanation of the Leontief paradox is that the apparent relative labour intensity of US exports is due to a comparative US abundance of natural resources. It would indeed seem paradoxical, for example, if Japan were to be found to export beef to the US.

But Leontief's finding appears paradoxical only in the context of the comparative advantage framework. If there are other forces that also drive trade flows, then his results may not be so surprising.

The *Leontief Paradox*: statistical studies show that the capital-rich US imports goods that are more capital-intensive, on average, than the goods it exports.

Input-Output Tables

Since François Quesney and the *tableau économique*, economists have visualized the economy as an intricate mechanism linking markets in which we all buy from and sell to each other, combining labour and physical capital—commodities produced by commodities, in Sraffa's terminology—in the production of goods for final consumer demand.

A *circular flow diagram* (Figure 7.1) illustrates these relationships, but at a very aggregate level. *Input-output tables*, the development of which is associated in particular with the

---

[4] Some statistical tests find results that are consistent with the predictions of comparative advantage trade theory; see Davis et al. (1997), who study the location of production.

work of Nobel-prize-winning economist Wassily Leontief, untangle interindustry relationships in a much more detailed way.

Table IO-1 is a simple input-output table for a three-sector economy. Rows identify
input shipments, and columns identify receiving sectors. The first column shows that the
inputs to production in the food industry are 30 units of food (seed corn), 15 units of
machinery, and 60 person-years of labour. The first row shows that the food industry
produces 80 units of output, of which 30 units are shipped to firms in the food industry
itself and 10 units to the machinery industry, leaving 40 units of food for final
consumption.

In the same way, reading down column 2, the inputs to the machinery industry are 10
units of food, 10 of machinery, and 120 person-years of labour. Reading across row 2, 15
machines are used in the food industry and 10 in the machinery industry, leaving 15 for
final consumer demand.

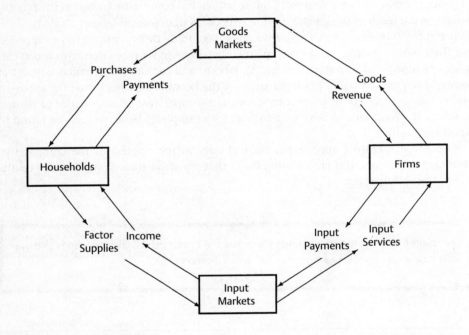

Fig. 7.1 Circular flow diagram

Table IO-1: 3-sector input-output table

	Food	Machinery	Final Consumption	Total
Food	30	10	40	80
Machinery	15	10	15	40
Labour	60	120		180

Table IO-2 Input-output coefficients, 3-sector economy

	Food	Machinery
Food	0.375	0.125
Machinery	0.375	0.250
Laboaur	0.75	3.00

Dividing the input flows in Table IO-1 by the corresponding outputs yields a table of input-output coefficients, as shown in Table IO-2. Each unit of food produced requires 0.375 units of food, 0.125 machines, and 0.75 person-years of labour; each machine requires 0.375 units of food, 0.25 machines, and three person-years of labour. These coefficients describe the technical production relationships among the industries that make up the economy and between industries and the labour market.

Like the circular flow diagram, this example is highly aggregated. The input-output tables that are produced by the governments of most major economies collect and report data at a much finer level. The OECD produces input-output tables for 10 industrialized countries that classify output and shipments in 36 industrial sectors. The most detailed version of input-output tables for the US divides the productive activity of the US economy into more than 500 industries.

Input-output tables are rich in descriptive information about the economy. The shipments of the advertising industry to other industries, for example, give information about the advertising intensity of different industries. Demand categories include final consumer demand, as in the above example, as well as exports (i.e. foreign demand) and government demand. Imports, the supply of goods by foreign producers, are also reported.

By working backward from input-output coefficients of the kind illustrated in Table IO-2, it is possible to calculate the direct (for final consumption) and indirect (for use as an input by other industries) output required from every industry to produce any menu of final consumer demand (Problem 7–4). The wish to make such calculations for planned economies was a main motive behind the early development of input-output tables. The calculation of direct and indirect input requirements is also part of testing comparative advantage trade theory.

References for further reading:

- Dorfman, Robert, Paul A. Samuelson, and Robert M. Solow *Linear Programming and Economic Analysis*. New York: McGraw-Hill Book Company, 1958.

- Leamer, Edward E. "Leontief paradox", in John Eatwell, Murray Milgate, and Peter Newman, editors, *The New Palgrave A Dictionary of Economics Volume* 3, pp. 166–7. London: The Macmillan Press, 1987.

- Leontief, Wassily "Input-Output Analysis", in John Eatwell, Murray Milgate, and Peter Newman, editors, *The New Palgrave A Dictionary of Economics Volume* 2, pp. 860–4. London: The Macmillan Press, 1987.

- Sraffa, Piero *Production of Commodities by Means of Commodities*. Cambridge: Cambridge University Press, 1960.

7.3 **Intraindustry trade**

Comparative advantage trade theory explains the exchange of the products of different industries by different countries in international markets. It seems clear, however, that much trade, especially among developed countries, involves two-way flows of goods that are close substitutes, products of the same industry.

Figure 7.2 shows the value of trilateral trade flows between the EC, Japan, and the US in 1994 for two important industries: motor vehicles and aerospace manufacturing. Japan is a net exporter of motor vehicles to both the US and the EC, and a net importer of aerospace manufactures from both. The US is a net importer of motor vehicles from the EC, and a net exporter of aerospace equipment to the EC. There is substantial *intraindustry trade*—two-way trade flows of products of the same industry—between the three regions for these two industries. Two-way trade is an important characteristic of trade flows among industrialized countries for many industries.

If it is comparative advantage alone that drives trade flows, this kind of intraindustry trade should not take place. To understand what lies behind the exchange of products of the same industry among industrialized economies, we must look elsewhere than comparative advantage.

One of the central assumptions of classical trade theory is that input markets and output markets are perfectly competitive. Relaxing this assumption generates models of trade that do not depend on relative factor endowments, but simply on the exercise of market power in the export market.

> *Two-way or intraindustry trade* in substitute products is a major part of trade among industrialized countries.

7.3.1 **Quantity-setting firms**

Conditions for interindustry trade

Recall the distinction made in Chapter 2 between markets in which firms set quantities and markets in which firms set price. Quantity-setting models describe markets where the nature of the technology dictates that production decisions be taken in advance of sales; the automobile market is an example.[5] Price-setting models describe markets where production takes place at the time of sale. Markets for services are good examples. We begin by showing that with quantity-setting firms the condition for intraindustry trade to take

---

[5] It is worth noting that the Toyota company claims to extend its *just-in-time* production method all the way forward to the final consumer, producing a car only after the car had already been ordered. Effectively, this would make Toyota a price-setting automobile manufacturer.

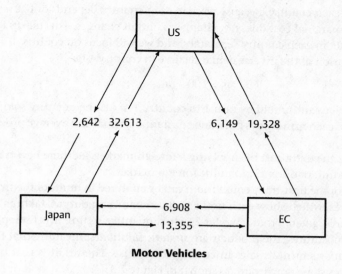

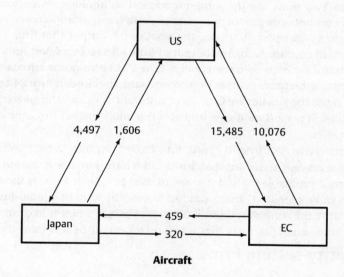

Fig. 7.2 Trilateral trade flows, motor vehicle and aircraft industries, EC, Japan, and US, 1997 (million dollars). Source: OECD Bilateral Trade Database, 1999

place in an imperfectly competitive market is simply that the monopoly price-cost margin be greater than transportation cost from one market to the other.

Consider a Cournot duopoly model, reinterpreted now by assuming that each of the two firms is located in a different country—firm 1 is based in country 1, firm 2 is based in country 2.

We will work with a linear demand, constant marginal and average cost example. With linear demand curves and constant marginal and average cost, output decisions are taken separately for each country, because price in each country depends only on sales in that country, and marginal cost does not change as output changes. This makes it possible to treat the market in each country separately, and we will focus on country 1.[6]

Let the equation of the inverse demand curve in country 1 be

$$p_1 = 100 - (q_{11} + q_{21}),\tag{7.1}$$

where q_{11} is the quantity sold by firm 1 in country 1, q_{21} is the quantity sold by firm 2 in country 1, and each firm enjoys the same constant marginal and average production cost, 10 per unit.[7]

To allow for the extra cost of supplying a foreign market, let there be a transportation cost t for each unit of output sold in the foreign market.

The nature of the post-trade equilibrium can be analyzed in terms of the two firms' best response curves, which show each firm's profit-maximizing output, taking the output of the other firm as given. From Chapter 2, when quantity-setting firms sell products that are demand substitutes, the products are *strategic substitutes*, meaning that firm 1's marginal profit falls as firm 2's sales in country 1 increase. The result is that quantity best response curves slope downward, as shown in Figure 7.3.

Although the two firms use the same production technology, when firm 2 sells in country 1, it incurs not only production cost c but also transportation cost t for every unit sold. The greater is transportation cost, the smaller the output that firm 2 will find it profitable to sell in country 1, for any output of firm 1. In terms of best response curves, the greater is transportation cost, the closer is firm 2's best response curve to the origin. Because quantity best response curves slope downward, the closer is firm 2's best response curve to the origin, the smaller are firm 2's equilibrium sales and the greater are firm 1's equilibrium sales. Transportation cost insulates the home market from the competition of foreign suppliers.

If transportation cost is sufficiently great, firm 2's best response curve moves below firm 1's best response curve. This means that firm 1 can sell the monopoly output in market 1 without making it profitable for firm 2 to sell in market 1. Such a case is shown in Figure 7.4. As shown in Problem 7–1, the condition to rule the kind of equilibrium shown in Figure 7.4—that is, the condition for firm 2 to sell a positive amount in country 1, so that intraindustry trade takes place—is that transportation cost be less than the monopoly price-cost margin:

$$t < \tfrac{1}{2}(a_1 - c).\tag{7.2}$$

Intraindustry trade: with imperfect competition, it will be profitable for producers of substitute goods to sell in several countries if equilibrium price is greater than marginal production plus transportation cost, even without a comparative advantage in production.

---

[6] This kind of separation would not be possible if there were economies of scale, and we will consider this case in Chapter 8, Section 8.1.3.

[7] For the moment, we ignore the fact that different countries typically use different currencies. The impact of exchange rate fluctuations in imperfectly competitive markets is taken up in Chapter 8.

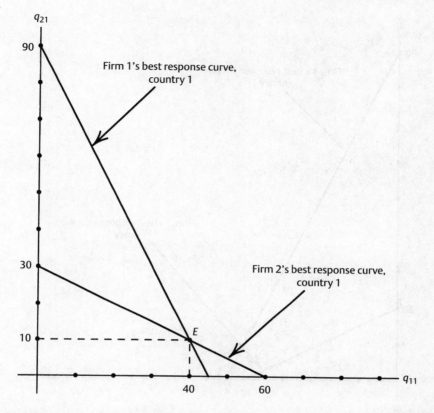

Fig. 7.3 Cournot duopoly trade model with intraindustry trade, country 1, unit transportation cost = 30; q_{11} = firm 1's sales in country 1; q_{21} = firm 2's sales in country 1.

If the foreign firm can profitably sell in country 1 when firm 1 sets the monopoly price, then it will enter the country 1 market, leading to a post-trade price below the monopoly level but high enough to cover production and transportation cost for the foreign firm.

Welfare consequences

We know from our previous discussions of Cournot oligopoly (Chapter 2, Section 2.2.10) that equilibrium market performance ranges from monopoly to perfect competition as the number of firms rises from one to infinity. One might expect, therefore, that the opening up of previously closed markets to foreign suppliers leaves consumers better off. This is indeed the case: if it is profitable for firm 2 to sell in country 1, then with trade the equilibrium price in country 1 is lower, and consumers' surplus larger, than without trade. Trade leaves consumers better off because the rivalry of foreign suppliers improves market performance in imperfectly competitive markets.

The impact of trade on profit, and the impact of trade on net social welfare—consumers' surplus plus profit—is not so clear-cut.

Trade leaves the home country firm worse off in its home market: with trade, it faces

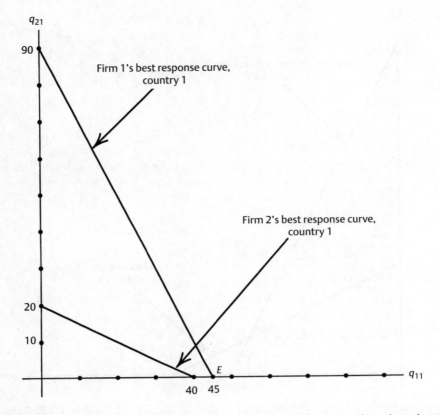

Fig. 7.4 No trade equilibrium in country 1, high transportation cost, Cournot duopoly trade model, unit transportation cost = 50; q_{11} = firm 1's sales in country 1; q_{21} = firm 2's sales in country 1.

competition from the foreign supplier that it would not otherwise face. But on the foreign market it is the new competitor, and it will earn some profit on the foreign market that it would not earn without trade.

The analysis of intraindustry trade arises particularly with respect to trade flows between countries at the same level of development. Consider first, then, a case of trade between identical countries, so that the markets in the two countries are the same size.

If the two markets are the same size, overall company profits fall with the opening of trade. This should be expected: considering only a single market, the combined profit of both firms in Cournot duopoly is less than monopoly profit. When trade is involved, each firm earns duopoly profit in two markets instead of monopoly profit in one market. Because Cournot duopoly profit is less than monopoly profit, the profit earned on the export market is not enough to make up for the profit lost on the home market. This result is reinforced by the cost disadvantage—transportation cost—that a firm has for sales in its export market.

When markets are the same size, then, trade makes consumers better off and firms worse off. For the linear demand, constant marginal cost model currently under consideration, the net effect is positive: intraindustry trade between countries of the same size raises net social welfare in both countries.

If trade is between markets of different sizes, the net welfare effect of trade may be positive or negative.[8] If a small country opens its home market to trade, its domestic firms will face foreign competition, and they will see their profits fall in their home market. If the home market is relatively small, lost profits will also be relatively small. If the foreign market is sufficiently large, the profits earned in the foreign market will more than offset the profits lost at home. If trade leaves home country firms with more profit, it is certainly beneficial overall, since the lower prices that result from trade leave consumers better off.

The other side of the coin is that if a large country opens its home market to trade, its domestic firms may lose more profit to firms from small countries than large-country consumers gain in increased consumers surplus, leaving net social welfare in the large country lower with trade than without trade.

7.3.2 Price-setting firms

Conditions for interindustry trade

For price-setting firms, it is most interesting to consider the case in which products are imperfect substitutes.[9] An example of linear inverse demand curves for country 1 that allow for product differentiation is

$$p_{11} = 100 - (q_{11} + \tfrac{1}{2}q_{21})$$

$$p_{21} = 100 - (\tfrac{1}{2}q_{11} + q_{21})$$

(7.3)

which describes a structure of demand in which sales of two units of variety 2 substitute for one unit of variety 1 in determining the price of variety 1, and two units of variety 1 substitute for one unit of variety 2 in determining the price of variety 2.[10]

Let the cost structure be the same as for the discussion of quantity-setting firms: constant average and marginal cost 10 per unit, transportation cost t for each unit sold in the export market.

From Chapter 2, when price-setting firms sell products that are demand substitutes, prices are *strategic complements*, meaning that it becomes more profitable for firm 1 to raise its own price, the higher is firm 2's price. Price best response curves slope upward, as shown in Figure 7.5.

The greater is transportation cost, the higher the price firm 2 will charge to maximize its own profit, for any price set by firm 1.[11] In terms of Figure 7.5, the greater is t, the higher is firm 2's price best response curve. Since price best response curves slope upward, if firm 2's best response curve is higher, firm 1's equilibrium price will be higher as well: greater transportation cost means greater equilibrium prices for both varieties.

---

[8] See Krugman and Venables (1990) for a model of trade between countries of different sizes.

[9] Recall the discussion in Section 2.3.1 of the Bertrand model with a standardized product. If price-setting firms produce a homogeneous product, the entire market demand will switch from one supplier to another in response to a negligible price difference. This is implausible in general, and particularly so in models of international trade.

[10] See Section 2.3.2.

[11] Problem 7–3 gives you the opportunity to formally demonstrate the results discussed in this section.

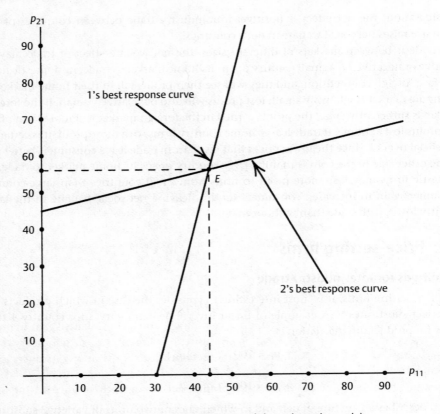

Fig. 7.5 Price best response curves, country 1, Bertrand duopoly trade model

It is generally the case in imperfectly competitive markets that a cost increase is partially passed on to consumers in the form of higher prices and partly absorbed by producers in the form of a reduced profit margin. In the present context, when transportation cost rises, firm 2's price in country 1 rises as well, but by less than the increase in transportation cost. For this example, the equation of firm 2's price best response curve is

$$p_{21} = 30 + \tfrac{1}{2}t + \tfrac{1}{4}p_{11}. \tag{7.4}$$

For any price of firm 1 in country 1, firm 2 maximizes its profit by picking a price that passes half of its transportation cost along to consumers in the form of a higher price. Firm 2's profit margin per unit goes down as transportation cost goes up:

$$p_{21} - 10 - t = 20 - \tfrac{1}{2}t + \tfrac{1}{4}p_{11}. \tag{7.5}$$

The condition for intraindustry trade to occur—for firm 2 to sell in country 1—is that the equilibrium price with trade be greater than $10 + t$, firm 2's marginal cost of selling in country 1. The condition for p_{21} to be greater than $10 + t$ is that transportation cost t not be too large—$t < 64\tfrac{2}{7}$ in this example.

In general, the upper limit on transportation cost for trade to take place is larger, the larger is market size and the greater is product differentiation (Problem 1–3). When the goods that are traded are poorer substitutes, each variety faces less competition from the other variety, and can cover higher levels of transportation cost before trade becomes unprofitable. Greater product differentiation promotes intraindustry trade.

Welfare consequences

The degree of demand substitutability affects the welfare impact of trade as well as whether trade is privately profitable.

Intraindustry trade leaves consumers better off when varieties are differentiated and firms set price, as when products are standardized and firms set quantities. Trade results in a lower price for variety 1, and with trade consumers have the possibility of acquiring a new variety.

In contrast to the homogeneous product case, with product differentiation firm profit may rise with intraindustry trade even if countries are the same size. This can occur if the varieties are poor substitutes.

The intuition behind this is clear if products are completely independent in demand: then the opening up of trade effectively means that a new market comes into being in each country. Each firm earns incremental profit in its export market, but does not lose any profit in its home market, because the two products are not demand substitutes. When substitutability is low, there is some loss of profit on the home market because of competition from foreign varieties, but not very much, and a considerable gain in profit in the export market. If varieties are poor substitutes one for another, intraindustry trade benefits firms as well as consumers. If trade benefits both firms and consumers, it is evidently beneficial overall.

We know from our previous discussions of imperfectly competitive price-setting olig-opoly markets that price tends to be near marginal cost when different varieties are close substitutes. If different varieties are close substitutes, the opening up of trade means substantially lower profits for firm 1 on its home market, and a low price-cost margin for sales in its export market. At this point the market size considerations that were present in the homogeneous good, quantity-setting model come into play. If markets are the same size, profit falls after trade opens, and the net effect of trade on national welfare depends on whether the increase in consumers' welfare exceeds domestic firms' lost profit.[12] If markets are of different sizes, intraindustry trade will be profitable for firms based in a small market that gain the chance to sell in a sufficiently large market, and trade will benefit the home country of such firms. But firms based in a large market that gain the chance to sell in a small market may be left worse off by trade.

[12] For example, a passenger flight between a city-pair on one airline is a close substitute for a passenger flight between the same city-pair on a rival airline. One should therefore expect that European airline deregulation would result in increases in consumer welfare but reductions in airline profits for city-pair routes served by one airline before deregulation, more than one airline after deregulation. Early evidence is certainly consistent with this.

7.4 **Trade and domestic market performance**

One implication of trade for domestic market performance follows immediately from Chapter 2's discussion of the Cournot model: domestic firms exercise less market power in the presence of foreign competition. The greater the number of suppliers in a quantity-setting market, the closer is equilibrium price to marginal cost.[13]

Chapter 4's discussion of collusion also suggests that the presence of foreign suppliers should be expected to improve domestic market performance. Since collusive agreements typically are not legally enforceable, all collusion is noncooperative in the sense that any firm can defect from a collusive strategy if it thinks it is in its interest to do so. In markets where firms differ in their costs, in their rates of time preference, and where interbrand substitutability is low, it will be more difficult to reach and maintain collusive agreements. Foreign suppliers are likely to differ from domestic firms in all these dimensions. This makes it less likely that foreign suppliers will adhere to a collusive output path, all else equal.

A large number of empirical studies confirm the prediction that imports temper the exercise of market power by domestic firms.[14] Jacquemin and Sapir (1991) study the impact of trade flows and other factors on industry price-cost margins in France, Germany, Italy, and the UK. Their results for the impact of elements of market structure on margins are consistent with those generally found in the literature: price-cost margins are greater where economies of scale and research and development are greater, and for consumer good industries. Price-cost margins are also higher, the greater are tariffs and when there are high non-tariff barriers to the movement of goods from one EC Member State to another.

Jacquemin and Sapir find that imports from outside the EC have a significant negative impact on price-cost margins. The average price-cost margin for German industries in their sample was 15.78 per cent (holding all other factors constant), and their results suggests that an increase of 10 percentage points in the share of imports from outside the EC would reduce an industry's price-cost margin by 4.3 percentage points, almost one-third of 15.78.

When markets are imperfectly competitive, an important benefit of foreign trade is that it limits the ability of domestic producers to earn economic profit and increases the extent to which the benefits of greater product variety and larger scale of production are passed on to domestic consumers.

In contrast to the results for extra-EC imports, Jacquemin and Sapir find that imports from other EC Member States have no statistically significant impact on price-cost margins. An important implication, to which we will return in Chapter 10, is that the competitive pressure of foreign suppliers may be necessary to fully realize the benefits of EC market integration.

---

[13] The same holds for a market in which firms set price, provided there is some product differentiation.

[14] For other such studies, see Esposito and Esposito (1971), Pagoulatos and Sorensen (1976), Caves (1980), Neumann, Böbel, and Haid (1985), Clark et al. (1990), Salinger (1990), Feinberg and Shaanan (1994), and Katics and Petersen (1994).

7.5 **Summary**

The new trade theory predicts that intraindustry trade flows will occur in imperfectly competitive industries, particularly if scale economies and product differentiation are important. It also predicts that foreign competition will improve domestic market performance.

These hypotheses have been subject to extensive empirical tests, and the predictions of the theory of trade in imperfectly competitive markets generally receive strong support. Imperfect competition emerges as a central factor in the explanation of trade flows among developed countries, and trade flows among developed countries limit the exercise of market power by domestic firms.

Study points

- mercantilism (page 140)
- interindustry trade (pages 142–3) v. intraindustry trade (page 148)
- Leontief paradox (page 145)

Problems

7-1 Let there be two countries, each home to one widget producer. The subscript 1 denotes both country 1 and its widget company; the subscript 2 denotes both country 2 and its widget company. Let the inverse demand curves in the two countries be

$$p_1 = a_1 - b_1(q_{11} + q_{21})$$
$$p_2 = a_2 - b_2(q_{12} + q_{22})' \tag{7.6}$$

where p_1 is the price in country 1, p_2 is the price in country 2, and q_{ij} is the quantity of widgets sold by firm i in country j, for $i, j = 1, 2$. The a and b parameters are respectively the price-axis intercept and the absolute value of the slope of the inverse demand curves.

Suppose also that widgets are produced at a constant marginal cost c per unit, and that there is a transportation cost t per unit to ship a widget from one country to another.

(a) write out the payoff functions of the two firms;

(b) show that the amounts the firms sell in one country are independent of the amounts they sell in the other country;

(c) find the equations of the best response functions for country 1;

(d) solve the equations of the best response functions for equilibrium outputs in country 1;

(e) show that inequality (7.2) is the restriction on transportation cost that must hold if firm 2 is to sell in country 1;

(f) what is equilibrium price in country 1? Compare the equilibrium price with each firm's marginal cost of supplying country 1. (This part of the exercise relates to the analysis of dumping.)

7-2 Analyze the Cournot duopoly trade model for general inverse demand curves,

$$p_1 = p_1(q_{11} + q_{21})$$
$$p_2 = p_2(q_{12} + q_{22}) \ . \tag{7.7}$$

7-3 (a) Answer Problem 7-1 if firms set prices rather than quantities. Suppose that products are differentiated, with demand curves in country i given by equations

$$p_{1i} = a_i - b_i(q_{1i} + \theta q_{2i})$$
$$p_{2i} = a_i - b_i(\theta q_{1i} + q_{2i}) \ , \tag{7.8}$$

where the first subscript denotes the firm and the second, $i = 1,2$, denotes the country, $0 \le \theta < 1$, with average and marginal cost c and transportation cost t per unit as in Problem 7-1.

(b) A representative consumer utility function that produces the demand curves (7.8) is

$$U = m + a_i(q_{1i} + q_{2i}) - \tfrac{1}{2}b_i(q_{1i}^2 + 2\theta q_{1i}q_{2i} + q_{2i}^2), \tag{7.9}$$

where m represents consumption on other goods.

(c) Analyze the welfare effects of trade.

7-4 What are the direct and indirect labour input requirements to produce one unit of food and one unit of machinery implied by the input-output table IO-1 (page 146)? If there are 100 units of labour in the economy, what is the equation of its production possibility frontier?

Chapter 8

Imperfect competition and international trade: II

Do unto others as you expect them to do unto you, only do it first.

Anonymous student of human nature

8.1 Trade policy

The classical case for free trade is one of efficiency. Viewed through the lens of comparative advantage theory, international trade is *not* a zero-sum game. In Ricardo's cloth–wine example, trade reduces output and employment in the English wine industry. But it expands output and employment in the English cloth industry. Trade is a way for countries to specialize in the production of things they are good at producing, increasing world output, and, by exchange, sharing the resulting output increases, to mutual advantage. The classical case for free trade, which traditionally assumes that markets are perfectly competitive, is that government policies interfering with this pattern of specialization also interfere with the efficient international allocation of production among countries and so leave all parties worse off.[1]

8.1.1 Strategic trade policy

Profit-shifting

The neo-Mercantilist argument for strategic trade policy takes off from the imperfect nature of competition in international markets. Firms that operate in imperfectly competitive markets may earn economic profits. If so, workers in such markets will be able to bargain for greater-than-competitive wages. If government policy can shift profit from

---

[1] It is possible to extend the theory of comparative advantage to models that allow for imperfect competition; see, for example, Helpman (1981).

foreign firms and workers to domestic firms and workers, the net effect on social welfare may be positive.

Quantity-setting firms To present this argument in the simplest possible setting, consider a case in which two firms, each based in a different country, are the only suppliers to a third country of a product that is not consumed in their home markets. This setting is very artificial, but because it rules out any negative impact of strategic trade policy on home-country consumer welfare by assumption, it highlights the potential for profit-shifting as a motive for strategic trade policy.[2]

Suppose also that the two firms have the same cost per unit of supplying the third-country market. This cost includes the expense of production, transportation, tariffs, and anything else, but whatever it is, it is the same for both firms. If firms set quantities, then the third-country market is a Cournot duopoly, supplied by two firms with identical marginal cost. As in Chapter 2 or in the discussion of Figure 8.1, equilibrium in this market is at the intersection of the best response curves of the two firms. This is point E_0 in Figure 8.1.

If a quantity-setting firm in an imperfectly competitive market somehow gets a lower unit cost, it will wish to expand output, taking rival output as given. For an oligopolist to maximize profit, it must be producing an output that makes its marginal cost equal to marginal revenue along its residual demand curve. If marginal cost falls, a profit-maximizing firm will expand output, so that marginal revenue falls as well. This means that with lower unit cost a firm's quantity best response curve shifts outward on the best response-curve diagram.

A key insight of the strategic trade policy literature is that an export subsidy has the same effect on firm behaviour as a cost reduction. If country 1 grants a subsidy s_1 on every unit of output exported by its firm to the third-country market, then as far as firm 1 is concerned, its cost of supplying that market falls by s_1 per unit.

The direct effect of the subsidy is that firm 1's best response curve shifts outward. If firm 2 were to maintain its output at the pre-subsidy level, firm 1's sales would go up. In terms of Figure 8.1, the market would move from point E_0 to point F.

But firm 2 will not maintain its output at the pre-subsidy level. When firms in imperfectly competitive markets set quantities and have constant marginal costs, their choice variables are strategic substitutes. The greater is firm 1's output, the lower is firm 2's marginal profitability. The result is that as firm 1's output expands, firm 2 reduces its own output. This indirect, strategic effect of the subsidy implies a further increase in firm 1's output, over and above the direct effect. The overall result of an export subsidy by country 1 is that the equilibrium moves down firm 2's best response curve from E_0 to E_1.

Firm 1 profits because of the direct effect of the subsidy, and it profits again because of the strategic effect. The overall result is that firm 1's profit increases by more than the amount of the subsidy,[3] making the net impact of the subsidy on country 1's welfare positive. A strategic trade subsidy increases firm 1's profit and country 1's welfare at the expense of its international rivals.

---

[2] Figure 8.1 is drawn for the inverse demand function $p = 100 - Q$, with marginal cost equal to 10 and an export subsidy equal to 30.

[3] See Problem 8–1 to show this formally.

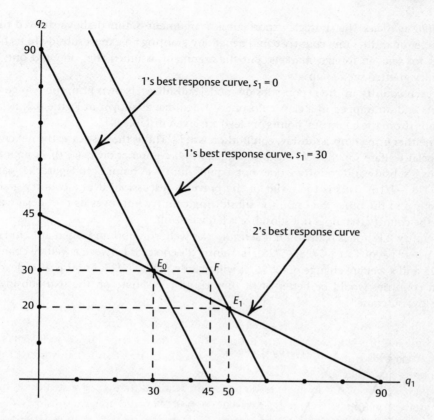

Fig. 8.1 Export subsidy and market equilibrum, Cournot duopoly trade model

Table 8.1 Payoff matrix, government export-subsidy games, quantity-setting firms.

		Firm 2	
		No subsidy	Subsidy
Firm 1	No subsidy	(0, 0)	(−7/16, 1/8)
	Subsidy	(1/8, −7/16)	(−7/25, −7/25)

Payoffs are proportional to the figures shown in the payoff matrix; see Problem 8-4.

> *Profit-shifting* export subsidies (I): when firms produce *strategic substitutes*, the direct (reaction of the subsidized firm) and strategic (reaction of other firms) effects of the subsidy are to increase the profit of the subsidized firm at the expense of rivals.

Duelling subsidies The strategic export subsidy argument outlined above showed that if firms set quantities one country could benefit by granting an export subsidy to its home firms for sales in foreign markets. But the argument assumed that one and only one country granted such a subsidy.

If each country in the export subsidy model subsidizes its own firm, the two governments end up trapped in a classic Prisoners' Dilemma, as shown in Figure 8.2. Relative payoffs (from the countries' points of view) are given in Table 8.1.

If neither firm grants a subsidy, equilibrium is at E_0. This is the base case: the net change in social welfare for the (No Subsidy, No Subsidy) combination is (0, 0). If country 1 grants a subsidy and country 2 does not, equilibrium is at point E_1 in Figure 8.1; payoffs are (1/8, −7/16). This is the result of the previous discussion: if one country grants a subsidy and the other does not, the subsidizing country improves its net social welfare and the country that does not subsidize is left worse off.

Country 2 is not as badly off if it subsidizes as well: equilibrium is then at E_2 in Figure 8.2, where payoffs are (−7/25, −7/25). If country 2's choice is between a welfare change of −7/25 and a welfare change of −7/16, it will plainly prefer −7/25. But it is also clear that both countries would be better off if they could coordinate on the (No Subsidy, No Subsidy) outcome.

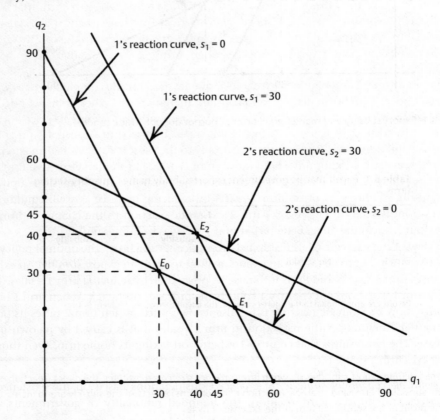

Fig. 8.2 Duelling subsidies, Cournot duopoly trade model

Adam Smith on Export Subsidies

But it is not the interest of merchants and manufacturers ... that the home market should be overstocked with their goods, an event which a bounty upon production might sometimes occasion. A bounty upon exportation, by enabling them to send abroad the surplus part, and to keep up the price of what remains in the home market, effectually prevents this. Of all the expedients of the mercantile system, accordingly, it is the one of which they are the fondest. I have known the different undertakers of some particular works agree privately among themselves to give a bounty out of their own pockets upon the exportation of a certain proportion of the goods which they dealt in. This expedient succeeded so well, that it more than doubled the price of their goods in the home market, notwithstanding a very considerable increase in the produce.

(*The Wealth of Nations*. Edwin Cannan, editor. New York: The Modern Library, 1937, p. 484.)

Price-setting firms In addition to the condition that rival countries not grant their own subsidies, an essential element of the argument in favour of export subsidies is that the strategic effect of the subsidy reinforce the direct effect—that when the firm that benefits from the subsidy changes its behaviour, its rival reacts in a way that is directly beneficial to the subsidized firm, and therefore indirectly beneficial to the country granting the subsidy. This is what happens when firms choice variables are strategic substitutes.

Matters are quite different if firms' choice variables are strategic complements, as when firms set prices with linear demand and constant marginal cost. When firms set prices, if firm 1 receives a subsidy from its home country, it responds by lowering its price, for any price set by firm 2. In Figure 8.3, this is illustrated by the shift of firm 1's price best response function to the left from the no-subsidy to the subsidy case. Were firm 2 to hold its price constant, equilibrium would move from E_0 to F. But in markets where firms set price and there is some product differentiation, best response functions slope upward. When firm 1 reduces its price, firm 2 reacts by reducing its price as well: equilibrium moves from E_0 to E_1 in Figure 8.3. Firm 2's strategic reaction to the change in firm 1's behaviour reduces the direct benefit that firm 1 receives from the subsidy.

In view of the strategic relationship between price-setting firms, the optimal policy for country 1 turns out to be to levy an export tax, not to grant an export subsidy. An export tax raises firm 1's costs and leads it to raise its price, thereby reducing firm 1's sales. This leaves firm 1 worse off, but country 1 collects the proceeds of the tax. When firm 1 raises its price, firm 2's strategic reaction is to raise its own price. When firm 2 raises its price, this partially neutralizes the reduction in firm 1's sales that is caused by its own price increase. The net result is that country 1 is better off taxing its home firm, even though this leaves firm 1 worse off.[4]

The political economy of strategic trade policy Considerations based on the existence of imperfect and impacted information, the bounded rationality of governments, the

---

[4] See Problem 8–2.

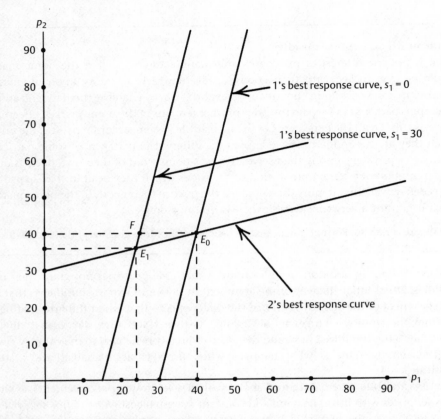

Fig. 8.3 Export subsidy and market equilibrium, Bertrand duopoly trade model

> *Profit-shifting* export subsidies (II): when firms' choice variables are *strategic complements*, the direct (reaction of the subsidized firm) and strategic (reaction of other firms) effects of a subsidy work in opposite directions, with the result that the socially optimal policy is to tax rather than subsidize exports.

expectation that companies will pursue their own self-interest, and the nature of the political process in representative democracies all suggest scepticism toward a policy of subsidizing exports.

Modern governments operate under increasingly severe budget constraints. If a government has an export subsidy programme, requests for subsidies from different industries will exceed the amount a government can grant. Firms and industry associations can be expected to make the strongest case they can for subsidies. Government agencies will normally have much less information at their disposal than the groups presenting requests for subsidies. Because these groups will pursue their own self-interest, governments will not be able to accept firms' arguments in favour of subsidies at face value. Assuming that the government seeks to maximize social welfare, how is the government to pick and choose which industries it will subsidize and which it will not? If the wrong industries are subsidized, the country could easily end up being worse off than with no subsidies at all.

But "government" is not a homogeneous entity, and it cannot be taken for granted that government will automatically seek to maximize social welfare. Government is the agent of society, and subgoal pursuit (Chapter 6) is a problem faced by governments as well as firms. Elected representatives will be influenced by campaign contributions as well as by objective assessments of the social benefits that can be expected to flow from export subsidies. Campaign contributions will be motivated by the benefits donors hope to obtain—and donors will include representatives of labour as well as of management. The result may well be that export subsidies are granted to protect jobs, wages, and profits in uncompetitive sectors where firms and workers are highly organized, not to shift profit from foreign to domestic markets.

Strategic trade policy: medium-size commuter aircraft

Baldwin and Flam (1989) study the impact of strategic trade policy on market performance in the market for 30–40 seat commuter aircraft. The market has three principal suppliers, each located in a different country (Brazil, Canada, Sweden). No one of these firms sells in the home market of the other, and all three compete in the potentially lucrative US market.

Baldwin and Flam present circumstantial evidence suggesting that trade barriers guarantee the Canadian firm privileged access to its home market, and that the Brazilian firm has received direct or indirect export subsidies, at least for its sales in the US market. They use simulation analysis to analyze the consequences of these policies, and their results are broadly consistent with the predictions of the strategic trade policy literature.

Reserving the Canadian market for the Canadian firm appears to increase the Canadian firm's profit and decrease the profits of the two other firms, which is the kind of rent-shifting that lies at the heart of the strategic trade policy literature. The increase in profits of the Canadian firm occur on its home market, at the expense of Canadian consumers, not on foreign markets. Alleged subsidies to the Brazilian firm increase its profit, but by much less than the simulated amount of the subsidy.

The Baldwin and Flam study suggests that strategic rent-shifting can occur in international markets. It does not suggest that such rent-shifting will increase the welfare of countries that implement strategic trade policy.

In February 1999, the World Trade Organization found that Brazil and Canada granted illegal export subsidies to their producers of medium-sized commuter aircraft.

> *Strategic trade policy*: under restrictive conditions—if firms' choice variables are strategic substitutes, if other countries do not grant subsidies of their own—export subsidies can improve domestic welfare by shifting profit from foreign to domestic firms. Otherwise, theory suggests that subsidies will benefit the firms that receive them but not the countries that grant them.

8.1.2 Tariffs and quotas

Export subsidies are an outward-looking policy. *If* they increase national welfare, it is because of their impact on equilibria in foreign markets. When returns to scale are constant, tariffs and quotas are inward-looking policies: they are undertaken because of their effects on the home market.[5] Any net national benefit from tariffs and quotas comes from the additional economic profit domestic firms are able to earn in their home market because of protection from foreign competition. Tariffs and quotas typically leave domestic consumers worse off.

The issues raised by tariffs and quotas are similar. We discuss quotas here, and leave the discussion of tariffs to Problem 8–3.

Suppose that the inverse demand curve in country 1 is

$$p_1 = 100 - (q_{11} + q_{21}),$$ (8.1)

that marginal and average cost are constant, 10 per unit, and that firms set quantities as in a Cournot duopoly. For simplicity, suppose also that there are no transportation costs.

Then Figure 8.4 illustrates the impact of a quota imposed on country 2 sales in country 1. Without a quota, equilibrium is at point E_0, at the intersection of the best response curves of the two firms. If a quota $\bar{q}$ restricts firm 2's sales to a level below its initial equilibrium output q_{12}^0, equilibrium moves along firm 1's best response curve from E_0 to E_1, the point that gives firm 1's profit-maximizing output if firm 2's sales are at the quota level $\bar{q}$.

Moving from E_0 to E_1, firm 1's output rises and total sales fall.[6] Since total sales fall, price rises: firm 1 exercises a greater degree of market power. Since firm 1 sells more and at a higher price, its profit definitely goes up. In the short run, a quota is privately profitable for the domestic firms it protects.

However, the price increase leaves consumers worse off. The change in net social welfare combines the profit increase enjoyed by firm 1 and the welfare loss of consumers. For the duopoly case (see Problem 8–3)—and more generally, if there are at least as many firms in the home country as there are foreign firms—the net effect of a quota on social welfare is positive. If the number of domestic firms is small relative to the number of foreign firms, a quota may allow domestic firms to exercise so much market power that the net welfare effect of the quota is negative.

---

[5] If returns to scale are not constant, then policy measures that protect the home market will have an impact on export markets as well; see Section 8.1.3.

[6] Total sales fall because the slope of the best response curve is less than one: firm 1's additional output is half the reduction in firm 2's output. See Problem 8–3.

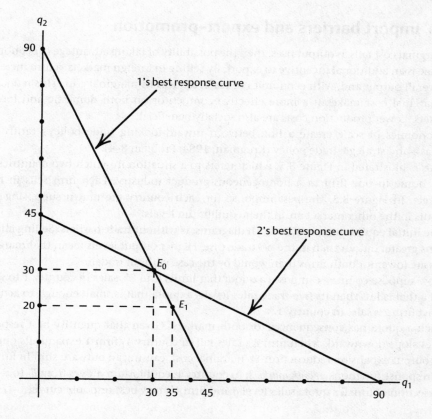

Fig. 8.4 Import quota and Cournot duopoly equilibrium, interindustry trade, constant returns to scale, $\bar{q} = 20$

A difference between tariffs and quotas is that tariffs automatically generate revenue for the government of the importing country. If the country that imposes the quota sells import licenses to foreign firms, and for a high enough fee, it can capture all or almost all of the economic profit foreign firms earn in its market.[7]

> *Quotas and tariffs*: protect domestic producers from foreign competition, increasing their profit and typically leaving consumers worse off.

---

[7] For a discussion of an import licensing scheme in New Zealand, see Pickford (1985). In the 1970s, sale of oil import licenses was proposed as a way of dealing with the OPEC oil cartel (Adelman, 1976). In that case, revenue-raising would have been incidental to the main purpose of cartel destabilization.

8.1.3 **Import barriers and export–promotion**

If marginal cost falls as output rises, then the possibility of taking advantage of economies of scale is an additional incentive to export. By selling in foreign markets, a firm increases its overall output and, with economies of scale, reduces its marginal cost. This reduction in marginal cost makes it a more effective competitor on both domestic and foreign markets. Lower production costs are also socially beneficial.

Economies of scale create a link between inward-looking trade policy—tariffs and quotas—and strategic trade policy (Krugman, 1984; Problem 8–4).

This is illustrated in Figure 8.5, which refers to a situation in which two countries are each home to one firm in a homogeneous-product industry. Each firm sells in both markets. In Figure 8.5, the best response for each country are drawn supposing that outputs in the other market are at their equilibrium levels.[8]

The initial equilibrium, at E_0 in both diagrams, is without trade barriers. Selling abroad means greater output than in the no-trade case. Higher output levels mean that marginal costs are lower for both firms than would be the case without trade.

Now suppose country 1 imposes a quota that limits firm 2's sales in country 1 to some level $\bar{q}$ that is less than its free-trade sales level—a quota that is small enough to actually restrict firm 2's sales in country 1.

Such a quota has consequences for both markets. Given that quantity best response curves slope downward, when firm 2's sales fall in country 1, firm 1 expands its output. This output expansion reduces firm 1's marginal cost, causing an outward shift in firm 1's best response functions *in both markets*. In country 1, equilibrium moves from E_0 to E_1, the intersection of firm 2's quota sales level $\bar{q}$ and firm 1's new best response curve.

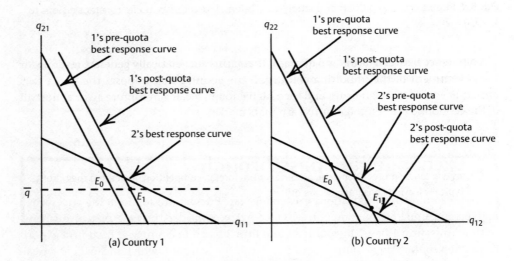

Fig. 8.5 Country 1 quota and Cournot duopoly equilibrium with economies of scale

---

[8] This is an expositional device. In contrast to the constant returns to scale case, when there are increasing returns to scale it is not possible to analyze the two markets separately. See Problem 8–4.

The reduction in firm 1's marginal cost causes an outward shift in its best response curve for country 2. The increase in firm 2's marginal cost causes an inward shift in its best response curve in country 2. The new equilibrium in country 2 is at E_1 in Figure 8.5(b): firm 1's equilibrium sales in country 2 rise, and firm 2's equilibrium sales in country 2 fall. In both cases, the changes in output reflect not only direct effects—movements along a fixed best response curve in response to the rival's output changes—but also indirect effects—shifts of the best response curves.

Empirical studies produce little evidence to suggest that such *internal* economies of scale are common (Chapter 6).[9] There is a dynamic equivalent, however, that may be important for some industries: *learning-by-doing*. Learning-by-doing arises if the cost of current production falls as cumulative production rises. Intuitively, learning-by-doing occurs if experience means that a firm becomes more efficient. Trade barriers that reduce rivals' cumulative outputs will have dynamic strategic effects—favourable to the home firms of the country imposing the barrier, unfavourable to other firms—like the static strategic effects of a quota in the presence of increasing returns to scale.

The analysis of this section is subject to the same general qualifications that apply to other types of strategic trade policy. If firms' outputs are strategic complements rather than strategic substitutes, then a quota forcing a reduction in firm 2's sales on the country 1 market would induce firm 1 to reduce its own sales. All else equal, this output reduction would lead to an increase in firm 1's marginal cost and cause inward shifts in its best response functions in both markets, making it strategically worse off.

Even if firms' outputs are strategic substitutes, as illustrated in Figure 8.5, a quota imposed by country 2 in reaction to the country 1 quota will create a Prisoners' Dilemma situation that is likely to leave both firms and both countries worse off.

> *Import barriers and export promotion*: if there are internal economies of scale or learning-by-doing, trade barriers that reduce rivals' outputs can benefit the export performance of firms based in the protected market, if outputs are strategic substitutes and if other countries do not retaliate with barriers of their own.

8.2 Exchange rate passthrough

We now examine the implications of exchange rate fluctuations for domestic prices when markets are imperfectly competitive. Once again, consider the case of two quantity-setting firms, firm 1 based in country 1 and firm 2 based in country 2. Each firm exports its product to the other country. Returns to scale are constant, which means that we can analyze each country separately.

---

[9] Economies of scale are internal to the firm if they depend on the output level of a specific firm and benefit only that firm. Economies of scale are external to the firm if they depend on industry output and benefit all firms in the industry.

Suppose that inverse demand curves are linear,

$$p_1 = 100 - (q_{11} + q_{21})$$

$$p_2 = 100 - (q_{12} + q_{22})$$

(8.2)

To keep the discussion as simple as possible, suppose also that there are no transportation costs, tariffs, or quotas.

The country 1 price p_1 is measured in country 1's currency, which we will call the dollar. Country 2's price p_2 is measured in country 2's currency, which we will call the euro. The exchange rate e gives the number of euros needed to buy a dollar. Higher values of e mean that more euros are needed to buy a dollar, and therefore represent lower values of the euro in terms of dollars.

Firm 1's profit on its sales in country 1 is

$$\pi_{11} = (p_1 - 10)q_{11} = (100 - 10 - q_{11} - q_{21})q_{11},$$

(8.3)

where firm 1's unit cost is $10. The exchange rate e does not directly affect firm 1's profit on its sales in country 1. The equation of firm 1's best response function for country 1 is found by maximizing firm 1's profit on its sales in country 1. Since e does not appear in (8.3), e does not affect firm 1's best response function for country 1, and changes in e do not cause shifts in firm 1's best response curve for country 1.

Firm 2's unit cost is €10, which is measured in terms of country 2's currency, the euro. Firm 2's profit on its sales in country 1, measured in euros, is

$$\pi_{21} = (ep_1 - 10)q_{21} = e(p_1 - \tfrac{10}{e})q_{21} = e(100 - \tfrac{10}{e} - q_{11} - q_{21})q_{21}.$$

(8.4)

Duelling trade barriers

There are arguments for free trade even if trade flows respond more to imperfect competition than to comparative advantage. One such argument is that protectionist trade measures backfire, because they evoke a self-defeating response in kind.

In the early years of the Great Depression, a desperate search for effective policy responses led many countries to implement strategic trade policies: competitive currency devaluations intended to promote exports and tariffs and quotas intended to reduce imports. Figure 8.6, Kindleberger's (1973, p. 172) spider-web graph of world trade flows shows the result: a thicket of trade barriers choked off export markets for all countries and left firms protected but also trapped in their own home markets.

Multiplying the dollar price p_1 by e converts the dollar price into euros. Dividing the euro cost €10 by e converts the euro cost to an equivalent dollar amount. An increase in e, which is a depreciation of the euro vis-à-vis the dollar, has the effect of a reduction in firm 2's unit cost relative to country 1's price p_1—if a dollar will buy more euros, then it takes fewer dollars to buy the euros needed to cover the cost of producing a unit of output in country 2.

The country 1 market is a Cournot duopoly with differences in unit cost. Firm 2's best response function for country 1 is found by maximizing (8.4). Since e enters directly in

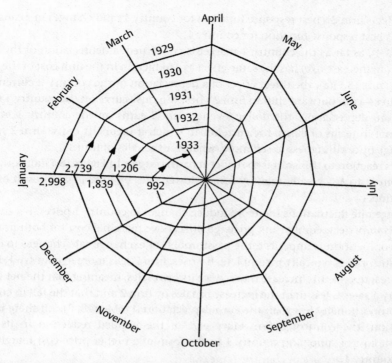

Fig. 8.6 Total imports of 75 countries, January 1929 to March 1933 (monthly values in US gold-standard dollars). Source: Kindleberger, 1973, p. 172

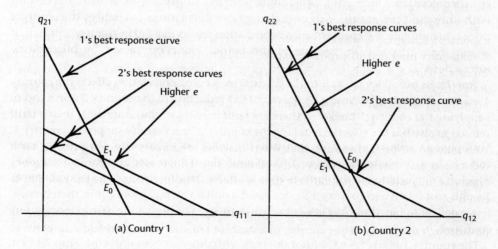

Fig. 8.7 Exchange rate fluctuations and Cournot duopoly equilibrium

(8.4), e affects firm 2's best response function for country 1, and changes in e cause shifts in firm 2's best response function for country 1.

From (8.4), as far as the country 1 market is concerned, a depreciation of the foreign currency (an increase in e) has the same effect as a reduction in the unit cost of the foreign firm. In Figure (8.7)(a), the direct effect of a depreciation of the country 2 currency—an increase in e—is an outward shift in firm 2's best response curve on the country 1 market. With a euro depreciation, the dollar revenue firm 2 earns on the country 1 market is worth more in terms of euros, the currency in which it incurs its costs. Firm 2 reacts to this change by a willingness to sell more, whatever the sales of firm 1.

Firm 1's reaction to this shift is to reduce its own output. In Figure (8.7)(a), equilibrium shifts from E_0 to E_1—greater sales by firm 2, lower sales by firm 1—as a result of a euro depreciation.

Exchange rate fluctuations therefore induce changes in country 1 prices. Because competition is imperfect, equilibrium price remains above marginal cost for both firms. And because competition is imperfect, the passthrough of exchange rate changes to changes in domestic price is typically incomplete. If e rises, firm 2 sells more in country 1. Firm 1's strategic reaction to this increase is to reduce its own sales, meaning that the net increase in country 1 sales is less than the increase in sales by firm 2 and that the fall in country 1 price is proportionally less than the euro depreciation (Problem 8–2).[10] If there is a euro depreciation, the country 2 firm takes part of the implied reduction in its dollar-equivalent cost of supplying country 1 in the form of a higher price-cost margin on its sales in country 1.

A euro depreciation also has an effect on the country 2 market, once again to the detriment of firm 1. An increase in e means that the euro revenue firm 1 earns in country 2 is worth less in terms of dollars. The direct effect of a euro depreciation is to cause an inward shift in firm 1's best response curve for country 2. Firm 2's strategic reaction to the shift in firm 1's best response curve is to expand its own output. In Figure (8.7)(b), equilibrium shifts from E_0 to E_1—greater sales by firm 2, lower sales by firm 1—as a result of a euro depreciation. Once again, equilibrium price in country 2 is above marginal cost for both firms, and the passthrough of exchange rate fluctuations to changes in country 2 price is incomplete: a 10 per cent euro depreciation results in a fall in country 2 price that is less than 10 per cent, because of the output reduction caused by oligopolistic interactions.

Now let us introduce tariffs into the discussion. A euro depreciation affects the country 1 market equilibrium because it is equivalent to a reduction in the country 2 firm's cost of supplying the country 1 market. If there are tariff barriers around country 1, then a tariff reduction also has the effect of reducing the country 2 firm's cost of supplying country 1. We ought to suspect, therefore, that when markets are imperfectly competitive, tariff reductions and foreign currency depreciations (tariff increases and foreign currency appreciations) will have qualitatively similar effects. This turns out to be the case (Problem 8–6).

A large number of empirical studies confirm the predictions of the exchange rate passthrough literature.[11] For example, in a study of Japanese motor vehicle shipments to

---

[10] In the international trade literature, this is called pricing-to-market (Krugman, 1987).

[11] See Knetter (1989, 1993); Marston (1990); Yang (1997); Lee (1997).

the US, Feenstra (1989) finds that tariff changes and exchange rate changes affect US prices in the same general way, and reports (1989, p. 43):

For trucks we have found a pass-through of about 0.6. This means that the increase in the tariff from 4 to 25 per cent in August 1980 raised consumer prices by an estimated 13 per cent, and lowered Japanese producer prices by about 8 per cent. In contrast, for heavy cycles, we found a pass-through of about unity, so the tariff increase in April 1983 and subsequent decreases had little effect on Japanese producer prices. These results have very [different] implications for trade policy. In trucks, the drop in the producer price corresponds to a terms of trade gain . . . this is a first step toward establishing a gain for the United States. For heavy cycles, the constant producer prices mean that the tariff led to a conventional deadweight loss.

Exchange rate passthrough: oligopolistic interactions and the reactions of firms in imperfectly competitive markets to the changes in own-currency value of revenue collected in other currencies means that only part of exchange rate fluctuations will be passed on to changes in domestic prices.

8.3 **Trade and market structure**

One of the most important lessons of modern industrial economics is that market structure is itself determined by market forces. We have explored the factors that shape domestic firm and market structure in Chapter 6; here we examine the determinants of firm and market structure when markets are international.

One aspect of this subject concerns how firms will choose to supply foreign markets, if they find it profitable to do so at all: by export, by licensing partners in local markets, by joint ventures, or by engaging in direct foreign investment and setting up their own production facilities in foreign markets.

We have seen that:

- the opening up of trade exposes firms to greater competition in their home market but gives them the opportunity to earn additional profit in foreign markets;
- the impact of trade on profits and on national welfare is in general ambiguous;
- but if the markets in different countries are of comparable size and product differentiation is not too great, profit is likely to fall, and welfare to rise, with the opening up of trade.

If the fall in profit that flows from the internationalization of markets is sufficiently great, some firms will go out of business. If a firm's gross profit is not sufficient to cover its fixed cost, then in the long run it must shut down. Such closures may take the form of bankruptcy; they may take the form of mergers that combine a larger number of parent firms into a smaller number of survivor firms. But they are unavoidable. Increasing competition improves market performance but also increases seller concentration, albeit in larger (world) markets (Problem 8–5). This *concentration effect* of trade is even greater if marginal cost falls as output rises.

Not only can internationalization cause some firms to shut down, but such closures are actually necessary if the full benefits of trade are to be realized. If production is concentrated in the hands of fewer firms, there is a social saving equal to the fixed costs of the firms that go out of business. In the long run, these fixed assets will be transferred to productive uses in other industries. But in the short run, the threat and the reality of bankruptcy will generate political pressure for subsidies and protection limit the gains from trade.

Concentration effect of intraindustry trade: lower price-cost margins with intraindustry trade raise the possibility that the equilibrium number of firms will fall because of free trade, economizing on fixed costs

---

8.3.1 **Mode of supply to a foreign market**

Consider an international market made up of two countries, each home to a single supplier. Given that both firms sell in both countries (we will return to this point shortly), the strategic situation of two firms can be described (following Veugelers, 1995) in terms of the game illustrated in Figure 8.8. A firm may choose to produce domestically—only in its home country—and export to the other. Alternatively, a firm may establish a production operation in the foreign market, becoming a multinational enterprise.

With two choices per firm, there are four possible strategy combinations and four possible payoff combinations. Depending on relative payoffs, any of the terminal nodes in Figure 8.8 might be an equilibrium.

Thinking of the domestic-multinational choice in these terms emphasizes that the equilibrium choice of investment strategy will depend not only on a comparison of the costs of the different modes of servicing the foreign market but also on the different strategic interactions that take place with each strategy combination, which will influence the revenue side of the payoffs received at the different terminal nodes. The equilibrium choice of investment strategy can also be influenced by policy measures. Tariffs, quotas, or voluntary export restraints (VERs) make export sales relatively less profitable, direct foreign investment relatively more profitable, and may alter the method foreign suppliers choose to supply the domestic market.

Each choice of method for entering a foreign market carries its own menu of implications for cost and revenue. On the cost side, export means the firm must bear transportation cost and exposes it to the risk of tariffs and other trade barriers. Opening up an operation in the foreign country means an extra investment in fixed and sunk costs. On the revenue side, the nature of strategic interactions between the two firms will generally

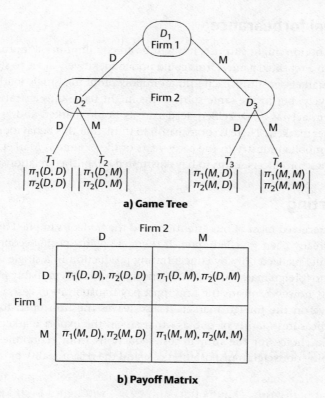

a) Game Tree

Firm 2

	D	M
D	$\pi_1(D, D), \pi_2(D, D)$	$\pi_1(D, M), \pi_2(D, M)$
M	$\pi_1(M, D), \pi_2(M, D)$	$\pi_1(M, M), \pi_2(M, M)$

Firm 1

b) Payoff Matrix

Fig. 8.8 Domestic (D) v. multinational (M) operation

differ across the four outcomes—establishing a foreign plant makes a stronger commitment to supply the foreign market than exports, since shutting down a foreign plant would entail the loss of sunk costs.

In fact, a firm with the possibility of operating in international markets faces more than two options. Ranked loosely from least direct to most direct involvement in a foreign market, a firm's possible strategies with respect to a foreign market include:

- not supplying the market;
- export;
- licensing a foreign firm to produce the product in a foreign market;
- establishing a joint venture with a local partner;
- purchasing an existing plant in a foreign market;
- setting up a new plant in a foreign market (greenfield investment).

This list is not exhaustive. Two foreign firms might form a joint venture to enter a third market; two foreign firms might set up a joint venture to produce an intermediate good (an automobile platform, for example) in a third market, but each sell their own final product in the third market and elsewhere.

8.3.2 **Mutual forbearance**

While the first option might surprise, it might be an equilibrium—a mutual forbearance equilibrium—in a repeated game. Firms could noncooperatively agree to stay out of each other's home markets, ensuring each firm monopoly profit in a single market.

Less restrictively, but in the same spirit, firms might settle into a strategic pattern in which each firm acts as a Stackelberg leader in its home market, and as a Stackelberg follower in other markets. There is some reason to think that this behaviour described the European automobile industry in the early years of the Common Market, although the arrival of Japanese producers seems to have disrupted established relationships.

8.3.3 **Exporting**

Exporting has received most of our attention, and the tradeoffs implied by a decision to export have already been touched upon. If there are plant-specific economies of scale, these can be fully realized only by concentrating production in a single domestic plant and exporting to foreign markets. Much of learning-by-doing is probably plant-specific as well. Exporting, however, means the firm must pay transportation cost, which makes it less competitive on the foreign market. It also leaves the firm open to the threat of protectionist measures—tariffs or quotas—that shield the export market. Export is the most profitable choice for the firm if cost reductions from economies of scale and learning-by-doing outweigh transportation cost and the risk or reality of trade barriers.

Table 8.2 Pluses and minuses of alternative strategies vis-à-vis international markets

Mutual Forbearance	Export	License/Joint Venture	DFI
Pluses			
avoid competition in home market	gain economies of scale, learning by doing	avoid transportation cost, tariffs, quotas	avoid transportation cost, tariffs, quotas
		gain information from local partner	possible economies of scope
			neutralize strategic advantage of host country firms with respect to host country government
Minuses			
forgo economies of scale, learning by doing	incur transportation cost	give up plant-specific economies of scale	sunk cost of setting up plant in host country
	exposure to possible tariff, quota barriers	transaction costs: possible opportunistic behaviour by local partner once sunk assets committed	

8.3.4 **Licensing/joint venture**

The mainstream approach to modeling international operations is an eclectic one, due to Hymer (1976) and Dunning (1980, 1988). This eclectic approach fits very well with the new industrial economics of international trade, since it begins with the premise that foreign direct investment would not occur in perfectly competitive markets.

The argument is that a foreign supplier will inevitably operate at a cost disadvantage with respect to domestic suppliers, if only because of its lack of familiarity with local market conditions. It follows that a firm establishing some sort of operation in a foreign market must possess a special advantage—based on product differentiation, operating efficiency, R&D competence—that compensates for its disadvantages in the foreign market.

Licensing a foreign firm or establishing a joint venture with a foreign partner are ways of dealing with informational problems. But they open the door to a variety of contracting problems, of the kind discussed in Chapter 6.

If the entering firm really does have an advantage, then at the moment it sets up a foreign arrangement, it is likely to have a choice among several local partners. Competition between the local partners will ensure that the balance of bargaining power lies with the licensing firm, that is to say, that it will be able to strike a bargain that allows it to appropriate most of the profit generated by exploiting its strategic assets in the foreign market.

Once a partner is selected and the project gets underway, the licensing firm will make a variety of sunk investments as part of its contribution to the licensing arrangement or joint venture. These sunk investments will lock it into a bilateral arrangement with the foreign partner. As the project develops, the balance of bargaining power will shift from the licensing firm to the foreign partner. The information advantage that the local partner brings to the arrangement means that the licensing firm will not be able to easily evaluate the reports it receives from the foreign partner about the way operations are developing. This exposes the licensing firm to the possibility of opportunistic behaviour by its foreign partner. If a dispute about the interpretation of the licensing contract should arise, it would most likely be adjudicated in the export market, where the foreign partner would have a home court advantage.

Licensing or forming a joint venture can be optimal strategies if transportation cost and/or trade barriers are sufficiently high and if the value of the foreign partner's information is so great that it outweighs the risk of future profit losses due to opportunistic behaviour.

8.3.5 **Direct foreign investment**

Setting up a wholly-owned plant in the foreign market means the domestic firm engages in direct foreign investment and transforms itself from a national firm that sells on world markets into a multinational firm.

We can think of the sunk investments of the firm as falling into two categories:

- sunk costs of operating the corporate headquarters;
- sunk costs of production plants.

A firm that sets up a wholly-owned plant in a foreign market avoids not only transportation costs but also any quotas or tariffs that have been erected around the target market. It also benefits from some economies of scale, since production in a foreign plant means that corporate overhead costs are spread over a larger corporate output. But it incurs the additional sunk cost of setting up a foreign plant.

Direct foreign investment has strategic advantages in the overseas market. In Figure 8.9, E_0 shows the Cournot duopoly equilibrium in country 2 if firm 1 (based in country 1) chooses the export route for supplying country 2. Its marginal cost, $c + t + \tau$, includes unit transportation cost t and a tariff τ per unit of output sold in country 2. If firm 1 sets up a plant in country 2 instead of exporting, its marginal cost falls from $c + t + \tau$ to c per unit. With this reduction in unit cost, firm 1's best response curve on the country 2 market shifts out from the origin. Since best response curves slope downward when products are demand substitutes and firms set quantities, equilibrium shifts from E_0 to E_1, moving down along firm 2's best response curve. The strategic impact of firm 1's direct foreign investment is an output reduction by firm 2 that improves firm 1's situation on the country 2 market.

This strategic reaction is greater, the greater is transportation cost and the higher is the

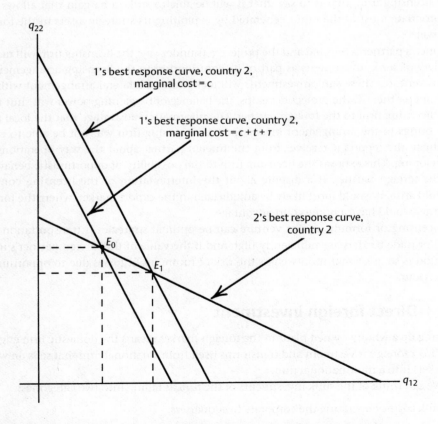

Fig. 8.9 Cournot duopoly equilibrium, country 2, export v. direct foreign investment

tariff rate. This creates the possibility of a long-run effect of trade barriers that may counteract their short-run protective effect.

Tariff-jumping DFI

We have seen that the impact of a quota or a tariff, taking market structure as given, is to protect the home firms of the country imposing the barrier from foreign competition. But in the long run, market structure is not given, and trade barriers may induce changes in market structure that work against the interests of domestic firms. Tariffs and quotas increase the profitability of direct foreign investment relative to exporting. If tariffs are high enough or quotas sufficiently restrictive, foreign firms may find that tariff-jumping direct foreign investment becomes the most profitable way of selling on the protected market (Problem 8–8). Such direct foreign investment makes the market more competitive. This is likely to benefit consumers in the target market, but it will leave the original domestic firms with lower profits.

Automobile industry transplants

Tariff- and quota-jumping direct foreign investment has indeed taken place in the world automobile industry. Restrictions on imports into European markets increased the incentives of Japanese firms to set up plants in the EC.[12] The presence of the plants increases rivalry in the host country markets. They also increase pressure on native firms to adapt and adopt high-productivity Japanese methods, and they alter traditional labour-management relations. These changes would have taken place without import restrictions, but at a slower pace.

8.3.6 Exports v. DFI: substitutes or complements?

From a static viewpoint, exporting and direct foreign investment appear to be alternative strategies: a firm will choose either one or the other, but not both. In a dynamic sense, the two approaches may be complements rather than substitutes. Many of the costs associated with direct foreign investment stem from imperfect information. Exporting can be a way to get information about a market before undertaking direct foreign investment (Veugelers, 1991). Exporting manufactured goods may also stimulate direct foreign investment in servicing, distribution, and finance operations that facilitate the marketing of the exported goods in the foreign market.

This seems particularly to have been the case with Japanese direct foreign investment in both the United States and Europe. Yamawaki (1991), for example, finds a mutually reinforcing relationship between Japanese exports to the United States and Japanese direct foreign investment in distribution activities.[13] His results also indicate that there are lower levels of Japanese exports and greater Japanese direct foreign investment in distribution for US industries that have high levels of research and development, which is consistent with the "special advantage" theory of direct foreign investment.

---

[12] Voluntary export restrictions had the same effect in the US.
[13] See also Wilkens (1990).

> *Direct foreign investment*: DFI is encouraged by high transport costs, tariffs, and other trade barriers, and by agency problems that make licensing of joint ventures risky. DFI normally improves market performance, leaving local consumers better off and reducing the profit of domestic firms.

8.3.7 Hysteresis

"Hysteresis" describes situations in which short-run phenomena have long-run effects, effects that persist even if the short-run phenomena reverse themselves.[14] In the present context, short-run exchange rate fluctuations may alter the entry decision of foreign suppliers, leading to changes in market structure and therefore in market performance that persist even if the exchange rate fluctuations are themselves only temporary.

If a firm decides to set up a plant in an overseas market, it commits itself to paying the fixed and sunk costs that go with setting up that plant. Some of these costs will be incurred in the home market—in particular, information processing costs associated with making decisions about the new plant. But many of the material costs will arise in the foreign market, with the result that in terms of the currency of the investing firm, the size of fixed costs changes with exchange rate fluctuations.

In terms of the previous example, if the euro-dollar exchange rate e rises the dollar is worth more in terms of the euro, reducing the dollar cost to a US-based firm of setting up a plant in Europe. As we have seen (in discussion of Figure 8.7(b)), a higher e also reduces the dollar value of the profit that is earned in the European market. The net impact of an increase in the value of the dollar on the foreign direct investment decision may be in either direction.

If the euro depreciates enough, direct foreign investment will become the most profitable choice for US firms.[15] If direct foreign investment occurs, the US firm will make a sunk investment in the European market. Once that sunk investment has been made, the US firm would not immediately withdraw from the market if the value of the dollar should fall relative to the euro—if e should decline. The US firm would withdraw from the European market if revenue earned there could not cover variable costs incurred there.[16] Revenue in the European market would be entirely, and variable costs almost entirely, denominated in euros, and to that extent would be little influenced by exchange rate fluctuations. The change in market structure, induced by exchange-rate fluctuations, will last much longer than the exchange-rate fluctuations themselves.

---

[14] Following Dixit (1989). Ansic (1995) offers experimental support for the hysteresis hypothesis.

[15] In general terms, this would occur when the exchange rate e has risen so much that it is profitable for US firms to invest abroad, and that further increases in e are unlikely; see Dixit and Pindyck (1994).

[16] Such withdrawals do occur. Volkswagen, which set up production in the US market in 1974, withdrew in 1989, citing among other factors high costs (Womak et al., 1990, p. 214).

8.4 **Summary**

The imperfectly competitive nature of international markets raises the possibility that a country can improve its own welfare through policies that allow its firms to earn greater monopoly profits in foreign markets. The conditions that must be satisfied to realize this result are stringent, and seem unlikely to be realized in practice. If foreign countries respond to strategic trade policies by adopting their own similar policies, the overall effect is to leave all trading parties worse off.

Strategic interactions in imperfectly competitive markets result in price and output changes that partially neutralize the effects of exchange rate movements. Exchange rates fluctuations are therefore only partially passed on to changes in domestic prices.

A variety of strategies are open to firms that supply international markets. Export exposes such firms to the risk that foreign governments will raise protective trade barriers. Licensing a foreign partner leaves the international firm open to the possibility of opportunistic behaviour once it has committed sunk investments to the local operation.

Tariffs and quotas give domestic producers short-run protection from foreign competition; they typically make consumers in the protected market worse off. Over the long run, tariffs and quotas may induce trade barrier-jumping foreign direct investment, eliminating their short-run protective effect.

Study points

- export subsidies (pages 160–5)
- tariffs and quotas (pages 166–9)
- import protection and export promotion (page 168)
- partial exchange rate passthrough in imperfectly competitive markets (pages 170–3)
- concentration effect of intraindustry trade (pages 173–4)
- tariff-jumping direct foreign investment (page 179)
- hysteresis (page 180)

Problems

8-1 Firm 1, based in country 1, and firm 2, based in country 2, sell quantities q_1 and q_2, respectively, in country 3. The demand curve in country 3 is

$$p = a - (q_1 + q_2), \tag{8.5}$$

and sales in country 3 have no impact on the country 1 and country 2 markets. The marginal and average cost of production and transportation, c, is constant and the same for both firms.

(a) Find equilibrium outputs and profits in country 3 if there are no export subsidies.

(b) Find equilibrium outputs and profits in country 3 if country 1 grants its firm a subsidy s_1 per unit sold in country 3. What subsidy is best for country 1?

(c) Find equilibrium outputs and profits in country 3 if country 1 grants its firm a subsidy s_1 per unit sold and country 2 grants its firm a subsidy s_2 per unit sold in country 3. What are the equilibrium subsidies if the two countries set subsidy levels noncooperatively (that is, if each country sets the best possible subsidy level for itself, taking the subsidy level of the other country as given)?

8–2 Answer question 8–1 if products are differentiated, with inverse demand curves

$$p_1 = a - b(q_1 + \theta q_2)$$
$$p_2 = a - b(\theta q_1 + q_2) , \qquad\qquad (8.6)$$

with $0 \le \theta < 1$, and firms set prices rather than quantities.

8–3 Return to Problem 8–1. Initially, let transportation cost t equal 0.

(a) Analyze the impact of a quota $\bar{q}$ that restricts firm 2's sales in country 1 below the Cournot equilibrium level on outputs, prices, profits, and net social welfare in country 1.

(b) Return to the model without a quota and with $t > 0$, but now interpret t as a tariff collected by country 1 on each unit of output sold by firm 2 in country 1. What is the impact of the tariff on country 1's net social welfare?

8–4 Let there be two countries with identical demand curves, each home to one widget producer. The subscript 1 denotes both country 1 and its widget company; similarly for the subscript 2. Let the inverse demand curves in the two countries be

$$p_1 = a - (q_{11} + q_{21})$$
$$p_2 = a - (q_{12} + q_{22}), \qquad\qquad (8.7a)$$

where p_1 is the price in country 1, p_2 is the price in country 2, and q_{ij} is the quantity of widgets sold by firm i in country j, for $i, j = 1, 2$. The parameter a is the price-axis intercept of the inverse demand curves, which are the same in both countries. The slope of the inverse demand curves is -1.

Let the cost function be

$$c(q_{i1} + q_{i2}) = \alpha(q_{i1} + q_{i2}) - \tfrac{1}{2}\beta(q_{i1} + q_{i2})^2 , \qquad\qquad (8.8)$$

where α and β are both positive and β is sufficiently small that marginal cost remains positive over the relevant output range. Assume there are no transportation costs or tariffs.

(a) write out the payoff functions of the two firms.

(b) find the first-order conditions to maximize the payoffs and solve them for equilibrium outputs.

(c) substitute equilibrium outputs for country 2 in the equations of the first-order conditions for country 1 outputs, and interpret the resulting expressions as equilibrium best response functions for country 1.

(d) Suppose now that country 1 imposes a quota that restricts the country 2 firm's sales in country 1 to a level $\bar{q}$ that is below the equilibrium level from (b). Find the new equilibrium outputs; describe the new equilibrium in terms of movements in the equilibrium best response functions.

8–5 (Concentration effect of trade) Suppose there are two identical countries, each with demand curve

$$p = a - bQ, \tag{8.9}$$

(where Q is total sales in the country) and that firms in each country operate with the cost function

$$c(q) = cq + F, \tag{8.10a}$$

where c is constant marginal cost, q is firm output, and F is fixed and sunk cost. Assume that firms behave as Cournot oligopolists.

  (a) What is the long-run equilibrium number of firms in each country if trade between the two countries is not possible?

  (b) Suppose trade opens up between the two countries (and for simplicity, assume there are no transportation costs or tariffs). What is the profit of each firm, after trade, if the number of firms in each country is the long-run equilibrium number of firms from (a)?

  (c) What is the long-run equilibrium number of firms (in both countries) after trade opens up?

  (b) What is the long-run number of firms if the two countries form a single market?

8–6 (Exchange rate passthrough, quantity-setting firms) Let markets for the same product in two different countries have the inverse demand curves (8.2).

  Let firm 1 be based in country 1 and firm 2 in country 2. Call the constant unit cost of firm 1 c_1 dollars and the constant unit cost of firm 2 c_2 euros. Let the exchange rate e be the number of euros required to buy a dollar on world currency markets. Assume firms compete by selecting outputs, and each firm exports to the other market if it is profitable to do so.

  (a) Find the equations of the quantity best response functions of each firm for each country.

  (b) Find equilibrium outputs in each country and discuss the way they are affected by changes in e.

  (c) Find equilibrium price in each country and discuss how they are affected by changes in e.

  (d) Compare the impact of exchange rate fluctuations with changes in

(i) a specific tariff t per unit paid by the country 2 firm on each unit of output sold in country 1;

(ii) an ad valorem tariff τ, a fraction of the country 1 price paid by the country 2 firm on each unit of output sold in country 1.

  Note: it is sufficient to write out the expression for firm 2's payoff in country 1 with a specific and alternatively an ad valorem tariff.

8–7 (Exchange rate passthrough, price-setting firms) Suppose that products are differentiated, with inverse demand curves

$$\begin{aligned}
p_{11} &= a_1 - b_1(q_{11} + \theta_1 q_{21}) \\
p_{21} &= a_1 - b_1(\theta_1 q_{11} + q_{21})
\end{aligned} \tag{8.11}$$

in country 1 and

$$p_{12} = a_2 - b_2(q_{12} + \theta_2 q_{22})$$
$$p_{22} = a_2 - b_2(\theta_2 q_{12} + q_{22})$$
(8.12)

in country 2. Assume firms compete by selecting prices, and each firm exports to the other market if it is profitable to do so. Let other aspects of the model be as in Problem 8-6.

(a) Find the equations of the price best response functions of each firm for each country.

(b) Find equilibrium prices in each country and discuss the way they are affected by changes in e.

Chapter 9

Trade policy and competition policy

And doleful dumps the mind oppress.

  Romeo and Juliet, Act IV, scene 5.

9.1 Introduction

Rivalry between domestic and foreign firms inevitably occurs in somebody's home market, raising the question of public policy toward such rivalry and more generally of the overlap between trade policy and competition policy.

A declared goal of EC competition policy is to make market performance as close to perfect competition as possible, subject to the constraints imposed by the overriding goal of promoting integration. The EC is also party to international agreements that commit it to a regime of free trade. Yet the evidence suggests that when trade policy and competition policy overlap, protectionist instincts emerge that lead the EC to circumvent its commitment to free trade and, in so doing, to adopt policies that not only distort trade on world markets but also worsen market performance within the EC.[1]

9.2 Export cartels

In most countries, competition policy forbids collusion. When consumers and producers are both from the same economy, collusion affects their interests in opposite ways, and the usual policy position is to resolve this conflict in favour of consumers.

---

[1] The EC is not distinctive in this respect; most other industrialized countries pursue a similarly schizoid policy mix.

From the point of view of national welfare, the conflict between producer and consumer welfare evaporates when the producers are located in the domestic market and the consumers are located in a foreign market. Perhaps for this reason, competition policy is often not hostile to collusion when it targets foreign markets. Here we analyze the welfare consequences of export cartels and examine how policy toward export cartels has been implemented.

9.2.1 Theory

An export cartel allows firms to eliminate competition among themselves, and this elimination of competition tends to reduce their combined sales on foreign markets. An export cartel may also allow firms to share the fixed costs of supplying a foreign market, increasing efficiency and therefore tending to increase sales on foreign markets. The net impact of an export cartel on the level of exports is therefore ambiguous.

If exports are reduced, price on the foreign market will rise. The amount of the increase will depend on the reactions of foreign firms to a reduction in exports. If the price increase is large enough, exporters' profits may rise, tending to increase the welfare of the exporting country. However, overt collusion on export markets may also facilitate tacit collusion on the home market. This will tend to reduce the welfare of the exporting country. The net effect of an export cartel on national welfare is therefore ambiguous as well.

Market power

Domestic suppliers only, no home-market effects An export cartel is socially beneficial in the context of the first model we used to discuss strategic export subsidies. Suppose two identical domestic firms are the only suppliers to a foreign market of a product that is not consumed in their home market. If they compete as quantity-setting Cournot duopolists, in equilibrium they each earn duopoly profit. If they are allowed to collude and maximize joint profit, then together they earn monopoly profit. Monopoly profit cannot be less than duopoly profit, and will in general be greater. Collusion on the export market will leave the two firms better off. Since the product is not consumed in their home market, there is no negative impact on home-market consumers. The export cartel thus leaves the home country of the two firms unambiguously better off.

International oligopoly, no home-market effects Leaving all other elements of the model the same, suppose now that there is a third firm that supplies the product, identical to the first two but based in the foreign market.[2] The result for this case, illustrated in Figure 9.1, differs from the previous one because of the way the equilibrium output of the third firm changes because of the export cartel.

If the two domestic firms form a cartel, they export less for any output level of the firm or firms outside the cartel than they would if they acted independently.

This is shown in Figure 9.1, where the "domestic firm" best response function shows

---

[2] It is not essential to the analysis that follows that the third firm be based in the export market. It could be based in the same market as the other two; it could be based in a third market. It is sufficient that the third firm not join the export cartel, but acts independently.

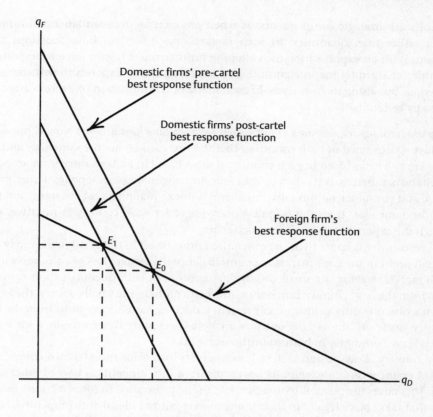

Fig. 9.1 Export cartel and Cournot triopoly reaction functions, export market

output per domestic firm when the two domestic firms produce identical output levels. This does not change the final result (see Problem 9–1), since the two domestic firms produce identical output levels in equilibrium, and it permits us to draw the best response functions on a two-dimensional graph. Formation of an export cartel means that the two firms produce less than they would with independent (noncooperative) output decisions; the best response function of domestic firms on the export market shifts inward.

When firms set quantities and products are demand substitutes, firms' choice variables are strategic substitutes: the reduction in output by colluding firms increases the marginal profitability of foreign firms, and they expand output. Equilibrium shifts from E_0 to E_1, moving up along the foreign firm best response function. Because domestic firms form a cartel, the firm that is outside the cartel takes a larger share of the market.

Unless domestic firms have a very large share of the export market, the reaction of foreign firms will typically mean that cartel members earn a lower profit after forming the cartel. When firms' choice variables are strategic substitutes, the presence of rivals outside the export cartel reduces, and may well eliminate, any incremental profit generated by the cartel.

The presence of suppliers outside the cartel has the opposite effect if firms' choice variables are strategic complements, as when products are differentiated and firms set prices rather than quantities. In such markets, price best response functions slope upward. With an export cartel, the colluding firms charge a higher price in response to any price charged by the foreign firm, and the foreign firm responds to this change in behaviour by raising its own price. In such markets, the formation of export cartels will generally be profitable.

Domestic consumption, duelling export cartels (and duelling jurisdictions) Now suppose the product is consumed in both countries, that the two markets are the same size, and that there are two firms based in each country. If firms based in each country form an export cartel, the national markets change from four-firm oligopolies to duopolies. Firms' profits go up, and consumer surplus falls. If demand is linear, marginal cost constant, and markets the same size, then the overall welfare effect for each country is negative, even though the export cartels leave firms better off.

If one country is larger than the other, then firms based in the small market may earn enough profit in the large market to counterbalance the welfare loss of consumers in the small market, leaving the small country better off even with duelling export cartels. If firms from the large country earn only a little extra profit in the small country, they could be left worse off with duelling export cartels. If duelling cartels leave firms from the large country worse off, the large country as a whole is certainly worse off, since the export cartels leave consumers in both countries worse off.

If a country allows export cartels, it exempts its own firms from its own competition laws. A country cannot exempt its own firms from the competition laws of other countries. This raises the possibility that firms might be prosecuted in foreign courts for conduct that takes place legally in their home market but has illegal anticompetitive effects on foreign markets. This happened in an early *Woodpulp* decision,[3] where producers' actions as part of an export cartel that was legal under US law were prosecuted as a concerted action in violation of Article 81 of the EC Treaty.

One country may also change its own competition law in reaction to a legal export cartel formed by firms from another country. For example, the UK changed its antimonopoly law to allow its sulphur producers to combine so they could bargain more effectively with an export cartel of US firms.

Domestic consumption, noncooperative collusion That competition policy allows domestic firms to overtly collude with respect to sales on foreign markets does not mean that export cartels have no implications for domestic market performance.[4] Explicit collusion on foreign sales may facilitate tacit collusion on the domestic market.

It is usually profitable in the short run for a firm to cheat on a collusive output pattern and expand output if all other firms restrict output. If all other firms restrict output, price is high, and the incremental profit to be gained by selling a little bit more than one is supposed to is great. If a firm persists in restricting output, despite the short-run profit that could be gained by defecting from a tacitly collusive output level, it must be because it expects that once other firms realize it has expanded output, they will expand output as

---

[3] *A. Ahlström Oy and others* v. *EC Commission* [1988] 4 CMLR 901 at 934.
[4] See also Auquier and Caves (1979).

well, leaving it worse off in the long run. If the present discounted value of the profit lost after other firms react is greater than the short-run profit that is gained by expanding output, firms will voluntarily select output levels that lead to collusive outcomes, although they are not obliged to do so (and although they are not colluding in a legal sense).

The essential element of models of noncooperative collusion is the trading off of the future profit that is lost once rivals realize that some firm has defected against the short-run profit that results from defecting. With this tradeoff in mind, what are the implications of the existence of a legal export cartel for the sustainability of tacit collusion on the domestic market? If firms form an export cartel, it is because they expect the cartel to raise their individual profits. This means that if the export cartel ends, the profit of individual firms goes down. It follows that the threat to break up a legal export cartel if tacit *domestic* collusion collapses can be used as part of the punishment strategy that makes single firms decide, in their own self-interest, to restrict output and raise price on the domestic market. The existence of export cartels makes it more likely that firms will be able to reach collusive outcomes (without colluding in a legal sense) on domestic markets.

If formation of an export cartel allows member firms to sustain noncooperative or tacit collusion on their home market, they will earn greater profits, but the welfare of domestic consumers will be reduced. In such cases, an essential element in the rationale for allowing export cartels, that they do not reduce the welfare of domestic consumers, fails.

Efficiency

An export cartel restricts sales on the foreign market, hoping to raise price. If there are increasing returns to scale, this output reduction means an increase in average cost. All else equal, this will translate into higher prices for domestic consumers, and reduced competitivity on foreign markets. Once again, the premise behind allowing export cartels—that there is no harm to domestic consumers—fails.

If there are constant returns to scale, formation of an export cartel does not affect the cost of producing for the domestic market. If there are decreasing returns to scale, then a reduction in output reduces unit cost, implying a cost saving on production for the domestic market.

In the same way, if learning by doing is important, then domestic interests are served by policies that increase output on foreign markets, not by policies that restrict such output. If an export cartel succeeds in restricting output and raising price on foreign markets, it will reduce the rate at which it accumulates knowledge and worsen technological performance at home and abroad.

9.2.2 Practice

The EC

The EC Treaty gives the European Community the responsibility and the authority to police trade among the Member States. As a matter of principle, therefore, the Article 81 prohibition of agreements and concerted practices that distort trade *within the common market* does not reach pure export cartels.

But EC competition policy is sceptical toward the possibility that firms could cooperate intimately with respect to export markets without having that cooperation also distort competition in the common market. This attitude is consistent with the economic theory of tacit collusion.

A leading Commission decision, *CSV*,[5] involved a joint sales agency and export cartel of Dutch fertilizer producers. CSV was a wholly owned subsidiary of two firms. One of these was the largest nitrogen-based fertilizer producer in the EC; the other was the leading world manufacturer of urea, an important input in the production of fertilizers. CSV allocated market shares within the Netherlands and outside the EC; it provided its parent firms with regular demand predictions for those markets. The parent firms provided CSV with detailed information about their inventories and their production plan. The parent firms' sales in the Netherlands and outside the EC, with minor exceptions, were made only through CSV. Representatives of the parent firms received regular reports comparing actual and predicted sales for the various markets.

CSV's activities were carried out under the supervision of a steering committee made up of representatives of both parent firms; the steering committee met monthly with CSV management.

For the European Commission, it was inevitable that these exchanges of information would affect the common market (§70):

decisions concerning the quantity or prices of products sold in one Member State can have repercussions not only in that Member State but in others too. Despite the parties' assertions it seems quite predictable that, faced with an unstable market, they should use their information exchange scheme to improve the coordination of their sales policies on other EEC markets.

The essential notion of noncooperative collusion, that the parent firms would hold off from hard competition in the common market to protect the profits they expected to inherit from the joint sales agency, also appeared in the Commission's decision (§68):

[The parent firms] must inevitably refrain from competing with one another on markets not included in their pooling arrangements in order to safeguard the joint sales policy they pursue through CSV.

The Commission concluded that CSV was the vehicle for concerted practices by the parent firms, that the concerted practices restricted trade within the common market, and that the arrangements had an appreciable effect on trade within the common market. The concerted practices were therefore inconsistent with the common market and in violation of the EC Treaty.

As a general rule, export cartels formed by EC firms are likely to be disapproved by the European Commission unless the market shares of the firms involved makes the likelihood of distortion of competition seem minimal.

---

[5] Commission Decision of 20 July 1978 OJ No L 242/15 4 September 1978. The full name of the joint sales agency was Centraal Stikstof Verkoopkantoor BV.

Japan

Japan's competition and industrial policy gives greater latitude to interfirm cooperation than either US antitrust policy or EC competition policy. This applies to export cartels as well. The Export and Import Trading Act of 1952 states:[6]

The purpose of this Act is to prevent unfair export trading and to establish order in export and import trading, and thereby to promote the sound development of foreign trade.

The Act provides that agreements must be notified to MITI, the Ministry of International Trade and Industry. It also requires that an export cartel not injure the interest of importers or enterprises at the destination; this provision would be quite restrictive if it were strictly interpreted, since there is a sense in which exports must injure firms in the destination market.

The Act also provides that export agreements should not restrict the possibilities of participation or withdrawal. This seems desirable, from the point of view of market performance. But the effect of this provision is weakened by the fact that the Minister of International Trade and Industry may issue orders that are binding on non-members of the export cartel.

A Fair Trade Commission interpretive memorandum of August 9, 1972 suggests that a Japanese export cartel cannot enter into agreements with non-Japanese producers without violating the Antimonopoly Law. Under some circumstances, Japanese firms may exchange information with foreign firms, and such instances are judged on a case by case basis.

Dick (1992b, 1993) reports empirical tests of Japanese export cartels.[7] He finds little evidence for effects of export cartels on export prices or volume.

The US

The Webb-Pomerene Act The US has a long history of a Mercantilist approach to cooperation by US firms on export markets, and there is little evidence that this approach accomplishes its stated goals or improves either export or domestic market performance.

The 1918 *Webb-Pomerene Act* allows US firms to collude with respect to export markets. Firms that exercise this option are obliged to register with the Federal Trade Commission. The law provides that cartel actions are permitted on the condition that they do not lessen competition on the US market. Further, an export cartel cannot restrict the export trade of a US firm that is not a member, and it cannot cooperate with foreign firms to restrict competition on world markets.

Motivation The Congress that passed the Webb-Pomerene Act was not (at least, not openly) motivated by the idea that the Act would make the US better off by allowing US firms to more effectively exercise market power in foreign markets. The stated rationale was defensive, to allow US firms to combine and bargain more effectively with large foreign buyers.

There was concern over the relative bargaining power of US and foreign firms because of cases, well known at the time, in which a product's price was lower in the foreign

---

[6] The translation is by Iyori and Uesugi (1983).
[7] See also Jacquemin et al. (1981).

market than in the US market. For example, copper mined in the US and sold both in the US and Germany had a lower price on the German market.

But a lower price need not mean that powerful buyers on foreign markets bargained for a lower price. It could just as well mean that the foreign market was more competitive than the US market, with the result that US firms charged a lower price in the German market because their most profitable price on the German market was lower than their most profitable price on the US market (Fournier, 1932, p. 19).[8]

Intended scope There is evidence in the legislative record that Congress intended the Webb-Pomerene Act to apply to joint selling agencies, which would generate the afore-mentioned increase in bargaining power and which might also result in cost savings and efficiency gains. But the 1924 "Silver Letter" of the Federal Trade Commission, so-called because it was issued in response to an inquiry from a group of silver producers, held that the Webb-Pomerene Act also applied to associations that fixed export prices and allocated export sales, without any combination of selling activities. Since that time, many Webb-Pomerene associations have operated as pure price-fixing groups, without any combination of exporting activity. This would seem to eliminate possible efficiency gains rooted in combination and rationalization of exporting operations.

Evidence Webb-Pomerene associations have been regularly studied, no doubt because the registration requirement permits identification of such cartels and facilitates the collection of data. They seem never to have accounted for a large part of US trade: less than 3 per cent of US merchandise trade in 1924, rising to 13.8 per cent in 1929 (Fournier, 1932). The increase was apparently related to the FTC's 1924 "Silver Letter", but it did not persist. In the first 50 years of the Act, Webb-Pomerene-related exports were 2.5 per cent of US exports (Dick, 1992a, p. 97).

Larson (1970) examines 47 Webb-Pomerene export associations that operated over the period 1958–62. Six of the 47 associations ran joint sales agencies, and thus had at least the potential to generate operating efficiencies. All of the associations with joint sales agencies were in concentrated industries, suggesting that their operation had more to do with the exercise of market power than with increasing bargaining power. Nine associations were price-fixing associations that also allocated export business; three others only fixed prices. The Webb-Pomerene associations included firms that were large in an absolute sense and were among the leading firms both in the US and the world.

Dick (1992a) examines the impact of 16 Webb-Pomerene cartels on market performance. He concludes that six of the 16 were efficiency generating, resulting in lower prices and expanded exports. Efficiency-enhancing cartels tended to occur in unconcentrated US industries and were made up of small firms that had a small share of world markets. These cartels often provided marketing and distribution services for members.

Two of the Webb-Pomerene cartels in the Dick sample (carbon black and crude sulphur) resulted in higher prices and reduced export volumes. Both were in concentrated industries, for which US firms were leading world suppliers.

On balance, the empirical evidence suggests that Webb-Pomerene cartels are not

---

[8] This possibility anticipates Section 9.4's discussion of dumping, where we will pursue the implications for prices of different degrees of rivalry in different markets.

formed very often, that those which are formed have little effect on export markets, and that those effects are what would be predicted based on domestic market structure: Webb-Pomerene cartels formed by large firms in concentrated industries facilitate the exercise of market power, Webb-Pomerene cartels formed by small firms in unconcentrated industries, and which involve the combination of export operations, generate efficiency gains.

An interpretation consistent with both theory and empirical evidence is that Webb-Pomerene cartels are not formed very frequently because

- they do not facilitate collusion on export markets very much, since large firms in concentrated industries are likely to be able to tacitly collude in any event;
- they do not allow small firms in unconcentrated industries to generate much in the way of incremental efficiencies, since the force of competition in unconcentrated markets compels firms to attain reachable efficiencies in any event, or go out of business.

One explanation for the formation of Webb-Pomerene cartels that appear to have no effect on export markets is that their purpose is to facilitate collusion with respect to the domestic market. We have seen (Chapter 3) that an important effect of collusion is to relax the force of competition and make it more likely that less than completely efficient firms will survive. Amacher et al. (1978) report that Webb-Pomerene cartels tend to form in declining industries, and this is consistent with the view that such cartels help less efficient firms to survive.

The Foreign Trade Act and the Export Trading Act The Webb-Pomerene Act has been largely ineffective in promoting export trade because it is motivated by a theory that is incorrect for most US industries. There are few if any US industries for which export performance is poor because small US firms suffer from a weak bargaining position vis-à-vis foreign buyers. In 1982, the US Congress supplemented the Webb-Pomerene Act with two laws based on this same mistaken Mercantilist view of the economics of international markets. There is little reason to think that these laws will be effective in promoting US export performance.

The *Foreign Trade Act* requires that actions have a "direct, substantial, and reasonably foreseeable" effect on US domestic commerce or on US import/export trade before the Sherman Act can be applied. Conduct that would otherwise violate the Sherman Act does not do so if it affects only foreign markets. The *Export Trading Act* allows the Secretary of Commerce to issue a Certificate of Review to a trading entity that protects it from criminal liability and treble damages under state and federal antitrust laws. The Secretary of Commerce must consult with the Department of Justice before issuing such a certificate.

In its first nine years, 127 Certificates of Review were issued under the Export Trading Act, which at a minimum suggests a slow start. The fundamental problem, however, is that the Foreign Trade Act and the Export Trading Act, like the Webb-Pomerene Act, are based on a mistaken theory. All this legislation views vigorous competition policy and tough domestic competition as factors that hold back the performance of US firms on export markets, thus justifying the relaxation of antitrust policy toward business actions aimed at foreign markets. All evidence suggests the contrary, that tough domestic competition improves efficiency and performance on export markets. The risks of allowing cooperation are that if by small firms it will reduce their efficiency and competitiveness, and that if by large firms it will make it easier for them to tacitly collude for the domestic market.

> *Export cartels*: like other types of strategic trade policy, these may improve national welfare under relatively restrictive conditions. Export cartels may also enhance the likelihood of (tacit or overt) collusion on domestic markets.

9.3 **Voluntary export restraints**

Governments that wish to defend a commitment to free trade often find themselves in the situation of wishing also to cushion, over the short- or perhaps not so short-run, the competition from foreign suppliers that comes with free trade. There is a long history of resort, in such circumstances, to informal understandings, reached with the tacit or overt participation of foreign governments, under which foreign suppliers agree to limit their exports. Such *Voluntary Export Restraints* have been used in a variety of industries—particularly textiles and clothing, but also automobiles, machine tools, steel, video cassette recorders, and others.[9]

Innovative Japanese methods of organizing production gave Japanese firms productivity advantages that made them formidable rivals on world markets in the automobile industry in the 1980s. As it happens, these productivity advantages were developed behind the protection of a variety of trade barriers, including tariffs (Table 9.1) and

Table 9.1 Japanese tariffs (per cent) on imported cars.

	Small Cars	Large Cars
1955	40.0	35.0
1965	40.0	35.0
1967	40.0	28.0
1968	36.0	28.0
1969	36.0	17.5
1970	20.0	17.5
1971	10.0	10.0
1972	6.4	6.4
1978	0.0	0.0

Source: US General Accounting Office, *US – Japan Trade, Issues and Problems*. September 1979, pp. 42 and 44, reproduced in Hadley (1984, p. 326).

[9] See Greenaway and Hindley (1985), Kostecki (1987), and Wolf (1991).

currency controls. These formal trade barriers were dismantled as Japan assumed its place among leading industrial nations.

The emergence of Japanese automobile manufacturers on world markets resulted, in turn, in the imposition of protective barriers—formal and informal—around Japan's export markets. Some of these barriers are described in Table 9.2.

The restrictions often took the form of "voluntary" limits agreed to by Japanese firms under pressure that came directly from the governments of export markets and indirectly from foreign firms and labour unions.[10]

The European Union took the view that the country-by-country limits to Japanese sales in individual EC Member States shown in Table 9.2 were in conflict with the 1992 Single Market programme. The EC therefore negotiated a far-from-transparent accord under which Japanese exports to the EC as a whole would be limited over the period 1993–99. Restraints were justified on the ground that they would allow EC producers to prepare themselves for effective competition in a fully open single market; part of the understanding was that the EC automobile market would be fully open to Japanese suppliers from the year 2000 onward.

The level of Japanese sales in the EC was initially set at 1.2 million cars a year. The agreement also provided that the ceiling on sales would be reevaluated regularly in the light of market conditions. Such reevaluations have in fact taken place, and pressure from EC producers is generally to reduce the ceiling.

The overall ceiling on Japanese sales was allocated across EC Member States. In general, the effect of this allocation was to permit greater Japanese sales in Member States that had previously had very low limits, and to reduce sales somewhat in other Member States.

One difficult point in the implementation of the agreement has been the treatment of vehicles produced by Japanese firms at plants located in the EC. Japanese automakers take the view that such vehicles are not covered by the agreement, while native EC

Table 9.2 Restrictions on Japanese imports, by country, 1992.

Country	Trade barrier	Japanese share, 1992 (%)
France	Limited historically to 3%	4.1
Germany	No restrictions	14.1
Italy	3,000 cars as direct imports	2.7
Netherlands	No restrictions	27.0
Spain	No imports	3.7
Sweden	No restrictions	29.7
Switzerland	No restrictions	30.0
United Kingdom	Imports limited to 11%	12.3
United States	Imports limited to 1.7 million	31.4

Source: "Motor vehicles" in EC Commission *Panorama of EU Industry 1994*. Brussels–Luxembourg 1996, pp. 11–15

[10] The very strict limit on sales of Japanese cars in Italy originated in a 1952 reciprocal agreement that was sought by Japan, which wished to limit the sale of small Italian cars in Japan (de Melo and Messerlin, 1988, p. 1529). For further discussion of Japanese VERs, see El-Agraa (1995).

automakers have argued that the limits apply to all automobiles produced by Japanese firms, regardless of the location of production.

Another difficult point in the implementation of the agreement has been the shipment of imported Japanese vehicles from one EC Member State to another. One the one hand, it is the essence of a single market that such shipments should be possible. On the other hand, cross-border shipments defeat the purpose of the agreement allocating permitted sales across Member States.

9.3.1 Quality upgrading

Voluntary export restraints typically take the form of an agreed number of units that may be sold in the protected market. When products are differentiated in terms of quality, as is almost always the case to some extent, quantity limits create an incentive for foreign suppliers to shift their product range to the high-profit, and this usually means high-quality, end of the market.

de Melo and Messerlin (1988) estimate quality indexes for Japanese automobiles sold in France in the early 1980s, a period when VERs limited the number of Japanese vehicles sold on the French market. They find that the quality index rose 29 per cent between 1981 and 1983, and a further 6 per cent between 1983 and 1985. Over the same periods, the value of Japanese cars sold in France rose 31 per cent and 6 per cent respectively. Under the constraint of VERs, Japanese firms limited the number of Japanese vehicles sold on the French automobile market, but they also concentrated those sales in the most profitable segment of the market.

9.3.2 Trade diversion

If the world were bilateral—one exporting country, one importing country—then VERs would benefit firms in the protected market, as exporting rivals restrict output and raise price in the importing market. Of course, the rivals benefit as well: from their point of view, the government of the importing country is establishing and enforcing a collusive agreement for them, an agreement that would normally be considered to violate competition policy if carried out by private firms on their own initiative.

In a multilateral world, however, some of the benefit of VERs will go to firms based in third countries. For example, Smith (1990) presents simulation results suggesting that one result of Japanese VERs for the French auto market was a larger share of the French market for German producers. In the same way, Dinopoulos and Kreinin (1988) present evidence that one consequence of Japanese VERs for the US auto market was higher prices for European vehicles sold in the US.

It seems, therefore, that VERs often act to shift sales from foreign firms that are covered by the VER to foreign firms that are not covered by the VER, not to increase the sales of domestic firms. Such trade diversions make VERs less effective as a protective device. They also reduce the consumer welfare loss caused by VERs.

9.3.3 **Welfare consequences**

de Melo and Messerlin (1988) estimate that French VERs for motor vehicles resulted in a welfare loss for France of approximately 320 million FF, while preserving at most 324 jobs in the French automobile industry.

Takacs and Winters (1991) analyze the impact of British VERs on footwear imports from Korea and Taiwan in the late 1970s and 1980s. They estimate that the VERs in place in 1979 caused an annual loss of consumers' surplus of £79 million and increased UK industry profit by £22 million, for an annual welfare loss of £57 million. Against this loss, they estimate that the VERs may have preserved jobs for as many as 1,064 workers and avoided labour market adjustment costs of £9.6 million.

Smith and Venables (1991) estimate the consequences of various changes in EC auto industry VERs. Their calculations suggest that removal of the French VER described in Table 9.2 would have given French consumers an increase in consumers' surplus equivalent to about 6 per cent of their spending on motor vehicles. At the same time, if the French VER had been removed, European auto producers would have suffered lost profits equal to almost half of the gain in consumers' surplus. The net welfare effect of removing the VER would have been positive.

Smith and Venables also estimate that if all EC VERs were removed, the result would be a net welfare gain of about 3 per cent of the value of EC motor vehicle sales. They estimate that if country-by-country VERs were replaced by an EC VER that left the overall level of Japanese sales in the EC unchanged,[11] the result would be to increase Japanese sales and improve market performance in Member States that previously had strict limits on imports, but to reduce Japanese sales in EC Members States that had been relatively open to imports. An EC VER benefits Japanese firms, which are able to reallocate sales across EC Member States to their own greater profit.

In the US, a VER limited sales of Japanese cars to 1.68 million vehicles per year beginning April 1981. This was increased to 1.85 million cars per year from April 1984 and to 2.3 million cars per year from 1985. The VER was continued by MITI (the Ministry of International Trade and Industry) at least through 1987–88. Feenstra (1988) estimates that by 1984 price increases due to the quota were over $1000 per vehicle. He also estimates incremental profits to retailers and producers of Japanese cars at $2 billion per year in 1983 and 1984, with an additional loss of consumers' surplus of around $300 million per year.

Dinopoulos and Kreinin (1988, p. 490) estimate that each US job saved in 1981 and 1982 because of the VER cost the US over $180,000 in lost welfare, at a time when the average annual wage in the automobile industry was around $35,000 (see also Crandall, 1984).

9.3.4 **VERs and the WTO Agreements**

The ground rules of international trade are laid out in the World Trade Organization Agreements. The WTO Agreements, reached in 1994 and effective from January 1, 1995, were the product of the seven-year long Uruguay Round of multilateral trade

---

[11] At least approximately, this is the policy that has been adopted.

negotiations. They established the World Trade Organization to guide international trade flows and reaffirmed the commitment of WTO member states to free trade. As part of that commitment, member states agreed to phase out the use of VERs over a five-year period.[12] As we will see, the WTO Agreements permit policy measures that allow a member state to neutralize its commitment to free trade.

> *Voluntary export restraints*: informal trade barriers, solicited by governments committed to free trade and inducing foreign suppliers to restrict sales and raise price in ways that would be considered illegal collusion if carried out entirely by private agents.

9.4 **Dumping**

Dumping is traditionally said to occur if a foreign firm sells in its export markets at a price that is below its home market price, taking account of transportation cost and other differences in the cost (for example, tariffs or marketing and sales efforts) of serving the two markets. An increasingly common alternative definition treats dumping as the practice of selling in a foreign market at a price below some measure of the unit cost of production, whether or not prices are different in the home and export markets.

The theory of international trade in imperfectly competitive markets suggests that dumping in the sense of international price discrimination should not be a matter of concern. Unless different markets are identical in every way—numbers of firms, patterns of consumer tastes, income distributions—profit-maximizing firms will generally set different prices in different markets. Such price discrimination may be profitable, but it does not generally reduce welfare or worsen market performance. Dumping in the sense of price discrimination is a normal outcome of independent behaviour in imperfectly competitive markets.

Turning to the second definition of dumping, in the absence of learning-by-doing or similar effects, profit-maximizing firms will not sell at a price below marginal cost. There are any number of reasons why profit-maximizing firms might sell at a price below average cost over a short-run time period—for example, an unexpected decline in demand—but this too is normal when markets are imperfectly predictable.

Pricing below average or marginal cost might occur as part of a predatory strategy to achieve or maintain market dominance. In an international market where there is a foreign-based dominant firm, where there are barriers to entry and reentry, and where the foreign firm could expect to raise price so high after acquiring market control to make predation a profitable strategy, this might be a concern. There are, however, few

---

[12] VERs were to be eliminated within four years from the entry into effect of the WTO Agreements (that is, by January 1, 1999), with the possibility of maintaining one VER through 31 December 1999. The EU and Japan motor vehicle VER takes advantage of this possibility (Hindley and Messerlin, 1996, p. 56).

international markets that meet these conditions. Abusive behaviour by a foreign-based dominant firm would in any case fall under Article 82, and the European Commission has not hesitated to apply Article 82 against non-EC firms (see the final footnote of Chapter 5).

These arguments indicate that from the point of view of the economics of market performance in imperfectly competitive markets, there is little reason to be concerned with international price discrimination (which does not reduce welfare) or international predation (which is unlikely to occur). But concern with dumping is deeply rooted in the forums that determine the institutional framework for international trade. There seem to be two main types of reasons for this concern, or at least, two types of reasons that are openly stated.

It is often claimed that dumping should be a matter of policy concern because it is unfair. Very often the argument stops at that point. It is not made clear why dumping is unfair, or to whom. Usually, it is simply taken for granted that if conduct were fair (if dumping did not occur), welfare and market performance would be improved. None of these points survive careful analysis.

The unfairness argument often seems to be based on an incorrect model of international markets. Policymakers who express concern about dumping seem to have a vision of international trade in which their home markets are basically competitive, with domestic firms pricing at marginal and average cost and earning only normal ("fair") profits, while foreign markets are imperfectly competitive, supplied by foreign firms that have protected positions of market power from which they can sally forth with impunity, engaging in a variety of ("unfair") strategic schemes. It is difficult to make a rational case for concern with dumping if instead one begins from the premise that home and domestic markets are both imperfectly competitive.

9.4.1 **Dumping as price discrimination: reciprocal dumping**

The first definition of dumping focuses on price discrimination—the selling of identical goods at different net prices[13] in different markets. We will see that such price discrimination is the natural outcome of noncooperative profit-maximizing behaviour in imperfectly competitive markets. It follows that when antidumping policy condemns international price discrimination, it condemns the natural outcome of market processes in imperfectly competitive industries (Brander and Krugman, 1983).

Dumping in the sense of price discrimination occurs if a firm exports its product for a lower net price, after subtracting transportation and other (such as tariff) incremental costs of serving the export market, than the price in its home market.

Dumping in this sense is the natural consequence of profit-maximizing behaviour in imperfectly competitive markets. At a fundamental level, it has in common with the partial passthrough of exchange-rate changes (Section 8.2) the fact that firms with market power pass part of cost increases or higher costs on to consumers in the form of higher prices, but also absorb part of such increases or differences in the form of lower profit margins.

---

[13] Net, that is, of differences in the costs of serving the markets.

To see this, consider the case of two national markets, each with a single domestic producer that sells in both markets. Suppose that the two firms sell slightly differentiated varieties of the same product; this makes it possible to talk about the prices of specific goods in the same national market, as is common in the antidumping literature.

For simplicity, let the structure of demand be the same in both markets, with inverse demand curves in country 1

$$p_{11} = 100 - \tfrac{3}{4}q_{21} - q_{11} \qquad (9.1)$$

for firm 1 and

$$p_{21} = 100 - \tfrac{3}{4}q_{11} - q_{21} \qquad (9.2)$$

for firm 2.

Let both firms have the same technology: constant marginal production cost 10 per unit of output and transportation cost t per unit to ship a unit of output from one country to the other.

Figure 9.2 illustrates firm 2's price and sales decision for country 1 if it maximizes profit as a Cournot quantity-setting oligopolist.[14] For any level of sales of firm 1 on market 1 (q_{11}), firm 2's residual marginal revenue curve is

$$MR_{21} = 100 - \tfrac{3}{4}q_{11} - 2q_{21}. \qquad (9.3)$$

Taking firm 1's sales on market 1 as given, the sales level that maximizes firm 2's profit from country 1 is the q_{21} that makes marginal revenue from (9.3) equal to firm 2's marginal cost, $10 + t$:

$$100 - \tfrac{3}{4}q_{11} - 2q_{21} = 10 + t. \qquad (9.4)$$

If we solve (9.4) for q_{21}, we obtain the equation of firm 2's best response function, which gives firm 2's profit-maximizing sales level for any level of sales by firm 1:

$$q_{21} = \tfrac{1}{2}(90 - \tfrac{3}{4}q_{11} - t), \qquad (9.5)$$

The corresponding price is

$$p_{21} = 10 + \tfrac{1}{2}(90 - \tfrac{3}{4}q_{11} + t). \qquad (9.6)$$

Only half of unit transportation cost is passed on to the price of variety 2 in market 1. Just as the passthrough of exchange fluctuations to export prices is incomplete in imperfectly competitive markets (Section 8.2), so the passthrough of transportation and other export costs to export prices is typically incomplete. Because marginal revenue is less than price, and because a profit-maximizing firm sells where marginal revenue equals marginal cost, it will pass only a portion of unit cost differences into price differences.

If we proceed as we did in Chapter 2, solving the equations of the firms' best response functions for equilibrium outputs (see Problem 9–2), we find that equilibrium prices in country 1 are

$$p_{11} = 42\tfrac{8}{11} + \tfrac{12}{55}t \qquad p_{21} = 42\tfrac{8}{11} + \tfrac{23}{55}t. \qquad (9.7)$$

[14] We apply Chapter 2's discussion of Cournot duopoly to the context of international markets.

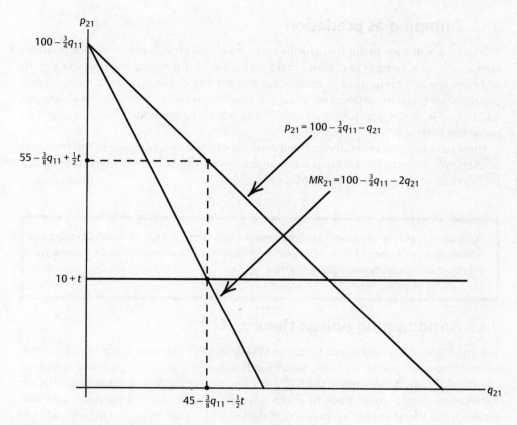

Fig. 9.2 Firm 2's price and sales decision, market 1

From (9.7), firm 2's net price in country 1, after subtracting unit transportation cost, is

$$p_{21} - t = 42\tfrac{8}{11} - \tfrac{32}{55}t. \tag{9.8}$$

As long as trade actually occurs, prices are above marginal production cost and both firms earn economic profits: in this example, p_{11} and $p_{21} - t$ are both greater than 10.

Because the countries are identical, in equilibrium $p_{22} = p_{11}$; then the difference between firm 2's price in country 2 and firm 2's net price in country 1 is

$$p_{22} - (p_{21} - t) = 42\tfrac{8}{11} + \tfrac{12}{55}t - (42\tfrac{8}{11} - \tfrac{32}{55}t) = \tfrac{4}{5}t \geq 0. \tag{9.9}$$

It follows that unless transportation cost is zero, when firm 2 independently maximizes its own profit, it is guilty of dumping.

Because we have used an example where the two national markets are identical, the same result holds for firm 1. As long as there are some differences in the unit cost of supplying imperfectly competitive export markets, dumping in the sense of net price discrimination is the normal outcome of independent, profit-maximizing behaviour in a market system.

9.4.2 **Dumping as predation**

The second definition of dumping focuses on predation. Few if any international markets appear to have structures that would make predation an interesting business strategy. In addition, few antidumping cases involve a dominant firm or group of firms: antidumping penalties are typically imposed on groups of small firms (often, based in less-developed countries). It is not plausible that such firms would either undertake or succeed in predatory schemes.[15]

There have been no generally accepted episodes of predatory dumping in international markets, and it seems unlikely that antidumping policy can be convincingly justified as a tool to combat international predation.

> *Dumping*: dumping as predation in international markets seems unlikely to occur. Dumping as international price discrimination is a normal consequence of independent profit-maximizing behaviour in imperfectly competitive markets.

9.4.3 **Antidumping policy: theory**

It is the General Agreement on Tariffs and Trade (GATT) that lays down rules for international trade in goods. In 1995, following the conclusion of the Uruguay Round of multilateral trade negotiations, the GATT became part of the World Trade Organization Agreements, which cover trade in goods, services, and intellectual property, and also establish the World Trade Organization as the permanent forum for the management of international trade flows.

The GATT commits the members of the World Trade Organization to free trade. We have seen (Section 9.3.4) that as part of the Uruguay Round, WTO members agreed to phase out the use of voluntary export restraints as a protective device. But the GATT allows protective measures if dumping occurs and causes or threatens material injury to domestic industries.[16]

Antidumping duties

An antidumping duty has the same effect as any other tariff. In the example of Section 9.4.1, if country 1 imposes an antidumping duty d on sales by firm 2, the resulting changes in equilibrium prices are less than the amount of the antidumping duty:

$$\Delta p_{11} = \tfrac{12}{55}d < d \qquad \Delta(p_{21} - t) = \tfrac{23}{55}d < d \tag{9.10}$$

(see Problem 9–3).

---

[15] In the US, the Antidumping Duty Act of 1916 controls dumping that is an attempt to monopolize. Before a finding of predatory dumping can be made under this law, it is necessary to show an intent to monopolize. Following the general development of US policy toward predation, it is also necessary to pass the recoupment test—to show that the predator firm(s) had the reasonable expectation of profitably raising price after injuring domestic firms. This law has been used extremely little, and no violation of the law has ever been found.

[16] The GATT also allows protective measures (countervailing duties) to neutralize subsidies to foreign suppliers.

An antidumping duty is essentially an artificial increase in firm 2's cost of supplying market 1. When firm 2's cost of supplying market 1 goes up, firm 2 reduces output somewhat, moving back and up along its marginal revenue curve until marginal revenue equals the now-higher marginal cost $(10 + t + d)$. Because of this movement up the marginal revenue curve, only part of the antidumping duty is passed along to consumers in the form of a higher p_{21}.

With an antidumping duty, firm 2 reduces its sales in country 1. This tends to increase p_{11} and p_{21}. Firm 1 reacts to firm 2's output reduction by expanding output (quantities are strategic substitutes, quantity best response curves are downward sloping) but the increase in firm 1's output is not so great that it reverses the upward increase in p_{11}.

Since firm 2's price increases by less than the amount of the antidumping duty, if country 1's government wished to impose a large enough duty to make firm 2's net price the same in the two markets (to make $p_{21} - t = p_{22}$), it would need to impose a duty that is greater than the price difference with an antidumping duty.

Undertakings

A foreign firm can avoid an antidumping duty if it charges the same net price in home and foreign markets. As our discussion of reciprocal dumping shows, profit maximization usually involves setting a lower net price in export markets, so setting the same net price in both markets will involve some sacrifice of profit. It will, however, avoid the payment of an antidumping duty to the government imposing protective measures. An undertaking to equalize net prices in this way is one of the avenues by which an EC antidumping procedure may be concluded.[17]

If the foreign firm undertakes to eliminate any difference in its net prices, it will generally change its prices in both markets, raising the net price in its export market (in our example, raising p_{21} by $\frac{2}{5}t$) but also lowering the price in its home market (reducing p_{22} by $\frac{2}{5}t$).

The increase in p_{21} makes firm 1 better off in country 1. The reduction in p_{22} makes firm 1 worse off in country 2. This means that the net benefit to firm 1 of an antidumping undertaking is less than the extra profit it earns in country 1.

With linear demand, constant marginal cost, and countries of the same size, an antidumping undertaking leaves each firm's total output unchanged (Problem 9–4). The antidumping undertaking causes a reallocation of sales, so that each firm sells more in its home market and less in its export market, but each firm produces the same total output as it would have produced without an antidumping undertaking.

Tacit collusion

If tacit collusion is to work, a firm that is tempted to defect from its part of an industry strategy that restricts overall output and allows greater economic profit to all firms must believe that such defection would result in such severe future punishment that defection is not profitable. Antidumping legislation gives domestic firms a credible way to have their government punish defection by foreign firms from a collusive output pattern.

---

[17] More than half of EU antidumping procedures between 1980 and 1987 ended in undertakings; since that time, the use of undertakings has declined and the use of duties has increased (Hindley and Messerlin, 1996, p. 40).

In one example of such official punishment, Hexner (1943, pp. 213–14) reports that in 1938 a publicly-owned South African steel firm, a member of the International Steel Cartel, complained to its government that US steel firms were dumping in South Africa. Antidumping duties were imposed for several months, then withdrawn.

Messerlin (1990) studies the systematic use of EC antidumping regulation (administered by DG Trade of the European Commission) by chemical industry firms that have themselves been fined for violating EC competition law (administered by DG Competition of the European Commission).[18] His case study evidence indicates that the opening of an antidumping investigation was sufficient to stabilize prices that had been going down, and that when the investigation was ended by an undertaking under which East European firms would end dumping, prices increased substantially. The estimated profits of EC firms due to successful collusion were substantially higher than the fines eventually paid by those same firms for colluding in violation of EC competition law.

The use of antidumping policy to enforce tacit collusion suggests that undertakings to end antidumping investigations result in outcomes under which foreign firms raise their prices in export markets even more than suggested by Section 9.4.3 and by Problem 9–4. Instead of behaving noncooperatively, subject to the constraint that they charge the same net price in both markets, foreign firms are likely to act in a way that is consistent with tacit collusion, restricting output because of the threat of punishment from government antidumping authorities.

9.4.4 EC antidumping policy: application

Under the World Trade Organization Agreements, a country may impose antidumping measures if dumping occurs and if dumping causes or threatens material injury to domestic industries. As it is administered, EC antidumping procedures are biased both in favour of finding that dumping has occurred and in favour of finding that it has injured EC firms.[19]

Occurrence of dumping

The conclusion that dumping has taken place depends on a comparison of the price of the foreign good when it is sold in the EC with its price or its cost of production (the so-called "normal value") in its home market.

To determine whether or not dumping has occurred over a given time period, antidumping authorities calculate the average of the prices over which the foreign good was sold in the EC during that period. If some sales took place above the normal value, those high prices are thrown out in calculating the average and the normal price is substituted for them. A rationale put forward for this procedure is that (Hindley and Messerlin, 1996, p. 62) "a high price should not be allowed to conceal dumped sales".

The result is that "the" price of foreign goods used by EC antidumping authorities to

---

[18] The EC chemical cases are reviewed by Hindley and Messerlin (1996, pp. 36–9).

[19] See Council Regulation (EC) No 384/96 of 22 December 1995 1996 OJ L 56/1. The same biases appear in US antidumping procedures; see Clarida (1996) (for a concise discussion of US antidumping policy, see Baldwin, 1998). The aspects of antidumping procedures that lead to these biases are consistent with the WTO Agreements. (The fault, dear Brutus, is not in the stars, but in the WTO Agreements.)

determine if the good has been sold below the normal price is an average of sales taking place below the normal price and other sales that are treated as if they had taken place at the normal price. It is a simple property of arithmetic that this average will always be below the normal price if even a single sale has taken place below the normal price.

When the determination whether dumping has occurred is made based on a comparison of prices and the cost of production, the methodology that is used to construct the cost figure is central to the outcome. In estimating cost of production, EC authorities have allocated fixed costs in ways that appear to inflate the resulting cost figure. For example, in a decision involving the alleged dumping of Japanese semiconductor chips, the Commission allocated the R&D costs of Japanese firms to the period covered by the Commission's investigation, even though the revenues generated by those R&D expenses would be collected over the entire product life-cycle of the chips in question (Tharakan, 1997).

The procedures that are used to construct cost-of-production and normal value figures result in estimates of dumping margins that seem indefensible.[20] In an anti-dumping decision involving Japanese semiconductors, the Commission's figure for the difference between estimated production costs and the average price of the Japanese chips on the EC market was 206.2 per cent (Tharakan, 1997, p. 11). In one chemical industry case, dumping margins (Messerlin, 1990, p. 478) "on imports from Czechoslovakia, Romania, East Germany and Hungary were, respectively, 53–68 per cent, 58–74 per cent, 26–37 per cent and 25–45 per cent".

The Commission has begun to suppress reporting its estimated dumping margin in published decisions. Nicolaides and van Wijngaarden (1993, p. 42) suggest that the dumping margin is not reported because "its revelation would be embarrassing".

Existence of injury or the threat of injury

Imposition of an EC antidumping duty requires not only the finding that dumping has occurred but also a finding that the dumping has injured or threatens to injure the competing EC industry. A decision whether such injury has occurred or not is to be based on the volume of imports and their impact on the EC industry. If it should develop that imports of like products from several different countries are the subject of antidumping proceedings, the injury determination may be based on impact of combined imports from all such countries.

If it has been found that products have been dumped, it might be thought that the occurrence of injury would follow automatically (Vermulst and Waer, 1996, p. 281): "every sale of imported products on the domestic market is by definition a potentially lost sale for the domestic industry and hence a cause of injury".

For the purpose of EC antidumping procedures, an injury finding seems to require a showing that a group of EC firms are suffering economic distress, and that foreign firms selling similar products in the EC can be found to have dumped according to official definitions. There does not appear to be a need to show that the economic circumstances of the EC firms would be better if the dumping had not taken place.

For example, in a series of cases involving the EC chemical industry, the growing

[20] For further discussion, see Hindley (1988).

market share of foreign suppliers was taken to be evidence that dumping was causing injury to EC firms. An expanding market share of fringe foreign suppliers is exactly what would be expected if such firms reacted in an independent way to formation of a cartel by a dominant group of EC firms (Messerlin, 1990, pp. 480–1). The EC chemical firms were in fact found to have formed a cartel. Thus a finding of harm from dumping was based on the reaction that would be expected from independently-behaving profit-maximizing firms to a coordinated exercise of market power by EC firms.

Intermediate goods

Antidumping procedures are often opened against firms that produce intermediate goods. Antidumping penalties benefit EC firms that compete against foreign suppliers. But antidumping penalties harm EC firms that purchase the protected goods and use them as inputs to produce other goods that are then sold to final consumer demand. This raises the possibility that antidumping policy, far from merely (!) protecting EC firms at the expense of EC consumers, may in fact protect a subset of EC firms at the expense of other EC firms *and* EC consumers.

> *Antidumping measures*: policy tools that allow a government that is publicly committed to free trade to engage in selective protection that benefits some domestic firms to the injury of domestic consumers and, in many cases, to the injury of other domestic firms as well.

Case study: EC antidumping action: cotton fabrics

The European Commission's persistent efforts to impose antidumping penalties on unbleached cotton fabric imported from China, Egypt, India, Indonesia, Pakistan, and Turkey, over the opposition of a majority of EC Member States, illustrate the ease with which WTO-consistent antidumping procedures can be used for protectionist purposes, and demonstrate that antidumping policy not only harms consumers at the expense of favoured business interests, but may also harm segments of the business community.

The argument that fabric producers from the less-developed countries in question have dumped their products in the EC is that they have held their prices constant, even though their costs (as measured by the Commission) have gone up. The evidence that EC weaving firms have been injured by dumping is that their share of the EC market has gone down. This is true, but because total sales in the EC market went down, not because the sales of the non-EC firms (which were limited by quotas) went up.

It would seem difficult to establish that many small weaving firms, selling a largely standardized product, either entered on a predatory scheme against EC firms or were engaged in international price discrimination.

The dispute over whether or not to impose antidumping duties has pitted Member States (particularly France) that are home to declining textile sectors against Member

States (particularly Britain and Germany) that are home to clothing manufacturing firms, for which cotton fabric is a necessary input.

The European Commission rejected an antidumping complaint in 1995, but imposed temporary duties in 1996. In a closely divided vote, EC foreign ministers rejected a proposal to extend the temporary antidumping duties for five years. Despite this decision, the European Commission began another antidumping procedure less than two months later. EC textile importers unsuccessfully challenged this action before the European Court of Justice as an abuse of power by the Commission.

In March 1998, the Commission again imposed provisional antidumping duties on unbleached cotton imports from the six countries, although an advisory committee of Member State representatives voted 9–5 against imposing the duties.

In the run-up to a decision on whether to extend the temporary duties, EC weavers argued for protection against dumped imports, and clothing manufacturers and retailers argued that higher costs for imports would mean higher prices for consumers and could cost up to 200,000 lost jobs.

In October 1998, EC foreign ministers once again rejected a proposal to impose antidumping duties for five years.

9.5 **What is to be done?**

The protectionist impulse is deeply rooted. There is a broad consensus that free trade will maximize welfare in the long run, and for this reason most governments take the high road of public commitment to free trade. But free trade also requires costly structural adjustments in the short run, and resistance to such adjustments generates short-run political pressure to circumvent the commitment to free trade in ways that are superficially plausible but do not survive close examination.

Export cartels are defended on the ground that they increase the bargaining power of domestic firms against powerful foreign rivals. More often, it appears, they allow powerful domestic firms to exercise domestic market power.

Voluntary export restraints (set to disappear from the world stage under the WTO Agreements) are an opaque trade barrier and are, in effect, government-sponsored and policed cartels.

There is no convincing evidence that dumping in the sense of international predation has ever occurred. Dumping in the sense of international price discrimination seems likely to occur, but only in situations where domestic and foreign firms exercise some market power and where import competition improves market performance to the benefit of purchasing industries and final consumers. This improvement in market performance is one of the arguments in favour of a free-trade policy. In this context, anti-dumping policy is invoked by firms in declining and noncompetitive sectors to limit foreign competition, punish foreign rivals that compete too vigorously, and delay inevitable structural adjustments.

The negative impact of protectionist policies on market performance and national welfare could be controlled by administering such policies as part of national competition policy[21] and applying the guidelines about the determinants of market performance that have developed in the enforcement of competition policy to international markets.

Such an approach would require that firms seeking protection from international rivalry demonstrate that market structure suggested (a) that foreign firms were able to exercise market power and that (b) domestic firms in the import-competing industry could not. Export cartels involving the creation of joint-sales agencies would be allowed for small firms, not for large firms with market power. Domestic industries would not be able to invoke antidumping procedures against small foreign rivals based in several different countries.

Trade flows will continue to require adjustments in national market structures: some industries will decline, others will expand. In industrialized countries, industry segments that produce standardized, labour-intensive varieties will decline, industry segments that produce high-quality, differentiated, and capital-intensive varieties will expand. Rather than indirectly deliver adjustment aid to firms in declining sectors by means of export protection, it would be better to allow overt aid for industrial readjustment, subject to rules of the kind that have developed in administering EC state aid policy (Section 10.4) and the EC's own Structural Funds. In general, adjustment aid would be limited in time and conditional on the implementation of a programme of structural adjustment that would allow the industry receiving assistance to reposition itself so that it could eventually compete on international markets without public assistance.

Study points

- export cartels and tacit collusion on home market (page 189)
- competition policy toward export cartels
  - Article 81 (page 190)
  - Japan (page 191)
  - US (pages 191–3)
- voluntary export restraints (pages 194–5)
  - quality upgrading (page 190)
- dumping and antidumping policy (pages 198, 202, 204)
  - reciprocal dumping (pages 199–201)
  - antidumping duties (pages 201–2)

---

[21] In a longer run, protectionist trade policies might be subjected to the control of an international competition policy administered by the World Trade Organization.

Problems

9–1 Analyze the impact of an export cartel on national welfare:

(a) if two domestic firms are the only suppliers in a third market of a good which is not consumed on their home market;

(b) if there is a third firm supplying the product, based in the export market, that competes as a quantity-setting firm with the two domestic firms;

(c) if the product is consumed in both countries, if there are two firms based in each country, and if firms in each country are allowed to form an export cartel;

(d) if formation of an export cartel allows domestic firms to tacitly collude on the home market.

9–2 (VERs and direct foreign investment; see Flam, 1994).

There are three markets, each with a linear inverse demand curve

$$p_i = a - Q_i, i = 1, 2, 3 \tag{9.11}$$

for a homogeneous product.

Countries 1 and 2 form a custom union, which has aggregate inverse demand curve

$$p_U = a - \tfrac{1}{2}Q_U. \tag{9.12}$$

Countries 1 and 3 are each home to one automobile manufacturer, which we will call firm 1 and firm 3 respectively.

Only firm 3 sells in country 3; firm 3's cost function for its operations in country 3 is

$$C_{33}(x_3) = F_3 + c_3 x_3. \tag{9.13}$$

Firm 1's cost function for its operations in the custom union is

$$C_1(x_1) = F_1 + c_1 x_1. \tag{9.14}$$

The country 3 firm has lower marginal cost in country 3:

$$c_3 < c_1. \tag{9.15}$$

If firm 3 opens a plant in the customs union, its cost function at that plant is

$$C_{3U}(x_{3U}) = F_3 + c_1 x_{3U} \tag{9.16}$$

If firm 3 opens a plant in the customs union, it must pay an extra set of fixed costs. Its marginal cost is the same as firm 1: marginal cost is country specific. This is an assumption that simplifies the analysis of market equilibrium if there is foreign direct investment.

(a) Find Cournot equilibrium profits if there is free trade and firm 3 exports from country 3 to the customs union; find equilibrium consumers' surplus and net social welfare in the customs union.

(b) Suppose firm 3 is persuaded or constrained to limit its exports to a level v that is below its free trade equilibrium export level. Find Cournot equilibrium profits under this voluntary export restraint. Also find equilibrium consumers' surplus and net social welfare in the customs union.

(c) Find Cournot equilibrium profits, consumers' surplus and net social welfare in the customs union if firm 3 sets up a plant in country 1. What is the condition that must be satisfied for direct foreign investment to be the most profitable choice for firm 3? How is this condition affected by v? How is this condition affected by F_3?

9-3 (Reciprocal dumping) Consider two firms, firm 1 based in country 1 and firm 2 based in country 2. Markets in the two countries are identical. The two firms produce differentiated varieties of the same product. Inverse demand curves are

$$p_{11} = a - q_{11} - \theta q_{21} \tag{9.17}$$

$$p_{21} = a - \theta q_{11} - q_{21} \tag{9.18}$$

in country 1 (p_{21} is the price of variety 2 in country 1, and so forth) and

$$p_{12} = a - q_{12} - \theta q_{22} \tag{9.19}$$

$$p_{22} = a - \theta q_{12} - q_{22} \tag{9.20}$$

in country 2. The parameter θ lies between 0 and 1 and measures the degree of substitutability between the two varieties.

The cost of production is c per unit. Transportation cost to ship from one country to another is t per unit.

Calculate equilibrium prices and quantities in both markets. For the exported varieties, calculate price net of transportation cost (i.e. calculate $p_{21} - t$ and $p_{12} - t$). Compare export prices net of transportation cost with the price of the same variety in its home market.

9-4 (Antidumping duties) For the model of Problem 9-3, if country 1 imposes an antidumping dumping d on firm 2's sales in country 1, what is the impact on equilibrium prices in country 1? How great an antidumping duty would country 1 need to impose to make $p_{22} = p_{21} - t$?

9-5 (Antidumping undertaking) For the model of Problem 9-3, what is firm 2's profit-maximizing price if it agrees to charge the same price (net of transportation cost) in both countries? (Assume firm 1 continues to act as a Cournot firm in both markets.)

9-6 Answer Problems 9-4 and 9-5 as for the case in which firms' choice variables are prices rather than quantities.

Chapter 10

Market integration in the European Union

Consumption is the sole end and purpose of production; and the interest of the producer ought to be attended to, only so far as it may be necessary for promoting that of the consumer.

  Adam Smith (1937, p. 625)

10.1 Introduction

It is the ongoing process of EC market integration that makes the study of the organization of European industry such a fascinating exercise. Here we begin by using basic oligopoly models to seek insights into the consequences that ought to be expected when markets, particularly imperfectly competitive markets, merge. We follow this with a brief examination of the situation of the steel half of the EC's first exercise in market integration, the European Coal and Steel Community. Then we look at more recent progress and at the effect of the Single European Act on market performance and market structure. We conclude with a discussion of a unique and important part of EC competition policy, the control of Member State aid to business.

10.2 Market integration in theory

10.2.1 Market integration and market performance

Perfect competition

Identical costs, no taxes, no export costs The simplest possible case, perfect competition, serves as a starting point and is illustrated in Figure 10.1. Consider the case of two countries, homes to identical markets for a homogeneous product. In each country the market is perfectly competitive (in particular, firms are price-takers), and production costs are the same in both countries (constant marginal cost 10 per unit of output). Assume also that there are no taxes and no transportation or distribution costs if a firm located in one country sells to a consumer located in the other country.

Under these conditions, what are the consequences for market performance if all barriers to trade between the two countries are eliminated? Prices are the same in both countries, and equal to marginal cost, both before and after market integration. The model makes no predictions about trade flows: in the context of this model, no conclusions can be drawn about market integration by examining data about shipments between countries.

Perfect competition yields the best possible market performance, so it is not surprising that market integration brings no change in market performance if markets are perfectly competitive.

Taxes, no export costs How does this outcome change if we consider the case in which there is a per unit tax t_1 in country 1 and t_2 in country 2, with, for specificity, $t_1 < t_2$?

The pre-integration long-run equilibrium output is shown in Figure 10.2. In each

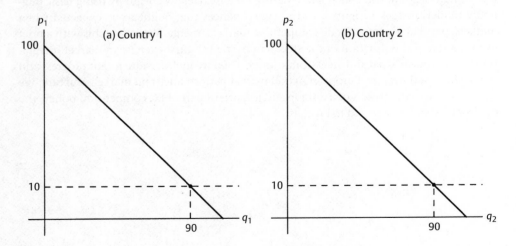

Fig. 10.1 Two countries, identical markets in each country, perfect competition, identical production costs, no taxes or distribution costs

country, the long-run perfectly competitive equilibrium price equals marginal production cost plus the per unit tax. Output in each country is less with the tax than it would be without a tax, and output is smaller in the country that has the higher tax rate.

If all barriers to trade are removed, one consequence of taxes is that firms must maintain records that treat sales in the two countries separately—a tax t_1 per unit sold must be paid to the government of country 1, a tax t_2 per unit sold must be paid to the government of country 2.

There is no incentive for supply-side arbitrage (as, indeed, is the case without taxes). Firms earn a normal rate of return on investment, net of taxes, on sales in either country, so firms have no particular incentive to seek sales in one country or the other.

There may be an incentive for demand-side arbitrage. Consumers in the low-tax country have no incentive to buy in the high-tax country. Consumers in the high-tax country have an incentive to buy in the low-tax country if the high-tax country does not control its borders and collect the difference in taxes at the border when returning residents bring in items purchased in the low-tax country. If the high-tax country does use such controls, then (neglecting the possibility of smuggling), consumers in the high-tax country have no incentive to buy in the low-tax country.

With economic integration, prices net of taxes are the same in both markets after formation of an economic union (as they were before). If countries prevent tax avoidance by cross-border purchases, the model makes no predictions about trade flows. If countries do not prevent tax avoidance by cross-border purchases, firms in the low-tax country supply all consumers in both markets. The total quantity demanded in both countries will go up (to twice the amount demanded in the low-tax country before integration). Consumers in country 2 will be better off, country 2 tax collections will fall to zero, and suppliers located in country 2 will go out of business.[1]

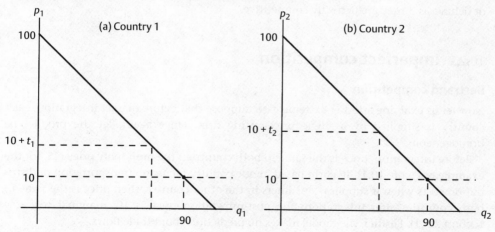

Fig. 10.2 Two countries, identical markets in each country, perfect competition, identical production costs, no export costs, different tax rates

[1] Given that there has been an economic union, these firms might, in principle, move to country 1 and continue operations from a new location. Since the industry is perfectly competitive and they are earning only a normal rate of return on their investment, they would be just as well off investing in some other perfectly competitive industry.

Export costs If in addition to taxes there is an export or distribution cost d per unit incurred by a firm from one country if it sells in the other country or by a consumer that purchases outside his or her home country, then the distribution cost tends to insulate each national market from the other.

A firm located in country 2 can supply a customer in country 2 at a cost $10 + t_2$ per unit. The cost to a country 1 firm of supplying a customer in country 2 is $10 + t_2 + d$. No country 1 firm would sell in country 2 for less than that amount; to accept a lower price would mean economic losses. No country 2 consumer would pay more than $10 + t_2$, since that is firm 2's price. Firms will sell only in their own market.

If a country 2 consumer buys in country 1, the cost of a unit of output is $10 + t_1 + d$, with the distribution cost d incurred by the consumer in going from one country to the other. If $10 + t_1 + d > 10 + t_2$, consumers from the high-tax market will buy in their home country. Prices net of taxes are the same, 10, in both countries. If $10 + t_1 + d < 10 + t_2$, that is, if $d < t_2 - t_1$, and the high-tax country does not collect the difference in taxes at the border, consumers from the high-tax country will buy in the low-tax country.[2] All sales will occur in the low-tax country. Firms in the high-tax country will go out of business.

With perfectly competitive markets, we should observe that prices net of taxes are the same in national submarkets after integration. However, these are markets where performance is optimal before and after formation of an economic union—which means they are not the kinds of markets where integration would be expected to bring improvements in market performance. For perfectly competitive markets, market integration need not lead to important trade flows between national markets. When the perfectly competitive model does yield a prediction about the direction of trade flows, the kind of prediction—all consumers from a high-tax country going to a low-tax country to buy—strikes us as being implausible. So it is, because not many real-world industries are or behave as if they are perfectly competitive.

10.2.2 Imperfect competition

Bertrand competition

Now let us examine another extreme case: suppose that before market integration, each country is supplied by a single price-setting firm. Once again, let the product be homogeneous.

Before integration, price is the same in both countries: the monopoly price (45, for the example of Figure 10.1). If a firm based in one country incurs no transportation or distribution costs when it supplies consumers in the other country, then price is the same in both countries after integration: the post-integration price is 10, marginal cost (see Section 2.3.1). Further, the model makes no prediction about trade flows.

Thus the fact that price is the same in both countries tells us nothing about the degree of market integration, since price is the same in both countries before and after integration. The sign that market integration has affected market performance is not that price is

---

[2] Consumer movements of this kind are common across the borders of countries where there are substantial differences in tax rates for particular products, as, for example, alcoholic beverages.

the same in both countries after integration, but that price is lower after integration than it was before.

Keeping all other aspects of the model unchanged, suppose now that a firm in one country incurs a distribution charge d if it supplies a customer located in the other market. Each firm acts as a price-setting and profit-maximizing oligopolist, which means that the post-integration market price is slightly less than $10 + d$ in each country. Each firm will set a price just below the level that would make it profitable for the other firm to enter its market. Once again, price is the same in both countries both before and after integration. Once again, the sign of market integration is that price is lower, market performance is better, after integration. With distribution costs, the model does yield a prediction about trade flows: they will not occur.

Cournot competition

Now turn to the case of quantity-setting oligopoly. Suppose that there are two countries, $i = 1, 2$, with markets for a homogeneous product, the equation of the inverse demand curve in country i being

$$p_i = 100 - Q_i. \tag{10.1}$$

Suppose further that before market integration, n_1 firms supply market 1 and n_2 firms supply market 2. All firms operate with the same cost function,

$$c(q) = 10q, \tag{10.2}$$

and there are no taxes or distribution costs.

If the preintegration markets are Cournot oligopolies, we can apply equations (2.60)–(2.62) to write out expressions for Cournot equilibrium output per firm, total output, and price in the two countries. These are

$$q_{1i} = \frac{90}{n_i + 1} \qquad Q_i = \frac{n_i}{n_i + 1}90 \qquad p_i = 10 + \frac{90}{n_i + 1}, \tag{10.3}$$

respectively, for $i = 1, 2$.

If the two countries form a single market, the equation of the aggregate inverse demand curve is[3]

$$p = 100 - \tfrac{1}{2}Q. \tag{10.4}$$

Proceeding in the usual way,[4] Cournot equilibrium output per firm and price in the single market are

$$q_{sm} = \frac{180}{n_1 + n_2 + 1} \qquad p_{sm} = 10 + \frac{90}{n_1 + n_2 + 1}, \tag{10.5}$$

where the subscript "sm" denotes "single market".

---

[3] If $p = 100$, the quantity demanded in each country is zero, so the aggregate quantity demanded is zero. If $p = 0$, the quantity demanded in each country is 100, and the aggregate quantity demanded is 200. (10.4) is the equation of a straight line connecting the points (0, 100) and (200, 0) in quantity-price space.

[4] That is, find the best response function of a single Cournot firm in a market with inverse demand curve (10.4) that is supplied by $n_1 + n_2$ identical firms. Using the fact that the firms are identical, impose symmetry on the equation of the best response function and solve for Cournot equilibrium output.

From (10.3) and (10.5), price falls in each country after integration:

$$p_i - p_{sm} = 90 \frac{n_j}{(n_1 + n_2 + 1)(n_i + 1)}, \tag{10.6}$$

for $i, j = 1, 2$ and $i \neq j$. The reduction in price in each country is proportional to the number of firms in the other: if there are more firms in country 1 than in country 2, then when the two firms form a single market, the number of suppliers goes up more, and price falls more, in country 2 than in country 1.

The change in output per firm after integration is

$$q_{sm} - q_i = \frac{180}{n_1 + n_2 + 1} - \frac{90}{n_i + 1} = \frac{90(1 + n_i - n_j)}{(n_1 + n_2 + 1)(n_i + 1)}, \tag{10.7}$$

again for $i, j = 1, 2$ and $i \neq j$. If the number of firms is the same in both countries, then output per firm rises in both countries after formation of a single market. In this case, firms in each country produce half of total output, and there are no net exports from one country to the other.

If n_1 is much greater than n_2 (to be precise, if $n_1 \geq n_2 + 1$), then before integration, each firm in country 1 was producing a relatively low output: after integration, equilibrium output of country 1 firms goes up, equilibrium output of country 2 firms goes down, and there are net exports from country 1 to country 2. If $n_2 \geq n_1 + 1$, formation of a single market means net exports from country 2 to country 1.

A Cournot model of market integration with linear inverse demand thus yields the predictions that if markets of equal size integrate, then holding the number of firms constant, consumers will be better off, and if the number of firms in each country is different, there will be net exports from the country with more firms to the country with less firms.

The consequences of market integration for market performance are of this same general type if markets are not too different in size and the nature of consumer demand in the integrating countries is roughly the same. Otherwise, it is possible for price to rise in some countries that join an integrated market.[5]

Suppose now that country 1 collects a tax t_1 on every unit sold by a country 1 firm, while country 2 collects a tax t_2 on every unit sold by a country 2 firm. The post-integration market is a Cournot oligopoly in which firms have constant but different average and marginal cost. We considered this kind of market for the duopoly case in Section 2.2.5. There we saw that higher-cost firms have smaller equilibrium sales and price-cost margins than lower-cost firms. In the present case if the number of firms is the same in each country (and leaving the derivation of the results to Problem 10–3), equilibrium price-cost margins in the post-integration market, net of taxes, are

---

[5] Suppose a single market is formed by two countries, a large country where demand is price inelastic and a small country where demand is price elastic. Before integration, price will be high relative to marginal cost in the large country, where demand is not very sensitive to price, and price will be low relative to marginal cost in the small country, where demand is very sensitive to price. The larger the country where demand is inelastic, the more will demand in the single market resemble demand in the large country, and the more likely that price will rise in the small country after integration. See also Problem 10–2.

$$p - t_1 = 10 + \frac{90 - t_1}{2n + 1} \qquad p - t_2 = 10 + \frac{90 - t_2}{2n + 1}. \qquad (10.8)$$

When there are regional tax differences in a single market, prices net of taxes will be different in different regions. When the number of firms is the same or approximately the same in different regions, prices after taxes are lower in the high-tax region: in an imperfectly competitive market, firms absorb part of a higher cost in the form of a lower price-cost margin, and pass only a portion of the tax on to final consumers in the form of a lower after-tax price.

> *Market integration, price, and market performance*: with imperfectly competitive markets, there is no reason to think that market integration will lead to identical prices, or identical net prices after allowing for unit tax and transportation cost, in different regional submarkets of an economic union. To determine the impact of market integration, it is necessary to analyze the way market performance is affected by the removal of barriers to trade. When countries with similar markets and market structures integrate, price in all regions should fall after integration. This may not be the case if regions are very different in size, if regional markets were supplied by quite different numbers of firms before integration, or if demand patterns are quite different in different regional submarkets.

10.2.3 **Market integration and market structure**

To this point, our discussion of the impact of market integration on market performance has taken supply-side market structure—the number of firms—to be given. In general, however, market integration will lead to a reduction in the number of firms. There is a concentration effect of market integration, just as there is a concentration effect of international trade (Problem 8–5).

To see this, suppose there are two identical markets, each with inverse demand curve of the form (10.1). Suppose also that all firms operate with the cost function

$$c(q) = 900 + 10q. \qquad (10.9)$$

From equations (2.60)–(2.62), Cournot equilibrium profit per firm in each market, when markets are separate, is

$$\pi = \left(\frac{90}{n + 1}\right)^2 - 900. \qquad (10.10)$$

It follows that equilibrium market structure in each market before integration is duopoly: with two firms supplying each market, economic profit per firm is zero, meaning each firm earns only a normal rate of return on investment and there is no incentive for entry or exit. The duopoly price in each market is

$$p = 10 + \tfrac{90}{3} = 40. \qquad (10.11)$$

In equilibrium, each firm produces 30 units of output, and average cost is also 40,

$$\frac{900 + 10(30)}{30} = 40. \tag{10.12}$$

This should be expected, since in equilibrium firms just break even.

If the two countries form a single market, the equation of the post-integration inverse demand curve is (10.4). Equilibrium profit per firm with n firms is

$$\pi = 2 \left(\frac{90}{n+1} \right)^2 - 900. \tag{10.13}$$

Equilibrium profit per firm is zero if

$$n = \frac{90\sqrt{2}}{\sqrt{900}} - 1 = 3.2426. \tag{10.14}$$

Taking into account that the number of firms must be an integer, the equilibrium market structure in the integrated market is a triopoly. If three firms supply the market, all will earn a rate of return on investment that is slightly greater than normal, but if a fourth firm were to come into the market, all would make losses.

Market integration leaves consumers better off: the post-integration price is lower than the pre-integration price:

$$p = 10 + \frac{90}{3+1} = 32.5. \tag{10.15}$$

In the integrated market, equilibrium triopoly output per firm is $\frac{180}{4} = 45$ and average cost is less than in the pre-integration market:

$$\frac{900 + 10(45)}{45} = 30. \tag{10.16}$$

A reduction in the number of firms is essential to obtain the full benefit of market integration. With fewer firms, each surviving firm produces more output in equilibrium, fixed cost per firm is spread over a larger number of units of output, and average cost falls.[6]

In practice, and with specific reference to the impact of market integration on EC market structure, the supply-side concentration effect of market integration will be most important in sectors where there are potential economies of large scale that extend to output levels sufficient to supply a market of European size. Consolidation on the supply side of such industries will reduce costs, by allowing some firms to reach a level of production not available in any one Member State market. If the production technology does not offer such economies of scale, or in markets where there is product differentiation based on distinctive national preferences, market integration is likely to have less of an effect in increasing supply-side seller concentration.[7]

---

[6] An additional efficiency gain may arise if large-scale operations make it optimal for firms to adopt a multi-divisional organizational form; see Section 6.6.

[7] More generally, see Buigues and Jacquemin (1989), Jacquemin (1992).

> *Concentration effect of market integration*: market integration will typically reduce the equilibrium number of firms in imperfectly competitive markets, increasing seller concentration, allowing greater exploitation of economies of scale, and improving noncooperative equilibrium market performance.

10.3 **Market integration in practice**

10.3.1 **Prologue: the ECSC**

The European Coal and Steel Community was established by the Treaty of Paris, signed in April 1951 and with effect for a period of 50 years from July 1952.[8] The economic provisions of the treaty were in many ways leading indicators of the provisions later incorporated in the 1956 Treaty of Rome, which established the European Economic Community. Both treaties took a harsh line against price discrimination, which was viewed as a business strategy that would have the effect of distorting competition among businesses purchasing inputs and as likely to undermine public support for the single market.[9]

The executive branch of the Coal and Steel Community was the High Authority, which enjoyed far more power over the two sectors of the economy that it was concerned with than its successor, the European Commission, does over a broader range of economic activity.

The ECSC Treaty prohibited price discrimination as being incompatible with a common market. It required that companies in the common markets for steel and coal publish price lists and related information on terms determined by the High Authority. In its implementation of these provisions, the High Authority required

- that steel producers publish their price lists and sell at published prices;
- that customers pay the published price for steel plus cost of shipping from the steel mill; and
- that transport rates be published.

Companies were, however, permitted to make sales at prices below published list prices if necessary to match a legal price of another firm.

In other words, the ECSC Treaty established a basing point system (Section 3.2.2) for distribution of steel in the ECSC, and this system, which had all the effects of a cartel, was enforced by the Community's High Authority.

The Treaty abhorred price discrimination for its feared effect on competition among

---

[8] On the ECSC generally, see Petzina (1981), Milward (1984, Chapter 12), Gillingham (1991), and Spierenburg and Poidevin (1994). On ECSC competition policy, see particularly Hamberger (1962) and Scheingold (1965).

[9] That is, the immediate concern was not with the impact of price discrimination on final consumers, but on rivalry between firms that purchased inputs at different prices.

The ECSC Treaty (1951):

Article 4

The following are recognized as incompatible with the common market for coal and steel and shall accordingly be abolished and prohibited within the Community, as provided in this Treaty: . . .

(b) measures or practices which discriminate between producers, between purchasers or between consumers, especially in prices and delivery terms or transport rates and conditions, and measures or practices which interfere with the purchaser's free choice of supplier;

(c) subsidies or aids granted by States, or special charges imposed by States, in any form whatsoever;

(d) restrictive practices which tend towards the sharing or exploiting of markets.

Article 5

The Community shall carry out its task . . . with a limited measure of intervention. To this end the Community shall . . . ensure the establishment, maintenance and observance of normal competitive conditions and exert direct influence upon production or upon the market only when circumstances so require . . .

Article 58

In the event of a decline in demand, if the Commission considers that the Community is confronted with a period of manifest crisis . . . it shall . . . establish a system of production quotas . . .

Article 60

1. Pricing practices contrary to Articles 2, 3 and 4 shall be prohibited, in particular:

* unfair competitive practices, especially purely temporary or purely local price reductions tending towards the acquisition of a monopoly position within the common market;

* discriminatory practices involving, within the common market, the application by a seller of dissimilar conditions to comparable transactions, especially on grounds of the nationality of the buyer.

2. For these purposes:

(a) the price lists and conditions of sale applied by undertakings within the common market must be made public to the extent and in the manner prescribed by the Commission.

Article 65

1. All agreements between undertakings, decisions by associations of undertakings and concerted practices tending directly or indirectly to prevent, restrict or distort normal competition within the common market shall be prohibited, and in particular those tending:

(a) to fix or determine prices;

(b) to restrict or control production, technical development or investment;

(c) to share markets, products, customers or sources of supply.

2. However, the Commission shall authorize specialization agreements or joint buying or joint selling agreements in respect of particular products, if it finds that:

> (a) such specialization or such joint buying or joint selling will make for a substantial improvement in the production or distribution of those products;
>
> (b) the agreement in question is essential in order to achieve these results and is not more restrictive than is necessary for that purpose; and
>
> (c) the agreement is not liable to give the undertakings concerned the power to determine the prices, or to control or restrict the production or marketing, of a substantial part of the products in question within the common market, or to shield them against effective competition from other undertakings within the common market. . . .

businesses that purchased steel as an input, not for the effect of price discrimination on final consumers. If (for example) German firms purchasing steel were able to buy at systematically lower prices than French firms, then German firms would have a systematic competitive advantage over French firms, and French political support for market integration would unravel.

Some contemporary observers recognized that the prohibition of price discrimination would facilitate tacit collusion (Hamberger, 1962, p. 357):

This rigid system of non-discrimination is likely to restrain competition and to be an incentive to keep prices on a high level as long as possible. The producer cannot reduce his price for a certain category of consumers where he is meeting an extraordinary form of competition, e.g., by a substitute product. He would be compelled in such a case to lower the price for all categories of consumers, which in many cases is too expensive.

Essentially, in order to avoid cases in which some purchasers closer to the final consumer would get lower prices than others, the ECSC put in place institutions that had the effect of ensuring that all customers closer to the final consumer would pay high prices.[10]

A theoretical basis for concern over different prices received by different consumers can be found in the comparative advantage theory of trade flows (Section 7.2.1). In a perfectly competitive free trade system, Germany, which is richly endowed with coal and iron ore, would be expected to specialize in the production of steel and export it to other ECSC Member States, which would specialize in the production of other goods, goods not covered by the ECSC Treaty.

An analysis of the same situation in terms of the "new trade theory" of imperfectly competitive international markets with product differentiation and economies of scale (Section 7.3) would instead predict that the different ECSC Member States would specialize in the product of different types of steel and steel products, and engage in intra-industry trade in steel.

It appears that it is the second outcome that actually occurred; Adler (1969–70, p. 180) writes that under the ECSC

---

[10] Price discrimination is a normal aspect of rivalry in imperfectly competitive markets. Lister (1960, p. 208, footnote 6) quotes a Herman Witte from the *Handelsblatt*, 12 December 1956, p. 6 to the effect that (emphasis added) "coal and steel producers experienced difficulty in *trying to understand* the concept of nondiscrimination in the early years of the ECSC".

First, there was no interindustry specialization in European steel. Steel production as a whole did not concentrate in a single country. Second, the process of intra-industry specialization remained incomplete.

Adler's own conclusion is that (p. 185) as "evidenced by the continuing exchange of physically identical steel products, the fifteen years between 1952 and 1966 constituted a transitional period too short for a new free-trade competitive equilibrium to be reached". It seems equally likely that the appropriate equilibrium concept for the EC steel industry was imperfect competition and intra-industry trade, not perfect competition and interindustry trade.

The fundamental goals of the ECSC were political rather than economic, and economic policies were seen as means to accomplish political purposes. The ECSC steel sector was set up in such a way as to promote rivalry by removing barriers to market access so that a producer based in one Member State could sell in another Member State if it found it profitable to do so but to prevent rivalry so intense that it would lead to politically unacceptable changes in the structure of the supply side of the market.

To the extent that there is a vision of the way markets work implicit in ECSC steel pricing policies, it seems to have been one of perfectly competitive markets. There is no price discrimination in a perfectly competitive market, so by forbidding price discrimination, policy will move the market toward perfect competition. There is complete and perfect information on the demand and supply sides of a perfectly competitive market, so by requiring price transparency on the supply side of a market, policy will move the market toward perfect competition. As the results show, policies motivated by ideas about perfectly competitive markets can be terribly misguided if applied to imperfectly competitive markets.[11]

Supply-side price transparency and market performance: complete and perfect information is one characteristic of a perfectly competitive market; supply-transparency in imperfectly competitive markets facilitates tacit collusion and worsens market performance.

10.3.2 Market integration: empirical evidence

Price dispersion

The Single European Act of 1986 aimed to create a single EC market by removing public barriers to intra-EC trade, harmonizing standards and regulatory structures, and

---

[11] In April 1965, Member States signed a treaty merging the ECSC, Euratom, and the EEC, with the Commission of the European Communities assuming the role of the ECSC High Authority. The Treaty went into effect in July 1967. As discussed in its *First Report on Competition Policy* (EC Commission, 1972, pp. 86–7), the Commission reinterpreted the concept of "price discrimination" for use in applying Article 60 of the ECSC Treaty so that it referred to differences in prices for comparable transactions, not to differences between transaction prices and published list prices; this ended the ECSC's role as public policeman of a steel basing point system. With the economic collapse that came with the oil shocks of the 1970s, the steel sector entered into a long and managed decline.

promoting cooperation among EC firms, all to be accomplished by the end of 1992. It seems most useful to think of competition in the sense of rivalry when markets are imperfectly competitive, and as the discussion of Sections 10.2.1 and 10.2.2 suggests, it is in imperfectly competitive markets that market integration is likely to have its greatest effects. Removing barriers to trade across national borders was expected to simultaneously increase rivalry and boost economic growth while promoting economic integration.[12]

To the extent that segmented markets in individual Member States did not permit full realization of economies of scale, market integration should improve market performance by concentrating production in the hands of a smaller number of larger, and therefore lower cost, producers. Greater rivalry in imperfectly competitive markets can be expected to encourage firms to operate more efficiently.[13] In our discussion of entry (Section 6.3), we saw evidence that the entry process acts as a selection mechanism, sorting a few, efficient, entrants into markets and sorting most, inefficient, entrants out. More intense rivalry might make this selection process more effective. More competitive product markets can also be expected to stimulate firms to invest in innovation and, therefore, to increase the rate of technological progress.[14] These types of benefits from increased competition are difficult to measure, but there is good reason to think that they are real.[15]

Establishment of a single market in a legal sense does not mean that the European Union has become a single market in an economic sense. Indeed, for most consumer goods and many producer goods, transportation costs imply that even when all artificial

Table 10.1 Big Mac prices (including sales tax), selected regions.

Country	Big Mac	
	$	€
Denmark	2.88	3.32
Britain	2.85	3.24
France	2.49	2.83
Sweden	2.33	2.65
Germany	2.30	2.61
Euro area	2.27	2.58
Spain	2.09	2.38
Italy	1.96	2.23

Source: The Economist, 19 April 2001.

[12] For general discussions of the impact of competition in this sense on performance, see Vickers (1995), Nickell (1996), and Hay and Liu (1997).

[13] See Leibenstein (1966) on X-efficiency. Some formal models show such an efficiency effect, others do not. Hay and Liu (1997) present empirical work suggesting that greater competition stimulates efficiency.

[14] See Section 5.4.2, as well as Martin (2001c). Nickell (1996) reports the results of an empirical study suggesting that greater competition increases the rate of productivity growth.

[15] For a forward-looking attempt to quantify the benefits that might be expected from the Single Market Programme, see Emerson et al. (1988), and for a sceptical review, Peck (1989).

barriers to the movements of goods and services are removed, the EC will contain several distinct local or regional geographic markets.

As we have seen in Section 10.2.2, there is in general no reason to expect net prices in an imperfectly competitive single market to be the same in different regions, and indeed there is no uniform tendency toward price convergence in the EC. Table 10.1 illustrates that price differences persist across the EC for one common consumer item, an item sold in what is most likely a monopolisticly competitive[16] market.

In a general study of price convergence that distinguishes between sectors where there is a high, medium, and low degree of price dispersion across Member States the European Commission (1999c) writes:[17]

Fierce competition in European and world markets keeps pushing price variation down on such readily tradable products as cheese, data processing machinery, tv-sets, and underwear. These products fall in the low-dispersion group . . . Though prices are not uniformly converging, most of these products command high unit values, which is why they belong to the group of most tradable products.

Among the products . . . with a medium level of price dispersion, hotels and motels are an interesting example. On the one hand, location plays a decisive role in consumption, leading one to expect a high level of price dispersion. However, the growing selection of cities for large-scale conferences and tourist trips keep price differentials within bounds.

Inherent immovability of products like rents and railways effectively preclude tradability and consign these products to the group of high price dispersion . . . If working in London, then moving to Lisbon to exploit lower housing costs is not really an option, nor is riding trains in Italy a substitute when the daily commute is between two Swedish cities. For medicine, natural gas and general practitioners the substantial price dispersion is due in large part to government regulation . . .

It would be incorrect to conclude from evidence of this kind that the Single Market Programme has failed, or that progress toward market integration has not had the effects that were hoped for. Progress toward market integration should show up in improved market performance, and there is evidence that such improvements are taking place.

Market structure

The early years of the European Community (1959 through 1968) saw a phased elimination of tariffs on movements of goods between Member States. Sleuwaegen and Yamawaki (1988) examine the impact of this elimination of tariffs on changes in market concentration between 1963 and 1978 in 47 three-digit NACE industries for five Member States: Belgium, Italy, France, West Germany, and The Netherlands. They find that seller concentration increased following tariff reductions in four of the five cases, excepting only The Netherlands. This is exactly the kind of seller concentration effect of market integration that is expected in imperfectly competitive markets.

---

[16] In such a market, individual firms are aware of their oligopolistic interdependence (which is often thought of as being based on product differentiation), minimum efficient scale is small relative to market size, and entry and exit occur until profit is zero. See Chamberlin (1933). The model of monopolistic competition is probably appropriate for the fast food market in most regions.

[17] In addition to hotels and motels, other products with medium levels of price dispersion are beef, electric light bulbs, eyeglasses, and veal.

They also examine the determinants of changes in Member State price-cost margins. For France, West Germany, and Italy, increases in EC-wide seller concentration have a positive effect on price-cost margins, suggesting that in 1978 firms in these countries were already, to some extent, operating in an EC-wide market: seller concentration at the EC level had an impact on price-cost margins because the geographic scope of the relevant market, in many industries, was larger than any one Member State.

Market performance

One aspect of the formation of the single market is the opening up to competition of product markets which historically, for reasons of tradition or technology, had been regarded as natural monopolies and in many Member States, supplied by a regulated state enterprise. Railroads, passenger airlines, telecommunications, electric power, natural gas, and postal services are examples. Entry into such markets often requires access to a physical distribution network,[18] and these networks have been controlled by the former state monopolist. For these sectors, therefore, the EC has issued directives to manage the liberalization process and ensure that entrants have access to distribution networks on terms that do not distort competition.[19]

In their review of the market integration process in EC network industries, Schmidt et al. (1999, p. 31) classify Member States in three groups, according to progress in opening up the telecommunications sector to competition:

- Competitive prior to Commission Directives: UK, Sweden, Finland, Denmark;
- Fully liberalized by January 1998: Germany, France, The Netherlands;
- Others: Austria, Ireland, Italy, Belgium, Spain, Portugal, Luxembourg, Greece.

Figure 10.3[20] plots the average cost of a standard package of telecommunications services to residential consumers against a crude measure of competition, the number of firms authorized to supply such services, for 14 Member States.[21] There is a clear pattern of rates falling as the number of suppliers rises, and rates tend to be lower, the farther along a Member State is in the liberalization process.

Bottasso and Sembenelli (2001) use data on a sample of 745 Italian firms over the period 1982–88 to analyze the impact of the Single Market Programme on firm and market performance. For firms operating in industries where the removal of non-tariff barriers to trade could be expected to make a significant increase in competition possible, they find that estimated price-cost margins (the Lerner index of market power (1.15) or (2.34)) range from 15.8 per cent to 19 per cent for the years 1982–7 and from 6.6 per cent to 10.7 per cent for the years 1988–88. They also find an increase in productivity growth for the same firms in the years 1985–87, which is (p. 184) "consistent with the idea of sensitive firms anticipating an increase in competitive pressure by reducing inefficiencies".

[18] Pipelines for natural gas, wires for electric power, landing slots for passenger airlines. Some (for example, telecommunications) but not all of these industries exhibit network externalities (Section 6.5).
[19] See, for example, the draft telecommunications directive of 12 July 2000 (OJ C96/2, 27 March 2001) or the electricity directive of 19 December 1996 (OJ L27 30 January 1997, p. 20).
[20] Figure 10.3 is an updated version of figures presented by Schmidt et al. (1999).
[21] The number of authorized suppliers is not available for Greece.

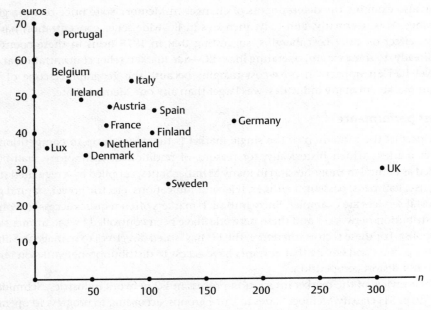

Fig. 10.3 Average monthly telecommunications expenditures for a standard basket of calls, residential users, *v.* number of authorized operators

Source: EC Commission, Sixth Report on the Implementation of the Telecommunciations Regulatory Package

Rivalry and market performance: early empirical evidence suggests that the EU Single Market is delivering the increased efficiency and improved market performance that it was intended to produce.

10.4 State aid and state aid policy[22]

10.4.1 The extent of state aid

The evidence that we have on the actual impact of EC market integration on EC market performance is that market integration is accomplishing its avowed purpose of increasing competitive pressure on firms, inducing greater efficiency gains than would otherwise take place, delivering better market performance for consumers, and making EC firms more competitive on world markets. As we have emphasized above (Section 10.2.3), for

---

[22] See Schina (1987), Evans and Martin (1991), and Beasley and Seabright (1999). This section draws on Martin and Valbonesi (2000).

market integration to have its full effect, supply-side market structure in many sectors will need to become more concentrated, as surviving firms take advantage of economies of large scale and as other firms go out of business. The danger is that the Member State governments will resist this kind of structural reorganization (Peck, 1989, pp. 290–1, footnotes omitted):

The history of industrial policy shows that European national governments have not passively accepted the closing of firms, but rather have devised state aids to rescue some of the losers. Indeed, Europe has a tradition of rescuing national firms in trouble, though in some industries the decline in the number of firms has been accepted, particularly for low-technology industries made up of small firms. Still, it is state aids of various sorts that explain why Europe has 12 manufacturers of industrial boilers or 16 manufacturers of electric locomotives compared with 2 firms in each industry in the United States.

It is to guard against this type of protectionist reaction that EC competition policy includes provisions to attempt to control Member State aid to business (and, in principle at least, such rules existed in the ECSC as well). Like the more traditional aspects of EC competition policy, the basis of EC state aid policy is contained in Articles 87 to 89 of the EC Treaty. The framework laid out in these articles includes a basic prohibition of state aid that distorts competition and affects trade (Article 87(1)), with some mandatory exceptions (Article 87(2)), and discretionary exceptions (Article 87(3)).

The provision for discretionary exceptions to the Article 87(1) prohibition makes it possible for the Commission to permit various types of aid, including regional aid (87(3)(a) and (c)), aid to combat unemployment (87(a)), aid to advance important EC goals (87(b)), aid to specific economic activities (87(c)), aid to deal with serious economic disturbances (87(b)), and other aid, with authorization of the Council. Aid granted under all these categories may, directly or indirectly, be aid to business, and so affect both market performance and the process of market integration.

As suggested by Table 10.2, the overall trend in Member State aid to manufacturing is downward. To place the figures in Table 10.2 in perspective, the EC commitments for agricultural spending and for the EC's own Structural Funds for the year 2000 were 40.9 billion euros and 32.0 billion euros, respectively.[23] State aid to manufacturing is thus of the same order of magnitude as two of the EC's major programmes.

Table 10.3 gives some indication of the different avenues by which aid is channelled to the manufacturing sector. Horizontal aid is, in principle, available to all firms, without regard to location or sector. The three major types of horizontal aid are aid to promote research and development, aid to small- and medium-size firms, and the catchall category "Other". Some sectors, either industries in long-term secular decline or recently liberalized industries struggling with the throes of competition, are covered by specific aid codes. Regional aid is the largest single type of aid to manufacturing.

Finally, as shown in Table 10.4, state aid to manufacturing is about one-third of all state aid.

---

[23] Both figures are adjusted for inflation and measured in 1999 euros.

Article 87

1. Save as otherwise provided in this Treaty, any aid granted by a Member State or through State resources in any form whatsoever which distorts or threatens to distort competition by favouring certain undertakings or the production of certain goods shall, in so far as it affects trade between Member States, be incompatible with the common market.

   2. The following shall be compatible with the common market:

(a) aid having a social character, granted to individual consumers, provided that such aid is granted without discrimination related to the origin of the products concerned;

(b) aid to make good the damage caused by natural disasters or exceptional occurrences;

(c) aid granted to the economy of certain areas of the Federal Republic of Germany affected by the division of Germany, in so far as such aid is required in order to compensate for the economic disadvantages caused by that division.

   3. The following may be considered to be compatible with the common market:

(a) aid to promote the economic development of areas where the standard of living is abnormally low or where there is serious underemployment;

(b) aid to promote the execution of an important project of common European interest or to remedy a serious disturbance in the economy of a Member State;

(c) aid to facilitate the development of certain economic activities or of certain economic areas, where such aid does not adversely affect trading conditions to an extent contrary to the common interest. . . .;

(d) aid to promote culture and heritage conservation where such aid does not affect trading conditions and competition in the Community to an extent that is contrary to the common interest;

(e) such other categories of aid as may be specified by decision of the Council acting by a qualified majority on a proposal from the Commission.

Article 88

1. The Commission shall, in cooperation with Member States, keep under constant review all systems of aid existing in those States. . . .

   2. If, after giving notice to the parties concerned to submit their comments, the Commission finds that aid granted by a State or through State resources is not compatible with the common market having regard to Article 92, or that such aid is being misused, it shall decide that the State concerned shall abolish or alter such aid within a period of time to be determined by the Commission.

. . .

On application by a Member State, the Council may, acting unanimously, decide that aid which that State is granting or intends to grant shall be considered to be compatible with the common market, in derogation from the provisions of Article 92 . . . if such a decision is justified by exceptional circumstances. . . .

   3. The Commission shall be informed, in sufficient time to enable it to submit its comments, of any plans to grant or alter aid. If it considers that any such plan is not compatible with the common market having regard to Article 92, it shall without delay initiate the procedure provided for in paragraph 2. The Member State concerned shall not put its proposed measures into effect until this procedure has resulted in a final decision.

Table 10.2 State aid to manufacturing in the Community, 1994–98, annual values, million 1997 euros.

	EUR 12	EUR 15
1994	40341	
1995	38441	39615
1996	33357	34486
1997	32470	33730
1998	28400	29702

Source: European Commission (2000a)

Table 10.3 State aid to manufacturing by type, 1996–98, EUR 15.

	%
Horizontal aid	**35**
R&D	11
Environment	2
Small & medium-size enterprise	9
Trade	2
Energy saving	3
Other (includes rescue & restructuring)	8
Sectoral aid	**8**
Shipbuilding	5
Other	3
Regional aid	**57**
Article 88(a) (promote economic development)	46
Article 88(c) (facilitate development of certain activities or areas)	11
Total	**100**

Source: European Commission (2000a)

10.4.2 Economic analysis of state aid

The EC Treaty provides for control of state aid to guard against the distortions of competition that would arise if more-developed Member States were able to systematically grant more aid to their firms than are less-developed states. Such distortions would not only worsen market performance, they would also undermine political support for the process of market integration.

In a market system, the general economic justification for state aid (and other types of public intervention in the marketplace) is the existence of some type of market failure. One can then interpret Article 87(3) as giving the Commission the option of permitting aid that not only benefits firms or regions but also corrects some market failure, and therefore benefits the Community as a whole as well as the immediate recipients of the aid.

Table 10.4 Average annual EU state
aid, 1996–98, million euros.

	1996–8
Manufacturing	32639
Agriculture	13339
Fisheries	260
Coal mining	7227
Transport	32193
Financial services	3283
Tourism	229
Media & culture	748
Employment	1616
Training	900
Other services	892
Total	88127

Source: EC Commission (2000a); footnotes
omitted

Horizontal aid

Horizontal aid targets market failures that affect firms independently of their location or
sector of activity. We have seen (Chapter 5) that a market system may underinvest in
innovation, relative to the socially desirable level. Direct or indirect subsidies may help
correct this. We have also seen (Section 6.3) that a variety of barriers to mobility, including financial market imperfections, affect the ability of small firms to grow from the
fringe of an industry to its core of established firms. Direct subsidies to firms, indirect
subsidies by way of support for venture capital markets or (for example) industrial parks
may improve the process of entry and growth.

These and other types of horizontal aid carry with them the danger that what is put
forward as aid to correct a market failure will in fact deliver operating aid, aid that covers
normal and routine expenses of operation, to recipient firms. It is operating aid that
short-circuits the supply-side concentration effect of market integration, and prevents
market integration from yielding its full potential benefits.

In an integrating market, if one Member State subsidizes its firms and others do not, the
subsidized firms benefit and firms based in other Member States are hurt. If several Member States each subsidize their own firms, the result can be an outcome in which subsidies
neutralize each other, so that funds are transferred from the rest of society to firms,
leaving recipient firms better off but without giving any one firm a competitive
advantage over its rivals (Collie, 2000).[24]

---

[24] The same effect arises with export subsidies; see Figure 8.1 and the accompanying text.

Regional aid

In the *First Report on Competition Policy*, the Commission highlighted the themes that have animated policy debates about regional aid ever since (EC Commission, 1972, pp. 116–17.)

National initiatives for regional development are becoming more and more costly. Part of the aid granted at present only achieves reciprocal neutralization with unjustified profits for the benefiting enterprises as the only counterpart. In fact, this process of outbidding cannot appreciably affect the aggregate flow of investments, which, at the Community level, can be mobilized for the purpose of regional investment.

The rate of aid and the means employed no longer correspond to the relative seriousness of the situation in the various regions when assessed at Community level. The choice of the location of investments tends to be made at the expense of the less-favoured regions and against the distribution of activities required by the common interest.

. . . In order to attract investments, the advantages offered often exceed the compensation for material inconvenience imposed on the benefiting enterprises as a result of the particular choice of location it is hoped to bring about. Under cover of worthwhile regional objectives, artificial sectoral development can be brought into being . . .

If regional aid attracts investment from outside to inside the EC, the net gain to the region and the net gain to the EC are the same. If regional aid attracts investment from elsewhere in the EC, the net benefit of the aid to the EC is the incremental development in the aided region, minus the reduction in development that would have taken place in other EC regions if the aid had not been granted. Aid may have positive effects on the aided region, yet have negligible or negative effects on the EC as a whole.

Sectoral aid

Some sectors of the EC economy are in secular decline and carry large amounts of excess capacity. Adjustment to equilibrium market structures in these sectors requires a substantial reduction in the number of firms, often accompanied by a reorientation of production toward specialized market segments. State aid to retrain workers that have been made redundant, or to facilitate restructuring, may be justified on social grounds, but there is a sense in which adapting business operations to changing market conditions is part of normal business operations, so that aid to sectors in secular decline has an unavoidable element of operating aid.

Economic efficiency requires that resources be transferred out of declining industries and into sectors where they can find productive use. There is always the danger that subsidies granted with the intention of easing the transfer of resources out of a declining sector will instead be used to delay inevitable and socially desirable adjustment.

As we have emphasized, market integration often implies a reduction in the equilibrium number of firms. To realize the greatest gains from market integration, it should be the most efficient firms that stay in the market, while less efficient firms exit. Subsidies can distort the selection function of the market by allowing less efficient subsidized firms to survive while more efficient but unsubsidized firms exit. Such outcomes reduce the gains from formation of the single market for all concerned.

10.4.3 **The application of state aid policy**

Administrative framework

The 1999 Regulation on state aid procedures[25] summarizes the procedures for application of state aid policy that have developed over the years. State aid can take a wide variety of forms, including cash subsidies, tax credits, loan guarantees, financial investment by the state in a firm, and many others, but state aid is considered to be present if public policy directly or indirectly gives a firm an economic advantage it would not otherwise have (Morch, 1995). Member States must notify the Commission in advance of aid projects. Aid cannot be granted unless and until it is approved by the Commission. Aid that is not notified to the Commission cannot receive an exemption under Article 87(3), and if aid is granted without receiving an exemption, it must be recovered.

The 1999 Regulation toughens the Commission's investigatory powers and establishes that legal appeals before national courts are not to delay recovery of aid that has been denied an exemption. But the record of Member States in following state aid rules is not a good one: 21 per cent of 1997 aid cases involved aid not notified to the Commission, and "Nearly 10 per cent of the recovery decisions are not executed *10 years* after they have been taken, in the majority of cases because of pending procedures before national courts" (Sinnaeve, 1998, p. 80).

Case study: Boch/Noviboch[26]

The European Commission became aware that a Belgian public enterprise had invested 475 million Belgian francs in a local firm that manufactured ceramic sanitary ware. In April and June 1982, the Commission contacted the Belgian government to point out that the EC Treaty required prior notification before state aid payments could be made. The Belgian government did not respond to these contacts.

The Commission issued a decision finding that the recipient firm had made substantial losses for several years, so that no private investor would have made investments comparable to those made by the Belgian public sector; the investment was therefore a state aid. The Commission also found that the firm sold a substantial portion of its output in other Member States, so the aid would affect trade between the Member States. As regards the impact of the aid on market performance the Commission wrote (OJ L91, p. 339, April 1983),

The purpose of the aid is to permit the maintenance of production capacity and this is likely to strike a particularly grave blow at conditions of competition since free market conditions would normally require the closure of the firm in question so that, in a situation in which the industry is faced with over-capacity, more efficient competitors could expand.

The Commission declined to permit the aid under any of the Article 87(3) exemptions and required that it be withdrawn.

Shortly thereafter, the Commission learned that the Belgian public sector had invested 83 million Belgian francs in the same company. The Commission contacted the Belgian

---

[25] Council Regulation (EC) No 659/1999 of 22 March 1999 OJ L 83/1.
[26] See Commission Decisions Boch I, Boch II, Boch III Noviboch.

government a number of times about the matter, eventually receiving a reply that the decision to grant the aid had been taken in 1981 and was not new. Relying on arguments much the same as those in the first decision, the Commission found that the aid would affect trade among the Member States, was incompatible with the common market, did not qualify for exemption, and should be withdrawn.

The Commission then learned that the Belgian government had invested 295.3 million Belgian francs in the recipient firm. After being contacted by the Commission, the Belgian government confirmed the nature of the investment, but took the view that it was not state aid, being comparable to an investment decision of a private stockholder, so that no notification was in fact necessary.

The Commission relied on the same arguments it had used in previous decisions: the firm had a series of substantial losses, and a private investor would not have made the kind of investment undertaken by the Belgian government.

The Belgian government reported to the Commission that the aid had not been paid and that regional authorities had decided "to wind up the firm". The Commission determined that 104 million Belgian francs had been paid to the firm, rescue aid which permitted the firm to continue operations until its sanitary ware division was taken over by a new firm set up on behalf of the regional authorities. Subsequent arguments by the Commission (as to the impact of the aid on trade between Member States and incompatibility with the common market) were essentially the same as those relied upon by the Commission in earlier decisions. The Commission found the aid to be incompatible with the common market and ordered the Belgian government to recover the aid, insofar as possible given that the firm had been liquidated.

In 1985, Belgian regional authorities arranged for the original firm, Boch, to be closed. It endowed a new firm, Noviboch, with a capital investment of 400 million Belgian francs. Noviboch acquired the assets of the old firm, but not its debts.

Once again the Commission reminded the Belgian government of its treaty obligations to notify aid in advance, and the Belgian government replied that the decision to invest in the new company was not state aid. The Commission's arguments that the investment constituted state aid and that it distorted competition in the common market were much the same as those presented in the previous decisions. Finally, however, the Commission was willing to grant an exemption for the aid (OJ L228, 15 August 1987, p. 41)

As to the exception in Article 92(3)(c) for aid to facilitate the development of certain economic activities or certain economic areas, Noviboch produces and markets quality ceramic sanitary ware on a fairly modest scale . . . its output is currently 20 to 30% lower than that of its predecessor Boch . . .

. . . Noviboch's operations are profitable. . . .

The restructuring stemming from the winding-up of Boch has therefore contributed to the reorganization of a Community industry suffering from surplus production capacity, namely the ceramics industry.

The Boch/Noviboch decisions illustrate the tenacity with which Member State governments have sought to deliver operating aid to domestic firms,[27] and the equal tenacity

---

[27] It should not be thought that Belgium's track record in state aid cases is qualitatively different from that of other Member States; it is not.

with which the Commission has sought to enforce the EC Treaty, the terms of which have been agreed to by all Member States. At different times, Members States have tried to deliver aid to private and public or formerly public firms in a wide range of markets: steel, shipbuilding, coal, banking, passenger airlines, and many others. Often the Commission has managed to block or reduce the aid; often it has not.

10.5 **Summary**

Market integration may lead to increased trade flows between formerly independent markets. It need not lead to identical net prices in different regions, if markets are imperfectly competitive, if regional demand characteristics differ, and if the legal single market contains several geographic submarkets in an economic sense.

Market integration should be expected to lead to improved market performance, in the static sense of reduced price-cost margins and greater consumers' surplus and also in the dynamic senses of greater efficiency, more extensive exploitation of whatever economies of scale are potential in the technology, and more rapid technological progress.

The rivalry- and performance-enhancing effects of market integration will reduce the long-run equilibrium number of firms in many industries. Member State governments will seek to improve the chances that their native firms survive the structural readjustment process. It is by the application of state aid control that the Commission seeks to ensure that more efficient firms survive, delivering the maximum benefit from market integration.

Study points

- market integration and market performance (pages 212–17, pages 222–6)
- market integration and market structure (pages 217–19, pages 224–5)
- the ECSC: price transparency and basing point steel pricing (pages 219–22)
- state aid and state aid control (pages 226–34)

Problems

10-1 Evaluate the consequences of market integration using the model of Section (10.2.2), that is, two countries $i = 1, 2$ each with an inverse demand curve with equation (10.1)

$$p_i = 100 - Q_i, \tag{10.17}$$

n_1 firms in market 1 and n_2 firms in market 2, and all firms operating with the cost function (10.2),

$$c(q) = 10q,$$ (10.18)

if country i collects a per-unit tax t_i on each unit sold within its territory.

10-2 Suppose n_1 Cournot oligopolists supply the market in country 1, where the equation of the inverse demand curve is

$$p_1 = 100 - Q_1,$$ (10.19)

while n_2 different Cournot oligopolists supply the market in country 2, where the equation of the inverse demand curve is

$$p_2 = 100 - \tfrac{1}{2}Q_2.$$ (10.20)

Compare equilibrium prices and outputs before and after market integration, holding the number of firms fixed.

10-3 Verify (10.8).

References

Acs, Zoltan and David B. Audretsch *Innovation and Small Firms*. Cambridge, Massachusetts: MIT Press, 1990.

Adelman, M. A. 'Oil import quota auctions', *Challenge*, January–February 1976, pp. 17–22.

Adler, Michael 'Specialization in the European Coal and Steel Community', *Journal of Common Market Studies* Volume VIII, 1969–70, pp. 175–91.

Albæk, Svend, Peter Møllgaard, and Per Balzer Overgaard 'Government-assisted oligopoly coordination? A *Concrete* Case', *Journal of Industrial Economics* 45(4) December 1997, pp. 429–43.

Amacher, Ryan C., Richard James Sweeney, and Robert D. Tollison 'A note on the Webb-Pomerene law and the Webb-cartels', *Antitrust Bulletin* 23(2), 1978, pp. 371–87.

American Economic Association 'Consensus report on the *Webb-Pomerene* law', *American Economic Review* 37, 1947, pp. 848–63.

Amir, Rabah 'Modelling imperfectly appropriable R&D via spillovers', *International Journal of Industrial Organization* 18(7), October 2000, pp. 1013–32.

Ansic, David 'Note: a pilot experimental test of trade hysteresis', *Managerial and Decision Economics* 16(1), January–February 1995, pp. 85–91.

Arrow, Kenneth J. 'Economic welfare and the allocation of resources for invention', in *The rate and direction of inventive activity: economic and social factors*. Princeton: NBER, Princeton University Press, 1962, pp. 609–25.

Arthur, W. Brian 'Competing technologies, increasing returns, and lock-in by historical events', *Economic Journal* 99, 1989, pp. 116–31.

d'Aspremont, Claude and Alexis Jacquemin 'Cooperative and noncooperative R&D in duopoly with spillovers', *American Economic Review* 78(5) December 1988, pp. 1133–7.

Audretsch, David B. *Innovation and Industry Evolution*. Cambridge, Massachusetts: MIT Press, 1995.

Auquier, Antoine A. and Richard E. Caves 'Monopolistic export industries, trade, taxes, and optimal competition policy', *Economic Journal* 89, 1979, pp. 559–81.

Bain, Joe S. 'A note on pricing in monopoly and oligopoly', *American Economic Review* 39(1) March 1949, pp. 448–69.

— *Barriers to New Competition*. Cambridge, Massachusetts: Harvard University Press, 1956.

Baldwin, Richard and Harry Flam 'Strategic trade policies in the market for 30–40 seat commuter aircraft', *Weltwirtschaftliches Archiv* 125, 1989, pp. 484–500.

Baldwin, Robert E. 'Imposing multilateral discipline on administered protection', in Anne O. Krueger, editor. *The WTO as an International Organization*. Chicago: University of Chicago Press, 1998, pp. 297–327.

Baumol, William J., John C. Panzar, and Robert D. Willig *Contestable Markets and the Theory of Industry Structure*. New York: Harcourt Brace Jovanovich, Inc. 1982.

Beasley, Timothy and Paul Seabright 'The effects and policy implications of state aids to industry: an economic analysis', *Economic Policy* 28, April 1999, pp. 15–53.

Beath, John, Yannis Katsoulacos, and David Ulph 'R&D rivalry v. R&D cooperation under uncertainty', *Recherches Economiques de Louvain* 54(4), 1988, pp. 373–84.

Berle, Adolf A. and Gardiner C. Means *The Modern Corporation and Private Property*. New York: Harcourt, Brace & World, Inc., 1932; New York and London: Transaction Publishers, 1968.

Bertrand, Joseph 'Review', *Journal des Savants* 68 1883, pp. 499–508; reprinted in English translation by James W. Friedman in Andrew F. Daughety, editor. *Cournot oligopoly*. Cambridge: Cambridge University Press, 1988, pp. 73–81 and by Margaret Chevaillier in an Appendix to Magnan de Bornier (1992).

Blitz, Rudolph C. and John J. Siegfried 'How did the wealthiest Americans get so rich?', *Quarterly Review of Economics and Finance* 32(1) Spring 1992, pp. 5–26.

Bottasso, Anna and Alessandro Sembenelli 'Market power, productivity and the EU Single Market programme: evidence from a panel of Italian firms', *European Economic Review* 45, 2001, pp. 167–86.

Bowley, A. L. *The Mathematical Groundwork of Economics*. Oxford: Oxford University Press, 1924.

Brander, James A. and Paul R. Krugman 'A reciprocal dumping model of international trade', *Journal of International Economics* 1983, pp. 313–21.

Bresnahan, Timothy F. 'Departures from marginal-cost pricing in the American automobile industry: estimates for 1977–1978', *Journal of Econometrics* 9, 1981, pp. 1010–19.

— 'Sutton's *Sunk Costs and Market Structure: Price Competition, Advertising, and the Evolution of Concentration*', *Rand Journal of Economics* **23(1)** Spring 1992, pp. 137–52.

Buigues, Pierre and Alexis Jacquemin 'Strategies of firms and structural environments in the large internal market', *Journal of Common Market Studies* **28**, 1989, pp. 53–67.

Bulow, Jeremy, John Geanakoplos, and Paul D. Klemperer 'Multimarket oligopoly: strategic substitutes and complements', *Journal of Political Economy* **93(3)** 1985, pp. 488–511.

Burton, Daniel F. and Kathleen Hansen 'German technological policy: incentive for industrial innovation', *Challenge* **36(1)**, January–February 1993, pp. 37–47.

Caves, Richard E. (editor) *Symposium on International Trade and Industrial Organization*. *Journal of Industrial Economics* **29(2)**, December 1980.

— 'Industrial organization and new findings on the turnover and mobility of firms', *Journal of Economic Literature* **36(4)** December 1998, pp. 1947–82.

Caves, Richard E. and Michael E. Porter, 'From entry barriers to mobility barriers: conjectural variations and contrived deterrence to new competition', *Quarterly Journal of Economics* **91**, May 1977, pp. 241–61.

Caves, Richard E., Michael D. Whinston, and Mark A. Hurwitz 'Patent expiration, entry, and competition in the US pharmaceutical industry', *Brookings Papers on Economic Activity* Microeconomics 1991, pp. 1–48.

Chadwick, Edwin 'Results of different principles of legislation and administration in Europe of competition for the field, as compared with competition within the field, of service', *Journal of the Royal Statistical Society* **22**, September 1859, pp. 381–420.

Chamberlin, Edward H. *The Theory of Monopolistic Competition*. Cambridge, Massachusetts: Harvard University Press, 1933.

— , editor. *Monopoly and Competition and their Regulation*. London: Macmillan, 1954.

Chandler, Alfred D., Jr. *Strategy and Structure: Chapters in the History of Industrial Enterprise*. Cambridge, Massachusetts: MIT Press, 1962.

— *The Visible Hand: The Managerial Revolution in American Business*. Cambridge, Massachusetts: Harvard University Press, 1977.

— *Scale and Scope The Dynamics of Industrial Capitalism*. Cambridge, Massachusetts and London: The Belknap Press of Harvard University Press, 1990.

Christensen, Peder and Philip Owen 'Comment on the Judgment of the Court of First Instance of 25 March 1999 in the merger case IV/M.619—Gencor/Lonrho', *Competition Policy Newsletter* 1999 Number 2, June 1999, pp. 19–23.

Clarida, Richard H. 'Dumping: in theory, in policy, and in practice', in Jagdish Bhagwati and Robert E. Hudec, editors. *Fair Trade and Harmonization*. MIT Press, 1996, pp. 357–89.

Clark, Don P., David L. Kaserman, and John W. Mayo 'Barriers to trade and the import vulnerability of US manufacturing industries', *Journal of Industrial Economics* **38(4)**, June 1990, pp. 433–47.

Coase, R. H. 'The nature of the firm', *Economica* New Series IV, 1937, pp. 386–405, reprinted in George J. Stigler and Kenneth E. Boulding, editors. *Readings in price theory*. Chicago: Richard D. Irwin, Inc., 1952, pp. 331–51 and in Oliver E. Williamson and Sidney G. Winter, editors *The Nature of the Firm*. Oxford: Oxford University Press, 1991, pp. 18–33.

Cohen, Wesley M. and Daniel A. Levinthal 'Innovation and learning: the two faces of R&D', *Economic Journal* **99(397)** September 1989, pp. 569–96.

Collie, David R. 'State aid in the European Union', *International Journal of Industrial Organization* **(18)6**, 2000, pp. 867–84.

Comité Intergouvernemental créé par la Conférence de Messine *Rapport des Chefs de Délégation aux Ministres des Affairs Etrangères (Spaak Report)*. Brussels, 21 April 1956.

Cook, P. Lesley *Effects of Mergers*. London: George Allen & Unwin Ltd, 1958.

la Cour, Lisbeth Funding and Peter Møllgaard 'Testing for (abuse of) domination: the Danish cement industry', Department of Economics,

Copenhagen Business School, Working Paper 10–2000,

Cournot, Augustin *Researches into the Mathematical Principles of the Theory of Wealth*. Original Paris: L. Hachette, 1838. English translation by Nathaniel T. Bacon. New York: The Macmillan Company, 1897; reprinted 1927 by The Macmillan Company, New York with notes by Irving Fisher; reprinted 1960, 1964, 1971 by Augustus M. Kelley, New York.

Cowling, Keith and Dennis C. Mueller 'The social costs of monopoly power', *Economic Journal* **88**, December 1978, pp. 727–48.

Crandall, Robert W. 'Import quotas and the automobile industry: the costs of protectionism', *The Brookings Review* Summer 1984, pp. 8–16.

Cusumano, Michael A., Yiorgos Mylonadis, and Richard S. Rosenbloom 'Strategic maneuvering and mass-market dynamics: the triumph of VHS over Beta', *Business History Review* **66(1)**, Spring 1992, pp. 51–94.

Dasgupta, Partha and Eric Maskin 'The simple economics of research portfolios', *Economic Journal* **97**, September 1987, pp. 581–95.

David, Paul A. 'Clio and the economics of QWERTY', *American Economic Review* **75(2)**, 1985, pp. 332–7.

Davis, Donald R., David E. Weinstein, Scott C. Bradford, and Kazushige Shimpo 'Using international and Japanese regional data to determine when the factor abundance theory of trade works', *American Economic Review* **87(3)**, June 1997, pp. 421–46.

Davis, Ralph *The Industrial Revolution and British Overseas Trade*. Leicester: Leicester University Press, 1979.

Degryse, Hans and Frank Verboven 'Car price differentials in the European Union: an economic analysis', London: CEPR, November 2000.

de Melo, Jaime and Patrick A. Messerlin 'Price, quality and welfare effects of European VERs on Japanese autos', *European Economic Review* **32(7)** September 1988, pp. 1527–46.

Deneckere, Raymond J. and Carl Davidson 'Incentives to form coalitions with Bertrand competition', *Rand Journal of Economics* **16(4)** Winter 1985, pp. 473–86.

Dewey, Donald *The Theory of Imperfect Competition*. New York: Columbia University Press, 1969.

Dick, Andrew R. 'Are export cartels efficiency-enhancing or monopoly promoting?: evidence from the Webb-Pomerene experience', *Research in Law and Economics* 1992a, pp. 89–127.

— 'The competitive effects of Japan's export cartel associations', *Journal of the Japanese and International Economies* September 1992b, pp. 275–98.

— 'Japanese antitrust: reconciling theory and evidence', *Contemporary Policy Issues* **XI(2)**, April 1993, pp. 50–61.

Dinopoulos, Elias and Mordechai E. Kreinin 'Effects of the US-Japan auto VER on European prices and on US welfare', *Review of Economics and Statistics* **70(3)**, August 1988, pp. 484–91.

Dixit, Avinash 'A model of duopoly suggesting a theory of entry barriers', *Bell Journal of Economics* **10(1)** Spring 1979, pp. 20–32.

— 'Hysteresis, import penetration, and exchange-rate pass-through', *Quarterly Journal of Economics* **104(2)**, 1989, pp. 205–28.

Dixit, Avinash K. and Robert S. Pindyck *Investment Under Uncertainty*. Princeton: Princeton University Press, 1994.

Dowrick, Steve 'von Stackelberg and Cournot duopoly: choosing roles', *Rand Journal of Economics* **17(2)** Summer 1986, pp. 251–60.

Dunning, J. 'Towards an eclectic theory of international production: some empirical results', *Journal of International Business Studies* **11**, 1980, pp. 9–31.

— 'The eclectic paradigm of international production: a restatement and some possible extensions', *Journal of International Business Studies* **19**, 1988, pp. 1–31.

Duysters, Geert and John Hagedoorn 'Convergence and divergence in the international information technology industry', in John Hagedoorn, editor. *Technical change and the world economy*. Aldershot: Edward Elgar, 1995, pp. 205–34.

EC Commission *First Report on Competition Policy*. Brussels 1972.

— *14th Annual Report on Competition Policy* 1984. Brussels-Luxembourg, 1985.

— *24th Annual Report on Competition Policy* 1994. Brussels-Luxembourg, 1995.

— *NACE Rev. 1*. Luxembourg: Office for Official Publications of the European Communities, 1996.

— 'Measuring seller concentration in European industry', *Monthly Panorama of European Industry*, 1997a, pp. 69–84.

— *Commission Notice on the definition of the relevant market for the purposes of Community competition law*. OJ C 372 9 December 1997b; page references are to the version downloaded from the internet.

— *XXVIIth Report on Competition Policy 1997*. Brussels-Luxembourg, 1998.

— *White Paper on the Modernisation of the Rules Implementing Articles 81 and 82 of the EC Treaty*. Brussels, 28 April 1999a.

— *XXVIIIth Report on Competition Policy 1998*. Brussels-Luxembourg, 1999b.

— 'Market integration and differences in price levels between EU Member States', Study 4, *European Economy* 69, 1999c.

— *Eighth Survey on State Aid in the European Union*. COM(2000)205 final. 11 April 2000a.

— *Draft Guidelines on the Applicability of Article 81 to horizontal co-operation*. Brussels, 27 April 2000b.

— *Proposal for a Council Regulation on the implementation of the rules on competition laid down in Articles 81 and 82 of the Treaty and amending Regulations (EEC) No 1017/68, (EEC) No 2988/74), (EEC) No 4056/86 and (EEC) No 3975/87*. COM(2000) 582 final Brussels 27 September 2000c.

— *XXIXth Report on Competition Policy 1999*. Brussels-Luxembourg, 2000d.

Economides, Nicholas 'The economics of networks', *International Journal of Industrial Organization* 14(6), October 1996, pp. 673–99.

Economides, Nicholas and Frederick Flyer 'Compatibility and market structure for network goods', manuscript, Stern School of Business, New York University, November 1997.

El-Agraa, Ali 'VERs as a prominent feature of Japanese trade policy: their rationale, costs and benefits', *World Economy* 18(2), 1995, pp. 219–35.

Emerson, Michael, Michel Aujean, Michel Catinat, Philippe Goybet, and Alexis Jacquemin *The Economics of 1992: The EC Commission's Assessment of the Economic Effects of Completing the Internal Market*. Oxford: Oxford University Press, 1988.

Esposito, L. and F. F. Espositio 'Foreign competition and domestic industry profitability', *Review of Economics and Statistics* 53, November 1971, pp. 343–53.

Evans, Andrew and Stephen Martin 'Socially acceptable distortion of competition: EC policy on state aid', *European Law Review* 16(2), April 1991, pp. 79–111.

Farrell, Joseph and Garth Saloner 'Standardization, compatibility, and innovation', *Rand Journal of Economics* 16, 1985, pp. 70–83.

Farrell, Joseph and Carl Shapiro 'Asset ownership and market structure in oligopoly', *Rand Journal of Economics* 21(2) Summer 1990, pp. 275–92.

Feenstra, Robert C. 'Quality change under trade restraints in Japanese autos', *Quarterly Journal of Economics* 1988, pp. 101–46.

— 'Symmetric pass-through of tariffs and exchange rates under imperfect competition: an empirical test', *Journal of International Economics* 27, August 1989, pp. 25–45.

Feinberg, Robert M. and Joseph Shaanan 'The relative price discipline of domestic versus foreign entry', *Review of Industrial Organization* 9(2), April 1994, pp. 211–20.

Ferdinandusse, Ernst 'The Commission fines FEG, the Dutch association of electrotechnical equipment wholesalers and its biggest member', *Competition Policy Newsletter* 2000 No 1 February 2000, pp. 17–18.

Fingleton, John, Frances Ruane, and Vivienne Ryan 'Market definition and state aid control', *European Economy* 1999(3), pp. 65–88.

Finnegan, John 'Commission sets out its policy on commissions paid by airlines to travel agents', *Competition Policy Newsletter* 1999 No 3, October 1999, p. 23.

Fournier, Leslie T. 'The purposes and results of the *Webb-Pomerene* law', *American Economic Review* 22, 1932, pp. 18–33.

Friedman, James W. 'A non-cooperative equilibrium for supergames', *Review of Economic Studies* 38(1) January 1971, pp. 1–12, reprinted in Andrew F. Daughety, editor. *Cournot oligopoly: characterization and applications*. Cambridge: Cambridge University Press, 1988, pp. 142–57.

Galbraith, John K. *American Capitalism: The Concept of Countervailing Power*. Boston: Houghton–Mifflin, 1952.

Gaskins, Darius W. Jr. 'Dynamic limit pricing: optimal limit pricing under threat of entry', *Journal of Economic Theory* 3, September 1971, pp. 306–22.

Geroski, Paul A. 'Some data-driven reflections on the entry process', in Geroski, Paul A. and Joachim Schwalbach. *Entry and Market Contestability*. Oxford: Blackwell Publishers, 1991a, pp. 282–96.

Geroski, Paul A. *Market Dynamics and Entry*. Oxford, UK and Cambridge, USA: Basil Blackwell, 1991b.

Geroski, Paul A. and Joachim Schwalbach. *Entry and Market Contestability*. Oxford: Blackwell Publishers, 1991.

Ghemawat, Pankaj and Barry Nalebuff. 'Exit', *Rand Journal of Economics* **16(2)** Summer 1985, pp. 184–94.

— 'The devolution of declining industries', *Quarterly Journal of Economics* **105(1)** February 1990, pp. 167–86.

Gibrat, Robert *Les Inégalités Économiques*. Paris: Sirey, 1931.

Gillingham, John *Coal, Steel, and the Rebirth of Europe, 1945–1955*. Cambridge: Cambridge University Press, 1991.

— 'The European Coal and Steel Community: an object lesson?' in Barry Eichengreen, editor. *Europe's post-war recovery*. Cambridge: Cambridge University Press, 1995, pp. 151–68.

Greenaway, D. and B. Hindley, editors. *What Britain pays for voluntary export restraints*. Thames Essay 43. London: Trade Policy Research Centre, 1985.

Griliches, Zvi 'The search for R&D spillovers', *Scandinavian Journal of Economics* 94, 1992, pp. 29–47.

Grossman, Sanford J. and Oliver D. Hart 'The costs and benefits of ownership: a theory of vertical and lateral integration', *Journal of Political Economy* **94(4)**, 1986, pp. 691–719.

Hadley, Eleanor 'Counterpoint on business groupings and government-industry relations in automobiles', in Masahiko Aoki, editor. *The Economic Analysis of the Japanese Firm*. Amsterdam: North-Holland, 1984, pp. 319–27.

Hall, Bronwyn 'The relationship between firm size and firm growth in the US manufacturing sector', *Journal of Industrial Economics* **35(4)**, June 1987, pp. 583–606.

Hamberger, Richard A. 'Coal and Steel Community: rules for a competitive market and their applications', in John Perry Miller, editor. *Competition, Cartels, and their Regulation*. Amsterdam: North-Holland Publishing Company, 1962, Chapter 9, pp. 347–77.

Hamilton, J. H. and S. M. Slutsky 'Endogenous timing in duopoly games: Stackelberg or Cournot equilibria', *Games and Economic Behaviour* 2 1990, pp. 29–46.

Harberger, Arnold C. 'Monopoly and resource allocation', *American Economic Review* **44(2)**, May 1954, pp. 75–87.

Hart, Oliver 'An economist's perspective on the theory of the firm', *Columbia Law Review* 89, November 1989, pp. 1757–74.

— *Firms, Contracts, and Financial Structure*. Oxford: Oxford University Press, 1995.

Hart, Oliver D. and John Moore 'Property rights and the nature of the firm', *Journal of Political Economy* **98(6)**, 1990, pp. 1119–58.

Hart, P. E. and S. Prais 'The analysis of business concentration: a statistical approach', *Journal of the Royal Statistical Society*, Series A, 119, 1956, pp. 150–81.

Hay, Donald A. and Guy S. Liu 'The efficiency of firms: what difference does competition make?', *Economic Journal* 107, 1997, pp. 597–617.

Hazledine, Tim and John J. Siegfried 'How did the wealthiest New Zealanders get so rich?', *New Zealand Economic Papers* **31(1)**, 1997, pp. 35–47.

Helpman, Elhanan 'International trade in the presence of product differentiation, economies of scale and monopolistic competition', *Journal of International Economics* 11, 1981, pp. 305–40.

Henderson, Rebecca and Ian Cockburn 'Scale, scope and spillovers: the determinants of research productivity in drug discovery', *Rand Journal of Economics* **27(1)** Spring 1996, pp. 32–59.

Herfindahl, Orris C. *Concentration in the steel industry*, unpublished Ph.D. dissertation, Columbia University, 1950.

Hexner, Ervin *The International Steel Cartel*. Chapel Hill: University of North Carolina Press, 1943.

Hicks, John R. 'Annual survey of economic theory: the theory of monopoly', *Econometrica* **3(1)**, January 1935, pp. 1–20.

— 'The rehabilitation of consumers' surplus', *Review of Economic Studies* 9, 1941, pp. 108–16; reprinted in Kenneth J. Arrow and Tibor Scitovsky, editors *Readings in Welfare Economics*. London: George Allen and Unwin, 1969, pp. 325–35; page references are to reprinted version.

Hindley, Brian 'Dumping and the Far East trade of the European Community', *World Economy* **11(4)**, 1988, pp. 445–63.

Hindley, Brian and Patrick A. Messerlin *Antidumping Industry Policy: legalized protectionism in the WTO and what to do about it*. Washington, DC: AEI Press, 1996.

Hirschman, A. O. *National Power and the Structure of Foreign Trade*. Berkeley and Los Angeles: University of California Press, 1945.

— 'The paternity of an index', *American Economic Review* **54(5)**, September 1964, pp. 761–2.

Hotelling, Harold H. 'Stability in competition', *Economic Journal* **39** March 1929, pp. 41–57, reprinted in George J. Stigler and Kenneth E. Boulding, editors. *A. E. A. Readings in Price Theory*. Chicago: Richard D. Irwin, 1952.

— 'Edgeworth's taxation paradox and the nature of demand and supply functions', *Journal of Political Economy* **40(5)**, October 1932, pp. 577–616.

— 'The general welfare in relation to problems of taxation and of railway and utility rates', *Econometrica* **6(3)**, July 1938, pp. 242–69.

Hymer, Stephen H. *The international operations of national firms: a study of direct foreign investment*. Cambridge, Massachusetts: MIT Press, 1976 (reprint of 1960 dissertation).

Interparliamentary Union, 26th Conference, London, 1930: Resolution on The Control of International Trusts and Cartels.

Irwin, Douglas A. and Peter J. Klenow, 'High-tech R&D subsidies estimating the effects of Sematech', *Journal of International Economics* **40**, 1996, pp. 323–44.

Iyori, Hiroshi and Akinori Uesugi *The Antimonopoly Laws of Japan*. Federal Legal Publications, 1983.

Jacquemin, Alexis 'Corporate strategy and competition policy in the post-1992 Single Market', in William James Adams, editor. *Singular Europe*. Ann Arbor: University of Michigan Press, 1992, pp. 125–44.

Jacquemin, Alexis, Tsuruhiko Nambu and Isabelle Dewez 'A dynamic analysis of export cartels: the Japanese case', *Economic Journal* **91**, 1981, pp. 685–96.

Jacquemin, Alexis and André Sapir 'Competition and imports in the European market', in L. Alan Winters and Anthony Venables, editors. *European integration: trade and industry*. Cambridge: Cambridge University Press, 1991, pp. 82–95.

Jaffe, Adam B. 'The US patent system in transition: policy innovation and the innovation process', *Research Policy* **29(4–5)**, April 2000, pp. 531–57.

Jenks, Jeremiah W. *The Trust Problem*. New York: McClure, Philips, 1900.

Jones, Charles I. and John C. Williams 'Measuring the social return to R&D', Finance and Economics Discussion Series Staff Working Paper 1997–12, Federal Reserve Board, Washington, DC, February 1997.

Joskow, Paul L. 'Asset specificity and the structure of vertical relationships: empirical evidence', *Journal of Law, Economics and Organization* **4**, Spring 1988, pp. 95–117, reprinted in Williamson and Winter (1991).

Kaiser, Ulrich 'Research cooperation and research expenditures with endogenous absorptive capacity', *International Journal of Industrial Organization*, forthcoming, 2002.

Kamien, Morton I., Eitan Muller, and Israel Zang 'Research joint ventures and R&D cartels', *American Economic Review* **82(5)** December 1992, pp. 1293–306.

Kamien, Morton I. and Israel Zang 'Meet me halfway: research joint ventures and absorptive capacity', *International Journal of Industrial Organization* **18(7)** 2000, pp. 995–1012.

Katics, Michelle M. and Bruce C. Petersen, 'The effect of rising import competition on market power: a panel data study of US manufacturing', *Journal of Industrial Economics* **42(3)**, September 1994, pp. 277–98.

Katsoulacos, Yannis and David Ulph 'Endogenous spillovers and the performance of research joint ventures', *Journal of Industrial Economics* **46(3)**, September 1998, pp. 333–58.

Katz, Michael L. and Carl Shapiro 'Network externalities, competition, and compatibility', *American Economic Review* **75(3)**, June 1985, pp. 424–40.

Kindleberger, Charles P. *The World in Depression 1929–1939*. Berkeley: University of California Press, 1973.

Klein, Benjamin 'Vertical integration as organizational ownership: the Fisher Body–General Motors relationship revisited', *Journal of Law, Economics and Organization* **4(1)**, 1988, pp. 199–213, reprinted in Williamson and Winter (1991).

Klein, Benjamin, Robert G. Crawford and Armen A. Alchian 'Vertical integration, appropriable rents, and the competitive contracting process', *Journal of Law and Economics* **21(2)**, 1978, pp. 297–326.

Klemperer, Paul D. 'Entry deterrence in markets with consumer switching costs', *Economic Journal* **97** Conference 1987, pp. 99–117.

— 'Price wars caused by switching costs', *Review of Economic Studies* **56**, 1989, pp. 405–20.

Knetter, Michael M. 'Price discrimination by US and German exporters', *American Economic Review* **79**, March 1989, pp. 198–210.

— 'International comparisons of pricing-to-market behavior', *American Economic Review* **83**, June 1993, pp. 473–86.

Kostecki, Michel 'Export-restraint arrangements and trade liberalization', *World Economy*, December 1987, pp. 425–53.

Krause-Heiber, Ulrich 'Commission Decision of 20 September 2000 imposing a fine on Open Nederland and General Motors Nederland for obstruction of exports of new cars from the Netherlands', *Competition Policy Newsletter* 2001, No 1, February 2001, pp. 35–8.

Kreps, David M. and Robert Wilson 'Reputation and imperfect information', *Journal of Economic Theory* **27**, August 1982, pp. 253–79.

Krugman. Paul R. 'Import protection as export promotion', in Henryk Kierzkowski, editor. *Monopolistic competition and International Trade.* Oxford: Clarendon Press, 1984, pp. 180–93.

— 'Pricing to market when the exchange rate changes', in Sven W. Arndt and J. David Richardson, editors. *Real Financial Linkages Among Open Economies.* Cambridge, Massachusetts: MIT Press, 1987, pp. 49–70.

Krugman, Paul R. and Anthony J. Venables. 'Integration and the competitiveness of peripheral industry', in Christopher Bliss and Jorge Braga de Macedo, editors. *Unity with diversity in the European economy: the Community's Southern frontier.* Cambridge: Cambridge University Press, 1990, pp. 56–75.

Kumar, M. S. 'Growth, acquisition activity and firm size: evidence from the United Kingdom', *Journal of Industrial Economics* **33**, March 1985, pp. 327–38.

Larson, David A. 'An economic analysis of the Webb-Pomerene Act', *Journal of Law and Economics* **13(2)**, October 1970, pp. 461–500.

Lee, Jiawoo 'The response of exchange rate pass-through to market concentration in a small economy: the evidence from Korea', *Review of Economics and Statistics* **79(1)**, February 1997, pp. 142–5.

Lee, Tom and Louis L. Wilde 'Market structure and innovation: a reformulation', *Quarterly Journal of Economics* **94(2)**, March 1980, pp. 429–36.

Leibenstein, Harvey 'Allocative efficiency v. "X-efficiency,"' *American Economic Review* **56(3)**, June 1966, pp. 392–415.

— *Inside the Firm: the Inefficiencies of Hierarchy.* Cambridge, Massachusetts: Harvard University Press, 1987.

Leonard, Robert J. 'Reading Cournot, reading Nash: the creation and stabilization of the Nash equilibrium', *Economic Journal* **104**, May 1994, pp. 492–511.

Leontief, Wassily 'Domestic production and foreign trade: the American capital position re-examined', *Proceedings of the American Philosophical Society* **97**, September 1953, pp. 332–49; reprinted in Wassily Leontief, *Input-Output Economics.* Oxford: Oxford University Press, second edition, 1986.

Lerner, Abba P. 'The concept of monopoly and the measurement of monopoly power', *Review of Economic Studies*, 1 June 1934, pp. 157–75.

Levin, R. C., A. K. Klevorick, R. R. Nelson, and S. G. Winter 'Appropriating the returns from industrial R & D', *Brookings Papers on Economic Activity* 1988, pp. 783–820.

Liebowitz, Stanley J. and Stephen E. Margolis 'The fable of the keys', *Journal of Law and Economics* **33(1)**, April 1990, pp. 1–26.

Lipsey, R. G. and Kelvin Lancaster 'The general theory of the second best', *Review of Economic Studies* **24(1)**, 1956–7, pp. 11–32.

Lister, Louis *Europe's Coal and Steel Community.* New York: Twentieth Century Fund, 1960.

Loescher, Samuel M. *Imperfect Competition in the Cement Industry.* Cambridge, Massachusetts: Harvard University Press, 1959.

Loury, Glenn C. 'Market structure and innovation', *Quarterly Journal of Economics* **93(3)**, August 1979, pp. 395–410.

Lücking, Joachim 'Horizontal co-operation agreements: ensuring a modern policy', *Competition Policy Newsletter* 2000, No 2, June 2000, pp. 41–4.

Lücking, Joachim and Donncadh Woods 'Horizontal co-operation agreements: new rules in force', *Competition Policy Newsletter* 2001, No 1, February 2001, pp. 8–10.

Mansfield, Edwin 'How rapidly does new industrial technology leak out?' *Journal of Industrial Economics* **34(2)**, December 1985, pp. 217–23.

Mansfield, Edwin, John Rapoport, Anthony Romeo, Samuel Wagner, and George Beardsley 'Social and private rates of return from industrial innovations', *Quarterly Journal of Economics* **91(2)**, May 1977, pp. 221–40.

Mansfield, Edwin, Mark Schwartz and Samuel Wagner 'Imitation costs and patents: an empirical study', *Economic Journal* **91**, December 1981, pp. 907–18.

Marshall, Alfred *Principles of Economics*. London: The Macmillan Press Ltd, 8th edition, 1920.

— *Industry and Trade*. London: MacMillan and Co. Ltd. 4th edition, 1923.

Marston, Richard C. 'Pricing to market in Japanese manufacturing' *Journal of International Economics* **29**, 1990, pp. 217–36.

Martin, Stephen 'The measurement of profitability and the diagnosis of market power', *International Journal of Industrial Organization* **6(3)**, September 1988a, pp. 301–21.

— *Industrial Economics*. New York: Macmillan Publishing Company, 1988b.

— 'Sunk cost, financial markets, and contestability', *European Economic Review* **33(6)**, June 1989, pp. 1089–113.

— 'R&D joint ventures and tacit product market collusion', *European Journal of Political Economy* **11(4)**, April 1996, pp. 733–41.

— 'Competition policy: publicity v. prohibition & punishment', in Stephen Martin, editor. *Competition Policies in Europe*. Amsterdam: North Holland, 1998a.

— , editor. *Competition Policies in Europe*. Amsterdam: Elsevier Science B.V., 1998.

— 'Strategic research partnerships: evidence and analysis', paper presented at the National Science Foundation Workshop on Strategic Research Partnerships, Arlington, Virginia, 13 October 2000.

— 'Spillovers, appropriability, and R&D', forthcoming, *Journal of Economics*, 2001a.

— *Advanced Industrial Economics*, 2nd edition. Oxford, UK and Cambridge, Massachusetts: Blackwell Publishers, 2001b.

— 'Competition policy toward high-technology industries', 2001c.

Martin, Stephen and John T. Scott 'The nature of innovation market failure and the design of public support for private innovation', *Research Policy* **19(4–5)**, April 2000, pp. 437–47.

Martin, Stephen and Paola Valbonesi 'State aid in context', in Giampaolo Galli and Jacques Pelkmans, editors. *Regulatory Reform and Competitiveness in Europe*. Cheltenham, UK: Edward Elgar, 2000, Volume 1, pp. 176–201.

Matutes, Carmen and Pierre Regibeau 'Mix and match: product compatibility without network externalities', *Rand Journal of Economics* **19(2)**, 1988, pp. 219–34.

Messerlin, Patrick A. 'The EC antidumping regulations: a first economic appraisal, 1980–85', *Weltwirtschaftliches Archiv* **125**, 1989, pp. 563–87.

— 'Anti-dumping regulations or pro-cartel law? The EC chemical cases', *World Economy* **13**, 1990, pp. 465–92.

Milward, Alan S. *The Reconstruction of Western Europe 1945–51*. Berkeley and Los Angeles: University of California Press, 1984.

Morch, Henrik 'Summary of the most important recent developments', *Competition Policy Newsletter* Spring 1995, pp. 47–51.

Morelli, Carlo, editor. *Cartels and Market Management in the Post-War World*. London School of Economics Business History Unit Occasional Paper 1997 No 1.

Mowery, David 'The practice of technology policy', in Paul Stoneman, editor. *Handbook of the Economics of Innovation and Technological Change*. Oxford: Blackwell Publishers Ltd., 1995.

Mowery, David C. and W. Edward Steinmueller 'Government policy and industry evolution in the US integrated circuit industry: what lessons for newly industrializing economies?', CEPR Publication No 192, Center for Economic Policy Research, January 1990.

Nash, John F. Jr. *Non–cooperative Games*. Ph.D. dissertation, Princeton University, 1950.

Nelson, Richard R. 'Government stimulus of technological progress: lessons from American history', in Richard R. Nelson, editor. *Government and Technical Progress*. New York: Pergamon Press, 1982, pp. 451–81.

Nelson, Richard R. and Sidney G. Winter, *An Evolutionary Theory of Economic Change*. Cambridge, Massachusetts: Harvard University Press, 1982.

Neumann, Manfred, Ingo Böbel, and Alfred Haid 'Domestic concentration, foreign trade and economic performance', *International Journal of Industrial Organization* **3**, 1985, pp. 1–19.

Neven, Damien, Robin Nuttall, and Paul Seabright *Merger in Daylight*. London: CEPR, 1993.

Neven, Damien, Pénélope Papandropoulos, and Paul Seabright *Trawling for Minnows*. London: CEPR, 1998.

Nickell, Stephen J. 'Competition and corporate performance', *Journal of Political Economy* **104**, 1996, pp. 724–45.

Nicolaides, Phedon and Remco van Wijngaarden 'Reform of anti-dumping regulations: the case of the EC', *Journal of World Trade* **27**(3), June 1993, pp. 31–53.

Odagiri, Hiroyuki and Akira Goto 'The Japanese system of innovation: past, present, and future', in Richard R. Nelson, editor. *National Innovation Systems*. Oxford: Oxford University Press, 1993.

O'Hagen, H. Osborne *Leaves from My Life*, 1926.

Pagoulatos, Emilio and Robert Sorensen 'Foreign trade, concentration and profitability in open economies', *European Economic Review* **8**, 1976, pp. 255–67.

Peck, Merton J. 'Joint R&D: the case of Microelectronics and Computer Technology Corporation', *Research Policy* **15**(5), October 1986, pp. 219–31.

— 'Industrial organization and the gains from Europe 1992', *Brookings Papers on Economic Activity* **20**, 1989, pp. 277–99.

Peña Castellot, Miguel Ángel 'An overview of the application of the Leniency notice', *Competition Policy Newsletter* 2001 No 1, February 2001, pp. 11–15.

Petzina, Dietmar 'The origin of the European Coal and Steel Community: economic forces and political interests', *Journal of Institutional and Theoretical Economics* **137**, 1981, pp. 450–68.

Phlips, Louis 'Common markets: towards a theory of market integration', *Journal of Industrial Economics* **10**(2), March 1962, pp. 81–92.

— *The Economics of Price Discrimination*. Cambridge: Cambridge University Press, 1983.

— 'Basing point pricing, competition, and market integration', in Hiroshi Ohta and Jacques–François Thisse, editors. *Does Economic Space Matter? Essays in Honour of Melvin L. Greenhut*. London: The Macmillan Press Ltd., 1993, pp. 303–15.

Pickford, M. 'A new test for manufacturing efficiency: an analysis of the results of licence tendering in New Zealand', *International Journal of Industrial Organization* **3**(2), June 1985, pp. 153–77.

Reinganum, Jennifer F. 'A dynamic game of R and D: patent protection and competitive behaviour', *Econometrica* **50**(3), May 1982, pp. 671–88.

Ricardo, David *On the Principles of Political Economy and Taxation*. Piero Sraffa, Editor. Cambridge: Cambridge University Press, 1951.

Riordan, Michael H. and Oliver E. Williamson 'Asset specificity and economic organization', *International Journal of Industrial Organization* **3**(4), December 1985, pp. 365–78.

Robinson, Joan *The Economics of Imperfect Competition*, 2nd edition. London: Macmillan, St. Martin's Press, 1933.

Robinson, William T. and Jeongwen Chiang. 'Are Sutton's predictions robust? Empirical insights into advertising, R&D, and concentration', *Journal of Industrial Economics* **44**(4), December 1996, pp. 398–408.

Salant, Stephen W., S. Switzer, and Robert J. Reynolds 'Losses from horizontal merger: the effects of an exogenous change in industry structure on Cournot-Nash equilibrium', *Quarterly Journal of Economics* **98**(2), May 1983, pp. 185–213.

Salinger, Michael 'The concentration-margins relationship reconsidered', *Brookings Papers on Economic Activity*. Microeconomics 1990, pp. 287–321.

Salus, Peter H. *A Quarter Century of UNIX*. Reading, Massachusetts: Addison-Wesley Publishing Company, 1994.

Samuelson, Paul A. *Foundations of Economic Analysis*. Cambridge, Massachusetts: Harvard University Press, 1947.

— *Economics*, 7th edition. New York: McGraw-Hill, 1967.

Sappington, David E. M. 'Incentives in principal-agent relationships', *Journal of Economic Perspectives* **5**(2), 1991, pp. 45–66.

Scheingold, Stuart A. *The Rule of Law in European Integration*. New Haven and London: Yale University Press, 1965.

Scherer, F. M. *Industrial Market Structure and Economic Performance*. Chicago: Rand McNally: 1st edition, 1970, 2nd edition, 1980.

— 'Sunlight and sunset at the Federal Trade Commission', *Administrative Law Review* **42**, Fall 1990, pp. 461–87, reprinted in F. M. Scherer, editor. *Monopoly and Competition Policy*. Aldershot: Edward Elgar Publishing Limited, 1993.

— 'Professor Sutton's 'Technology and Market Structure', *Journal of Industrial Economics* **48**(2), June 2000, pp. 215–23.

Scherer, F. M., Alan Beckenstein, Erich Kaufer, and R. D. Murphy *The Economics of Multi-Plant Operation: An International Comparisons Study*. Cambridge, Massachusetts: Harvard University Press, 1975.

Scherer, F. M. and Dietmer Harhoff 'Technology

policy for a world of skew-distributed outcomes', *Research Policy* **29(4–5)**, April 2000, pp. 559–66.

Schina, Despina. *State Aids under the EEC Treaty Articles 92 to 94*. Oxford: ESC Publishing Limited, 1987.

Schmalensee, Richard C. 'Sunk Costs and Market Structure: a review article', *Journal of Industrial Economics* **40(2)**, June 1992, pp. 125–34.

Schmidt, Jan Host, Fabienne Ilzkovitz, Roderick Meiklejohn, and Ulrik Mogensen 'Liberalization of network industries: economic implications and main policy issues', *Economic Economy* 1999, No 4, pp. 11–55.

Schumpeter, Joseph A. *The Theory of Economic Development*. Cambridge, Massachusetts: Harvard University Press, 1934.

— *Capitalism, Socialism and Democracy*. London: Allen & Unwin, 1943; New York: Harper & Row, Colophon edition, 1975.

Schwalbach, Joachim 'Entry, exit, concentration, and market contestability', in Geroski, Paul A. and Joachim Schwalbach. *Entry and Market Contestability*. Oxford: Blackwell Publishers, 1991, pp. 121–42.

Selten, Reinhard 'The chain store paradox', *Theory and Decision* **9**, 1978, pp. 127–59, reprinted in Reinhard Selten *Models of Strategic Rationality*. Dordrecht: Kluwer Academic Publishers, 1988; page references are to reprinted version.

Siegfried, John J., Rudolph C. Blitz, and David K. Round 'The limited role of market power in generating great fortunes in Great Britain, the United States, and Australia', *Journal of Industrial Economics* **43(3)**, September 1995, pp. 277–86.

Siegfried, John J. and Alison Roberts 'How did the wealthiest Britons get so rich?', *Review of Industrial Organization* **6**, 1991, pp. 19–32.

Siegfried, John J. and David K. Round 'How did the wealthiest Australian get so rich', *Review of Income and Wealth* **40(2)**, June 1994, pp. 191–204.

Sigurdson, Jon *Industry and State Partnership in Japan: the Very Large Scale Integrated (VLSI) Project*. Lund: Swedish Research Policy Institute, University of Lund, 1986.

Simon, Herbert A. *Administrative Behaviour*. New York: Macmillan, 1947; 3rd edition, 1976.

— 'Organizations and markets', *Journal of Economic Perspectives* **5(2)**, Spring 1991, pp. 25–44.

Sinnaeve, Adinda 'The Commission's proposal for a Regulation on State Aid procedures', *Competition Policy Newsletter*, June 1998, pp. 79–82.

Sleuwaegen, Leo and Hideki Yamawaki 'The formation of the European common market and changes in market structure and performance', *European Economic Review* **32**, 1988, pp. 1451–75.

Smith, Adam *An Inquiry Into the Nature and Causes of the Wealth of Nations*. Edwin Cannan, editor. New York: The Modern Library, 1937.

Smith, Alasdair 'The market for cars in the enlarged European Community', in Christopher Bliss and Braga de Macedo, Jorge *Unity with diversity in the European Economy: the Community's Southern Frontier*. Cambridge: Cambridge University Press, 1990, pp. 78–103.

Smith, Alasdair and Anthony J. Venables 'Counting the cost of voluntary export restraints in the European car market', in Elhanan Helpman and Assaf Razin, editors. *International Trade and Trade Policy*. Cambridge, Massachusetts: MIT Press, 1991, pp. 187–220.

Spence, A. Michael 'Product differentiation and welfare', *American Economic Review* **66(2)**, May 1976, pp. 407–14.

Spencer, Barbara J. 'What should trade policy target?', in Paul R. Krugman, editor. *Strategic Trade Policy and the New International Economics*. Cambridge, Massachusetts: MIT Press, 1988, pp. 69–89.

Spierenburg, Dirk and Raymond Poidevin *The History of the High Authority of the European Coal and Steel Community*. London: Weidenfeld and Nicolson, 1994.

von Stackelberg, Heinrich *Marktform und Gleichgewicht*. Vienna: Julius Springer, 1934.

Steinmueller, W. Edward 'International joint ventures in the integrated circuit industry', CEPR Publication No 104, September 1987.

— 'Industry structure and government policies in the US and Japanese integrated-circuit industries', in John B. Shoven, editor. *Government policy towards industry in the United States and Japan*. Cambridge: Cambridge University Press, 1988, pp. 319–54.

Stigler, George J. 'The division of labor is limited by the extent of the market', *Journal of Political Economy* **59(3)**, June 1951, pp. 185–93, reprinted in George J. Stigler, *The Organization of Industry*. Homewood, Illinois: Richard D. Irwin, Inc., 1968.

Sutton, John *Sunk Costs and Market Structure*. Cambridge, Massachusetts: MIT Press, 1991.

— 'Gibrat's legacy', *Journal of Economic Literature* **35(1)**, March 1997, pp. 40–59.

— *Technology and Market Structure*. Cambridge, Massachusetts: MIT Press, 1998.

Symeonidis, George 'Price competition and market structure: the impact of cartel policy on concentration in the UK', *Journal of Industrial Economics* **48(1)**, March 2000, pp. 1–26.

Taft, William Howard *The Anti-trust Act and the Supreme Court*. New York and London: Harper & Brothers Publishers, 1914; New York: Kraus Reprint Co., 1970.

Takacs, Wendy E. and L. Alan Winters 'Labour adjustment costs and British footwear protection', *Oxford Economic Papers* **43**, 1991, pp. 479–501.

Tapon, Francis and Charles Bram Cadsby 'The optimal organization of research: evidence from eight case studies of pharmaceutical firms', *Journal of Economic & Behavioural Organization* **31**, 1996, pp. 381–99.

Teece, David J. 'Firm organization, industrial structure, and technological innovation', *Journal of Economic & Behavioural Organization* **31**, 1996, pp. 193–224.

Temin, Peter 'Two views of the British industrial revolution', *Journal of Economic History* **57(1)**, March 1997, pp. 63–82.

Tharakan, P. K. M. 'The Japan-EC DRAMs anti-dumping undertaking: was it justified? What purpose did it serve?', *De Economist* **145(1)**, 1997, pp. 1–28.

U.S. Department of Commerce, Bureau of the Census. *Standard Industrial Classification Manual, 1987*. Washington, DC: US Government Printing Office, 1987.

Vermulst, Edwin and Paul Waer *EC Antidumping Law and Practice*. London: Sweet & Maxwell, 1996.

Veugelers, Reinhilde 'Locational determinants and ranking of host countries: an empirical assessment', *Kyklos* **44(3)**, 1991, pp. 363–82.

— 'Strategic incentives for multinational operations', *Managerial and Decision Economics* **16(1)**, January–February 1995, pp. 47–57.

Vickers, John. S. 'Concepts of competition', *Oxford Economic Papers* **47(1)**, January 1995, pp. 1–23.

Viner, Jacob 'Cost curves and supply curves', *Zeitschrift für Nationalökonomie* **3**, 1931, pp. 23–46; reprinted in George J. Stigler and Kenneth E. Boulding, editors. *A. E. A. Readings in Price Theory*. Chicago: Richard D. Irwin, 1952.

Vonortas, Nicholas S. 'Inter-firm cooperation with imperfectly appropriable research', *International Journal of Industrial Organization* **12(3)**, September 1994, pp. 413–35.

Wallsten, Scott J. 'The effects of government-industry R&D programmes on private R&D: the case of the Small Business Innovation Research programme', *Rand Journal of Economics* **31(1)** Spring 2000, pp. 82–100.

Walsh, Paul Patrick and Ciara Whelen, 'Modelling firm size distribution in food and drink products', Department of Economics, Trinity College, Dublin, undated.

Werden, Gregory J. 'The divergence of SIC industries from antitrust markets', *Economics Letters* **28**, 1988, pp. 193–7.

Wilkins, Mira 'Japanese multinationals in the United States: continuity and change, 1879–1990', *Business History Review* **64(4)**, Winter 1990, pp. 585–629.

Williamson, Oliver E. 'Economies as an antitrust defense: the welfare tradeoffs', *American Economic Review* **58(1)**, March 1968, pp. 18–36.

— *Corporate Control and Business Behavior: an Inquiry into the Effects of Organization Form on Enterprise Behaviour*. Englewood Cliffs, New Jersey: Prentice-Hall, 1970.

— *Markets and Hierarchies*. New York: The Free Press, 1975.

— 'The modern corporation: origins, evolution, attributes', *Journal of Economic Literature* **19(4)**, December 1981, pp. 1537–68.

— *The Economic Institutions of Capitalism*. New York: The Free Press, 1985.

Williamson, Oliver E. and Sidney G. Winter, editors. *The Nature of the Firm*. Oxford: Oxford University Press, 1991.

Wolf, Martin 'Why voluntary export restraints: A historical analysis', in Ad Koekkoek and L. B. M. Mennes, editors. *International Trade and Global Development Essays in Honour of Jagdish Bhagwati*. Routledge: London and New York, 1991, pp. 83–104.

Womack, James P., Daniel T. Jones, and Daniel Roos *The Machine That Changed The World*. New York: Rawson Associates, 1990.

Yamawaki, Hideki 'Exports and foreign distributional activities: evidence on Japanese firms in the United States', *Review of Economics and Statistics* **73(2)**, May 1991, pp. 294–300.

Yang, Jiawen 'Exchange rate pass-through in US manufacturing industries', *Review of Economics and Statistics* **79(1)**, February 1997, pp. 95–104.

Index of Commission Decisions

Index of Court Decisions

Index of Names

Sorensen, Robert 156, 244
Spence, A. Michael 37, 245
Spencer, Barbara J. 245
Spierenburg, Dirk 219, 245
Sraffa, Piero 145, 147
Stackelberg, Heinrich von 71, 245
Steinmueller, W. Edward 96–7, 243, 245
Stigler, George J. 123, 237, 241, 245
Stoneman, Paul 243
Sutton, John 5, 116, 118, 128, 245, 246
Sweeney, Richard James 236
Switzer, S. 244
Symeonidis, George 58, 246

Taft, William Howard 79, 246
Takacs, Wendy E. 197, 246
Tapon, Francis 91, 246
Teece, David J. 97, 246
Temin, Peter 144, 246
Tharakan, P. K. M. 205, 246
Thisse, Jacques-François 244
Tollison, Robert D. 236

Uesugi, Akinori 191, 241
Ulph, David 94, 236, 241

Valbonesi, Paola 226, 243
Venables, Anthony J. 153, 197, 241, 242, 245
Verboven, Frank 135, 238
Vermulst, Edwin 205, 246
Versaevel, Bruno xv
Veugelers, Reinhilde 179, 223, 246

Vickers, John. S. 223, 246
Viner, Jacob 14, 246
Vonortas, Nicholas S. 97, 246

Waer, Paul 205, 246
Wagner, Samuel 242, 243
Wallsten, Scott J. 98, 246
Walsh, Patrick Paul 119, 246
Weinstein, David E. 238
Werden, Gregory J. 5, 246
Whelen, Ciara 119, 246
Whinston, Michael D. 237
Wijngaarden, Remco van 205, 244
Wilde, Louis L. 94, 242
Wilkins, Mira 179, 246
Williams, John C. 92, 241
Williamson, Oliver E. 73, 122, 124, 129, 237, 241, 242, 244, 246
Willig, Robert D. 236
Wilson, Robert 81, 242
Winter, Sidney G. 122, 237, 241, 242, 243, 246
Winters, L. Alan 197, 241, 246
Witte, Herman 221
Wolf, Martin 194, 246
Womack, James P. 180, 246
Woods, Donncadh 65, 242

Yamawaki, Hideki 179, 224, 245, 246
Yang, Jiawen 172, 246

Zang, Israel 97, 241

Index of Subjects

absolute capital requirements: EU merger policy 130; impact on seller concentration 118
absorptive capacity: R & D spillovers 97
antidumping policy: and tacit collusion 203; duties 202–3; European Community 204–7; cotton fabrics 206–7; undertakings 203
antitrust law, US 127: Sherman Act 63
appropriability, profit from innovation: patents and 97–8; price discrimination and 96
asset specificity: transaction costs 124
average cost 14, 107–8
average variable cost 14, 107

backward induction 81
barriers to mobility 115
basing point pricing 53–5; ECSC steel sector 53, 219
Bertrand oligopoly model: market integration 214–15; product differentiation 45–7; standardized product 43–5, 114
best response function: Bertrand oligopoly: product differentiation 45–6; standardized product 47; Cournot oligopoly 23–8: conjectural variations and 34–6, 111; diseconomies of scale 107–10; many firms 41–2; product differentiation 37; sales